How to Teach Elementary School Science

How to Teach Elementary School Science

Fourth Edition

Joseph M. Peters
University of West Florida

Peter C. Gega
Professor Emeritus
San Diego State University

Upper Saddle River, New Jersey
Columbus, Ohio

Library of Congress Cataloging in Publication Data

Peters, Joseph M.
    How to teach elementary school science / Joseph M. Peters, Peter C. Gega.—4th ed.
        p. cm.
    Gega's name appears first on the earlier edition.
    Includes bibliographical references and index.
    ISBN 0-13-016582-4
    1. Science—Study and teaching (Elementary) I. Gega, Peter C. II. Title.

LB1585.G39 2002
373.3'5044—dc21

2001030521

Vice President and Publisher: Jeffery W. Johnston
Editor: Linda Ashe Montgomery
Development Editor: Hope Madden
Editorial Assistant: Lori Jones
Production Editor: Linda Hillis Bayma
Copy Editor: Linda Poderski
Text Design: SettingPace
Design Coordinator: Diane C. Lorenzo
Photo Coordinator: Sandy Lenahan
Cover Designer: Diane Ernsberger
Cover photo: Pictor Uniphoto
Production Manager: Pamela D. Bennett
Director of Marketing: Kevin Flanagan
Marketing Manager: Krista Groshong
Marketing Coordinator: Barbara Koontz

This book was set in Berkeley Book by Carlisle Communications, Ltd. It was printed and bound by Courier Kendallville, Inc. The cover was printed by The Lehigh Press, Inc.

Photo Credits: Alan and Sandy Carey/PhotoDisc, p. 203; Scott Cunningham/Merrill, pp. 114, 184; Kenneth P. Davis/PH College, p. 105; Tim Daniel/ODNR/Division of Wildlife, p. 94; Richard Hoyt/Great Explorations in Math and Science, p. 120; T. Hubbard/Merrill, p. 156; Israel Office of Information, p. 21; Jet Propulsion Laboratory/NASA Headquarters, p. 38; Ken Karp/PH College, p. 30; KS Studios/Merrill, p. 194; James Kudlack and Barb Eldridge/Onekama Elementary School, p. 84; Anthony Magnacca/Merrill, pp. 130, 162, 166, 172, 179; Michael Newman/PhotoEdit, p. 73; Joseph M. Peters, pp. viii, 147; Barbara Schwartz/Merrill, p. 142; Silver Burdett Ginn Needham, p. 7; Cary I. Sneider/Great Explorations in Math and Science, p. 67; Stone/David J. Sams, p. 207; Courtesy of Uncle Milton Industries, Inc., p. 2; Anne Vega/Merrill, p. 48.

Prentice-Hall International (UK) Limited, *London*
Prentice-Hall of Australia Pty. Limited, *Sydney*
Prentice-Hall Canada, Inc., *Toronto*
Prentice-Hall Hispanoamericana, S.A., *Mexico*
Prentice-Hall of India Private Limited, *New Delhi*
Prentice-Hall of Japan, Inc., *Tokyo*
Prentice-Hall Singapore Pte. Ltd.
Editora Prentice-Hall do Brasil, Ltda., *Rio de Janeiro*

Merrill
Prentice Hall

10 9 8 7 6 5 4 3 2 1
ISBN 0-13-016582-4

This book is dedicated to David "Gus" Thomas, Mercyhurst College, whose desire for teaching inspired a love of science in all those with whom he came in contact.

Preface

Elementary school teaching is a challenging and exciting career. Your future as a professional educator includes the responsibility to meet the future demands and challenges of society, and the elementary classroom is where it all begins. The lifelong science-related attitudes of your elementary students will be shaped, for the most part, before they finish fifth grade. Along with these attitudes comes the desire to seek out new information about the world around them and to apply this knowledge in the form of technology. It is your job to build the skills, content knowledge, and desire for inquiry that will allow your students to function in a society that will be highly scientific and technologically developed. Your future as a teacher will include lifelong learning and research in your own classrooms. This text serves as a guide to start your journey as a professional educator.

New to This Edition —————

As you initiate your learning of elementary science education through the use of the fourth edition of this text, you will become acquainted with several features that will support you in your science education experiences. To help you think about the applications of what you are learning, you will find

- Vignettes opening each chapter that help introduce the concepts contained in the chapters and focus your thoughts

- Teaching tips for you to consider in your future instruction

- Companion Website references, which provide extensions to the chapter content

- CD-ROM connections, which help illustrate concepts in an actual classroom setting

- An entire chapter devoted to technology and science education

Organization of the Text —————

You will find that this book contains practical methods covering how to teach science to elementary through middle level learners. A companion paperback text, *Concepts and Inquiries in Elementary School Science,* Fourth Edition, as well as one hardcover text containing the complete content, *Science in Elementary Education,* Ninth Edition, also published by Prentice Hall, are also available.

How to Teach Elementary School Science focuses on the methods of teaching elementary school science. It centers on why science education is basic to children's schooling and explains the foundations that give it form and substance. Each of its eight chapters develops a broad concept or a cluster of related teaching skills through descriptions and the use of many real-life examples. The examples reflect our personal teaching experiences or ongoing, firsthand observations with elementary school children. The chapters and several of the included follow-up exercises should enable you to

- Decide what areas of science are basic, useful, and learnable for children
- Recognize and assess differences in children's thinking
- Use open-ended and closed-ended teaching activities in planning and implementing lessons and units
- Improve children's scientific skills
- Develop technological applications
- Locate and use a variety of resources to teach science
- Arrange and manage learning centers, microcomputer centers, and projects
- Assess science teaching

Each chapter focuses on an overall concept such as learning, assessment, or technology. To help summarize and extend the content, each chapter includes a summary, reflection, and additional readings. In addition, samples of the National Research Council's *National Science Education Standards* are cited throughout the text when applicable.

Supplements

- **CD-ROM**
  Containing classroom footage, this free supplement allows users to view, examine, and manipulate clips of elementary science classroom teaching. The CD is ideal for reflection and developing a deep, lasting understanding of text content.

- **Companion Website**
  A truly text-integrated supplement at **www.prenhall.com/peters** will provide users with access to research, meaningful activities, self-assessments, useful web links, chat areas, and a threaded message board. For the professor, the Syllabus Manager allows online creation and management of course syllabi.

- **Instructor's Manual**
  This useful tool provides additional support for instructors, test questions, and online integration.

- **NSE Standards Sampler**
  This document works in tandem with the text to help prospective teachers learn, fully understand, and apply the National Science Education Standards.

Acknowledgments

I wish to thank the many people who helped with this edition of *How to Teach Elementary School Science*. I especially wish to thank editors Linda Montgomery and Hope Madden of Merrill/Prentice Hall for their insight, encouragement, continued assistance, and constructive comments. I also want to thank those who reviewed the draft manuscripts and provided suggestions for the fourth edition. These include Kristin Devlin, Maro Foster, Tina Howard, Angela Kriner, Robin Loukota, Holly Nelson, and Misty Rawls, students at the

University of West Florida, who reviewed draft manuscripts and provided suggestions for clarifying concepts and improving the text for their colleagues, as well as my students at Mercyhurst College (see photo) who assisted with finalizing the content.

This edition of *How to Teach Elementary School Science* includes many vignettes. I extend my sincere thanks to Norman Lederman, Oregon State University; Ken Tobin, University of Pennsylvania; Jerry Mayernik, Northway Elementary School, North Hills School District, Pennsylvania; George O'Brien, Florida International University and Angela Alexander, Pine Villa Montessori School, Dade County (Florida) School District; Christine Peters, Harborcreek School District, Pennsylvania; Kata McCarville, South Dakota School of Mines and Technology; Pam Northrup and Charlotte Boling, the University of West Florida; and Sue Dale Tunnicliffe, International Council of Associations for Science Education Primary Projects and Homerton College, for sharing their experiences with us and reviewing chapters.

I would also like to acknowledge the external reviewers of this text: Andrea M. Guillaume, California State University–Fullerton; Eileen S. Kelble, The University of Tulsa; William C. Kyle, Jr., University of Missouri–St. Louis; Scott P. Lewis, Florida International University; Michael Meloth, The University of Colorado–Boulder; Brian Murfin, New York University; Michael Odell, University of Idaho; and John Shimkanin, California University of Pennsylvania.

Most important, I would like to show my heartfelt appreciation to my wife, Darlene, and to my children, Joe and Brenda, for their patience and guidance during the revision.

Joseph M. Peters

Discover the Companion Website Accompanying This Book

The Prentice Hall Companion Website: A Virtual Learning Environment

Technology is a constantly growing and changing aspect of our field that is creating a need for content and resources. To address this emerging need, Prentice Hall has developed an online learning environment for students and professors alike—Companion Websites—to support our textbooks.

In creating a Companion Website, our goal is to build on and enhance what the textbook already offers. For this reason, the content for each user-friendly website is organized by chapter and provides the professor and student with a variety of meaningful resources.

For the Professor

Every Companion Website integrates **Syllabus Manager**™, an online syllabus creation and management utility.

*   **Syllabus Manager**™ provides you, the instructor, with an easy, step-by-step process to create and revise syllabi, with direct links into the Companion Website and other online content without having to learn HTML.
*   Students may log on to your syllabus during any study session. All they need to know is the web address for the Companion Website and the password you've assigned to your syllabus.
*   After you have created a syllabus using **Syllabus Manager**™, students may enter the syllabus for their course section from any point in the Companion Website.
*   Clicking on a date, the student is shown the list of activities for the assignment. The activities for each assignment are linked directly to actual content, saving time for students.
*   Adding assignments consists of clicking on the desired due date, then filling in the details of the assignment—name of the assignment, instructions, and whether or not it is a one-time or repeating assignment.
*   In addition, links to other activities can be created easily. If the activity is online, a URL can be entered in the space provided, and it will be linked automatically in the final syllabus.
*   Your completed syllabus is hosted on our servers, allowing convenient updates from any computer on the Internet. Changes you make to your syllabus are immediately available to your students at their next logon.

Common Companion Website features for students include:

For the Student ———————

- **Chapter Objectives**—outline key concepts from the text
- **Interactive Self-quizzes**—complete with hints and automatic grading that provide immediate feedback for students

  After students submit their answers for the interactive self-quizzes, the Companion Website **Results Reporter** computes a percentage grade, provides a graphic representation of how many questions were answered correctly and incorrectly, and gives a question-by-question analysis of the quiz. Students are given the option to send their quiz to up to four email addresses (professor, teaching assistant, study partner, etc.).

- **Web Destinations**—links to www sites that relate to chapter content
- **Message Board**—serves as a virtual bulletin board to post—or respond to—questions or comments to/from a national audience
- **Chat**—real-time chat with anyone who is using the text anywhere in the country—ideal for discussion and study groups, class projects, etc.

To take advantage of the many available resources, please visit the text's Companion Website at

www.prenhall.com/peters

Brief Contents

Contents

NOTE: Every effort has been made to provide accurate and current Internet information in this book. However, the Internet and information posted on it are constantly changing, so it is inevitable that some of the Internet addresses listed in this textbook will change.

How to Teach Elementary School Science

Chapter 1

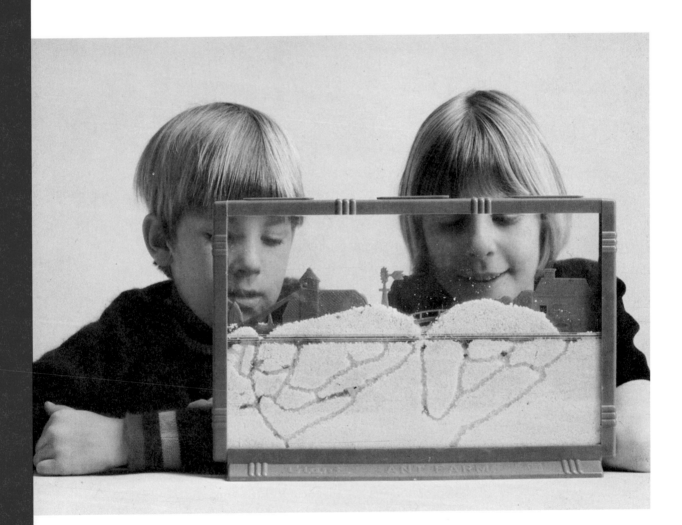

Science Inquiry and the Nature of Science

The Nature of Science

Dr. Norman Lederman
Oregon State University

Shedding Some Light on the Situation

The year is 1971, and Peter is a typically self-conscious high school sophomore. Like several of his friends, Peter has a slight acne problem. After trying several creams and ointments available at the local drugstore, he convinces his parents that the problem requires the help of the family physician. The physician tells Peter and his parents that the cause of his problem is an abundance of oil production by the glands on his face and that this extra oil provides a good nutritional source for common bacteria. She also tells Peter that eating less chocolate, among other things, might solve the problem but that there is a more reliable approach. Naturally, Peter and his parents are anxious to listen further. The physician recommends that Peter's parents purchase a sunlamp. The U.V. rays emitted by the sunlamp do an excellent job of "drying" the skin and eliminating acne problems. In fact, the physician adds, sunlamps are generally good for most people's skin regardless of whether they have an acne problem. Peter would only have to use the sunlamp about 10 minutes per day and, in addition to relieving his acne problems, he can have a desirable tanned look year-round. So, Peter, with his parents' permission, did what thousands of Americans did in the 1970s.

Thirty years later, the medical profession has recognized the possible carcinogenic effects of ultraviolet radiation. Acne patients are no longer advised to use sunlamp therapy. Indeed, the current advice regarding U.V. rays is to avoid them as much as possible. Consequently, the availability of sunscreen lotions and sunglasses designed to protect both the skin and the eyes from harmful light rays has increased significantly. The physician's advice to Peter and his parents in the 2000s would be much different from what it was in 1971.

How does the general public react to this "change of heart" by the scientific community? Although we have seen a proliferation of ointments and creams designed to block the harmful rays of the sun, tanning is as popular as ever in the United States and, indeed, around the world. A significant number of individuals have decided to ignore the advice of the scientific community. It is not uncommon to hear people say, "Why can't scientists make up their minds? One day something is good for you, and next day you hear that it causes cancer. It seems that everything causes cancer. I'm not going to do anything different until they decide once and for all."

3

The case of U.V. rays is not unique. "Flip-flops" in the opinions of scientists and physicians have occurred with respect to aspirin, alcohol, cold fusion, and Vitamin C. Indeed, such changes have become the object of jokes.

What does this have to do with teaching elementary-level students about the nature of science? These flip-flops we so often see are really not weaknesses of science. They are not reasons for the general public to disregard scientific knowledge or to lose faith in the scientific way of thinking. These flip-flops constitute one of the most important strengths of science—in fact, they *are* science. That is, scientific knowledge is self-correcting on the basis of new empirical evidence or new ways of interpreting data. The knowledge, though tentative, is based on volumes of data and should not be disregarded. Disregarding scientific knowledge severely limits the quality of decisions that we each make about our lives.

What is the nature of science? There are as many answers to this question as there are books; however, at the level of generality that will be useful to you as an elementary teacher there is a strong consensus. Strictly speaking, *science* can be defined as a body of knowledge, a process, and a way of knowing or constructing reality. *The nature of science* refers to those characteristics of scientific knowledge that derive directly from how the knowledge is developed. Of importance to you as an elementary science teacher are the following characteristics:

- There is no single set or sequence of steps in a scientific investigation (there is no such thing as the scientific method).
- Scientific knowledge (both theories and laws) is subject to change (all scientific knowledge is tentative).
- Scientific knowledge must be at least partially supported by empirical evidence (scientific knowledge must involve the collection of data, be consistent with what we "know" about the world, and be testable).
- Scientific knowledge is partially the product of the creative imagination of the scientist (all scientific knowledge combines both empirical evidence and the creative interpretation of data by scientists).
- Given the importance of scientists' individual creativity, scientific knowledge is necessarily subjective to some degree (scientific knowledge is not totally objective as is commonly believed).
- Scientific knowledge is a product of both observation and inference.

By carefully addressing these characteristics of scientific knowledge and by keeping in mind the developmental level of your students, you can help your students develop understandings that will help them in making decisions for the rest of their lives. In particular, your students will begin to develop a more balanced view of the "truth" of scientific knowledge. They will take "the truth" of science with an informed "grain of salt." This means your students will heed the notion that the sun's rays can cause cancer, and it also means they will not disregard all future knowledge about the effects of the sun's rays if the scientific community alters its current position.

As you begin to ponder your own teaching of the nature of science, keep in mind that developing content knowledge and inquiry skills with your students is facilitated by their inherent natural curiosity. Children intrinsically enjoy observing the world around them. Picture a group of students on a playground during lunch. They are watching ants move about on the pavement. Looking at the ants, they begin to ask questions like the following:

Why do ants follow each other?

Why do the ants live in the ground and not above the ground?

How can the ants carry things twice their size?

> ### Standards Link
>
> ## History and Nature of Science Standard
>
> As a result of activities in grades K–8, all students should develop an understanding of
>
> - **Science as a human endeavor**
> - **Nature of science**
> - **History of science**
>
> (Content Standard G, National Research Council, 1996, pp. 141 & 170. Reprinted with permission from *National Science Education Standards.* Copyright 1996 by the National Academy of Sciences. Courtesy of the National Academy Press, 1996)

How thoughtfully did your teachers handle questions you asked in school? Were you able to explore some of your own interests in the classroom, or was learning more restricted? Were you guided to think through some problems for yourself, or were standard answers always given?

How your teachers worked with you and your classmates reflected their notions about science and science teaching and how they thought it could benefit their students. We hope that what you learn through this methods course will affect how you will teach science.

Your school or district office will probably give you some instructional materials for teaching science. But your own concepts and values about science teaching will strongly affect what children actually learn in your science classroom. If you desire to understand **the nature of science, scientific concepts,** and **scientific processes,** this desire to learn more about the world around you will be transferred to your students.

How you and your students learn science will be related to your desire for inquiry and the nature of science. In the following sections, we use contrasting teaching approaches to show how your teaching can affect students' curiosity about the nature of science. As you read, think about the National Research Council's (NRC) History and Nature of Science Standard in the Standards Link box.

The nature of science means those characteristics of scientific knowledge that derive directly from how the knowledge is developed.

Scientific concepts relate to the knowledge of science, or what scientists have found out as a result of their work.

Scientific processes are the skills that students develop, such as observation, classification, inference, and measurement.

See *http://www.prenhall.com/peters* **for links to all the National Science Education Standards.**

The Nature of Science

Imagine that you are sitting in on three teachers as they use a teachable moment to engage students in the topic of "ants." Students from Martin Luther King Jr. Elementary School have just come back from their noon recess. While walking back from the playground, students from each of the three classes had discussed what they had witnessed: fire ants attacking a baby bird that could not fly. They are now wondering why ants behave the way they do, why they eat what they eat, and what their underground homes may look like.

Grade 3 Examples ─────────

Using the students' natural curiosity, three teachers use this time to introduce a lesson on ants. Compare each of the three approaches.

Mrs. Myers's Class

Mrs. Myers looks up ants in the classroom encyclopedia. She has one student read the passage aloud. After answering a few questions, she continues on with the reading lesson that she has planned for the afternoon.

Mr. Bryant's Class

In his early-elementary classroom, Mr. Bryant captures an opportunity to follow up the ant discussion with the classic story *A Bug's Life* (Steiner, 1998). Over the next few days, he reads *Ant Cities* (Dorros, 1987) and *It's an Ant's Life* (Parker, 1999) to the children. They discuss the anthills and tunnels and the worker ants, males, and queens. Later, they make a homemade Ant Farm®[1] as suggested in the *Ant Cities* book. Mr. Bryant introduces ants to the farm, and the children periodically feed them. During free time for the next few weeks, the students intermittently observe the ants just to see what they are doing.

See the Nature of Science section of the companion CD for teaching examples related to the nature of science.

Ms. Davis's Class

In the elementary classroom across the hall, Ms. Davis begins asking her students what they observed outside. She has students take turns recording this information on a flip chart. She also includes questions about what the students would like to know about ants. Later, she reads the fable *The Little Red Ant and the Great Big Crumb* (Climo, 1995) to begin a discussion on the foods ants eat. She then reads *The Magic School Bus Gets Ants in Its Pants* (Cole, 1996) and *Hey Little Ant* (Hoose, Tilley, & Hoose, 1998) to initiate conversation on ant behaviors and habitats. Her class discusses the anthills and tunnels and the worker ants, males, and queens. Next, the students set up an Ant Farm® as outlined in *The Practical Entomologist* (Imes, 1992). After they build the farm, she asks the students to predict what will happen as the ants are introduced to the Ant Farm® and what will occur over the next few weeks. They hypothesize that the ants will develop small sections of the farm into colonies.

Ms. Davis's students write these predictions and the accompanying observations on the flip chart. They also record brief daily observations and compare these against their predictions. Ms. Davis's students infer what kinds of food ants like. They place different containers of food (see Cole, 1996) near the ant mound outside the classroom to see what will happen. They predict which food will be found first and infer which food the ants will appear to like best. They periodically have class discussions to communicate the facts they find out about ants. Ms. Davis ends the lessons by returning to the students' questions to see if they were all answered. She also follows up to be sure the students have no **misconceptions** about ants.

Misconceptions are mistaken ideas that students have about how something works or how it is otherwise unlike what the scientific community has found to be true.

Comparing Classrooms ─────────

In the above three situations, all three teachers discuss ants. Mrs. Myers answers all the students' questions about ants. Mr. Bryant and Ms. Davis expand on the opportunity presented to them by the students. They answer questions about ants and integrate children's natural wonder with children's literature, activities such as building Ant Farms®, and opportunities

1. Ant Farm® is a registered trademark of Uncle Milton Industries, Inc. Used with permission.

Children discuss animals that live underground as part of their research related to the study of ants.

for observation. Mr. Bryant uses this activity as a fun way to see ants in their habitats and to learn about ants in general. Ms. Davis, however, sees this as not only a fun learning activity but also an opportunity for her students to make systematic observations of ants and to develop other related scientific skills. She wants her students to infer, predict, communicate, experiment, and form tentative theories as scientists would in similar situations. She also wants her students to understand that scientific knowledge is based on observation and inference as with their ant studies—all part of learning the nature of science.

Grade 5 Examples

Students in two fifth-grade classrooms at Martin Luther King Jr. Elementary School have also witnessed the ants. Their teachers are also preparing ant lessons.

Mrs. Brown's Class

Mrs. Brown begins with reading to the class *Life Story: Ant* (Chinery, 1991). They discuss anthills, ant life cycles, and ant food behaviors. She has Tanezia read *Those Amazing Ants* (Demuth, 1994). This book has a lot of interesting information, such as the mating dance, cleaning habits, and the way ants use secretions to mark food trails. The students discuss this information. Guided by the activity "A Special Plot" from the **AIMS** book *Field Detectives: Investigating Playground Habitats* (Gazlay, 1998), Mrs. Brown completes a skill-development activity with her students. They observe and sketch several ant mounds near the school and develop Venn diagrams of the commonalties and differences in the habitats. The students then discuss what they found out from their diagrams.

AIMS (Activities for the Integration of Mathematics and Science) are hands-on/minds-on integrated activities found in a series of books available from the AIMS Foundation. (See *http://www.prenhall.com/peters* for links and further information.)

Mrs. Malloy's Class

Mrs. Malloy's upper-elementary class decides on ants as a study theme for the next few days. Karolyn reads aloud the story *The 512 Ants on Sullivan Street* (Losi, 1997); Taylor, *A*

Remainder of One (Pinczes, 1995); and Rochelle, *One Hundred Hungry Ants* (Pinczes, 1993). These stories incorporate number sense and division to lay the foundation for related mathematics activities. Casen then reads aloud the story *Antics!* (Hepworth, 1992), and Hoa, *There's an Ant in Anthony* (Most, 1980). These are alphabetical anthologies that lend themselves to language activities during which Mrs. Malloy's students try to find as many words as possible with *ant* in them. Finally, they explore "Ants Around the World" from the *Ants* book (Teacher Created Materials, 1997).

Continuing the ant theme, Mrs. Malloy asks the students what they have already found out about ants and what else they would like to know about ants. They generate a list of topics such as the following to copy into their science journals:

How do ants tunnel? Are all tunnels alike?

What is the ant's body structure? Is it different for males, females, and queens?

How do ants reproduce and grow?

What is a scent trail, and how is it made?

Project WILD, Project Aquatic WILD, Project Learning Tree, and Project WET are national programs that enhance environmental education. (See *http://www.prenhall.com/peters* for links to these and related programs.)

See *http://www.prenhall.com/peters* for ant cam and related links.

Mrs. Malloy makes available for her students some resource materials, including the AIMS *Field Detectives* book (Gazlay, 1998), *Ant Homes Under the Ground* (Lawrence Hall of Science, 1996), and the *Project WILD* (Council for Environmental Education, 1992) guide. She also arranges a table with several other activity and field identification books and materials for making an Ant Farm®. Her students use these in small groups to plan science activities. She also bookmarks an Internet ant cam (online video camera) and movie site for her class to use in their studies.

Mrs. Malloy loads SimAnt (Broderbund/Maxis) onto the classroom computer. Students take on roles of ants with this program. They learn ant behaviors, including how to communicate with one another and how to avoid being "done in" by fierce red ants, ravenous spiders, and heavy human feet. Students use scientific information to develop strategies to survive, increase the size of their colony, and finally reach the ultimate reward—a safe home with a food supply.

Mrs. Malloy facilitates and provides other resources as her class works in small groups to plan and participate in numerous activities related to ants. Later, they share what they have found out about ants. They conclude when the questions in their science journals are answered.

Classroom Comparisons

As with our earlier example of the primary classrooms, there are differences in these upper-elementary classrooms. Mrs. Brown uses literature to initiate student interest in ants. She also provides concrete experiences for children to investigate the ant environments and develop process skills and concepts.

Mrs. Malloy also generates interest in ants through mathematics and language activities. She uses the ant theme as a starting point to help her students generate ideas for experiments and other hands-on activities. These activities will help her initiate student discussion, seek answers to their related questions, and develop scientific skills. In this less teacher-directed approach, the children act like scientists as they explore and experiment with ants—constructing understandings and answers to their questions. They find that there is no one correct way to explore ants. They also see that their theories related to ants often change with new observations and inferences that better explain things. In short, they not only are learning about ants but also are experiencing the nature of science through inquiry, a connection with other school subjects as suggested in the NRC's Science Program of Study Standard.

Questions as an Invitation to Learn

In two other classrooms at the school, teachers scheduled other ant lessons. Their students first made some preliminary observations of the ants. Compare the three sets of examples to see how each teacher began his or her lesson:

Teacher 1

- A queen ant is usually bigger than the other ants, and new queens and males have wings.
- Ants may eat honeydew from aphids or juices from insects and plants.
- An ant develops from an egg, to a larva, to a pupa, to an adult that will emerge from a cocoon.

Teacher 2

- Why did some ants look different from others in the ant nest we observed?
- I wonder if the ants we observed today and last week all eat the same food.
- Why did we find eggs, grubs, and cocoons in the ant nests?

The first teacher simply states what will be taught. For example, in her first lesson, children will learn that queen ants are bigger than worker ants and that new queens and males have wings and the lesson is completed.

The second teacher always begins his lessons with a question referring to children's everyday experiences. This teacher agrees with current reform efforts that ask teachers to base science on students' everyday lives. This method supports the notion that science is a human endeavor. Science principles, or concepts, typically have many real-life applications and are a result of the creative imagination of the scientist. Beginning and ending lessons with applications enables children to reflect on their own experiences, to interpret their observations creatively, and to construct new knowledge. The second approach also takes the pressure off the teacher to know everything about the topic under study. The teacher can explore the subject with his or her students.

You probably see by now that the second way of teaching is likely to be more interesting and productive to you and your students. Yet, if you're like most college students who select elementary teaching as a profession, science is probably not your strongest subject. You may not feel confident about teaching science. Do not worry about this; you and your class will learn together. The important point is that you begin to develop an awareness of the nature of science and

See the Planning and Management, Questioning section of the companion CD for examples of questions as an invitation to learn.

Standards Link

Science Program of Study Standard

The program of study in science for all students should be developmentally appropriate, interesting, and relevant to students' lives; emphasize student understanding through inquiry; and be connected with other school subjects.

- **The program of study should include all of the content standards.**
- **Science content must be embedded in a variety of curriculum patterns that are developmentally appropriate, interesting, and relevant to students' lives.**
- **The program of study must emphasize student understanding through inquiry.**
- **The program of study in science should connect to other school subjects.**

(Program Standard B, National Research Council, 1996, p. 212) how you can develop scientific skills and understandings with the students. Let's look at Vignette 1–2 for a view on teaching the nature of science.

How Can You Teach the Nature of Science?

Although the current reforms in science education place a strong emphasis on students' understandings of the nature of science, you will find very few resources containing classroom-tested teaching ideas. The following is an idea that I have found to be successful for teaching elementary students about each of the six characteristics of scientific knowledge. This activity requires virtually no scientific background on the part of the students. Consequently, it is relatively risk free.

1. Re-create the tube pictured in Figure 1–1. I suggest that you obtain a mailing tube from the post office, the map room at a local library, or a store that sells posters. You may also use a piece of PVC pipe. Clothesline, twine, or rope from a local hardware store will do for the rope. The ring holding the ropes together is plastic; you can buy one at a craft store. If a ring is not available, the lower rope can simply be looped over the upper rope. The ends of the tube can be sealed with rubber stoppers or be taped.

2. Make an overhead (and class set of handouts) of what is pictured in Figure 1–2.

3. Have the students carefully observe several sequential pulls of the various rope ends. It makes no difference which rope ends you choose to pull.

4. Have individual students, pairs, or groups speculate about what is inside the tube in an effort to explain what they have seen. After several minutes, allow several students to manipulate the ropes. At this point, they will be testing their hypotheses about the contents of the tube.

Figure 1–1

Figure 1–2

5. Allow the students several more minutes to revise their speculations on the basis of the additional data that they have just collected.

6. Allow several volunteers the opportunity to share their hypotheses with the rest of the class on the overhead diagram. There are a variety of workable explanations; allow the sharing of ideas until at least two alternatives are presented. If the students seem to be fixed on only one approach, be prepared to offer other possibilities. Be sure not to imply that any one of the explanations is correct or better than the others.

7. You and the students can discuss the ideas presented. Restrict the focus of the discussion to the relationship between the inferred ideas and the data that were collected through your demonstration.

8. Have the students construct models of the tube they developed, using a toilet paper or paper towel roll. Provide string, scissors, and paper tubes, or direct students to bring these from home.

9. After construction of the models, have the students follow along as you pull various ropes on your model. This gives the students a chance to see how consistent their models are with the actions of your model.

10. Some students' tubes will not "behave" the same way as yours, but most probably will. Stress two ideas at this point: First, lead the class to the idea that there are several ways to construct the tube so that it functions like yours. Second, ask the students if they can now know for sure what is in your tube, just because their model "behaved" the same as yours. The primary point is that we never really know for sure whether the proposed explanation is correct unless the tube can be opened.

See the Nature of Science section of the companion CD for examples of students collecting data.

Depending on the grade level of your students, the following ideas should be discussed:

1. The tube is analogous to the universe; what your students did is analogous to what scientists do. But we have no way of actually opening the universe to see how it really works.

2. Students collected empirical data and developed inferences to explain the data. These activities are similar to the way scientists collect data and develop inferences to explain the data. In essence, the speculations about the contents of your tube are theoretical models used to explain necessarily limited data. What your students have done is analogous to what a scientist does all the time. What your students have done is not very different from what the scientists of the 1970s did when they observed acne and inferred possible explanations and solutions for the problem.

3. Finally, explicitly discuss with your students how each of the six characteristics of scientific knowledge is evident in the activity.

Take a moment to see if you can identify the six characteristics of science in this activity.

Vignette 1–2 clearly points out some tenets of the nature of science. In *Benchmarks for Science Literacy* (American Association for the Advancement of Science [AAAS], 1993), the authors make the following point about the study of science:

See
http://www.prenhall.com/peters
**for a link to the Benchmarks
for Science Literacy.**

> When people know how scientists go about their work and reach scientific con-clusions, and what the limitations of such conclusions are, they are more likely to react thoughtfully to scientific claims and less likely to reject them out of hand or accept them uncritically. Once people gain a good sense of how science operates—along with a basic inventory of key science concepts as a basis for learning more later—they can follow the science adventure story as it plays out during their lifetimes. (p. 3)

This passage means that it is critical for students to understand how the scientific process works in order to be good science consumers and lifelong learners. Students must see science as a human enterprise and not as a body of knowledge to be memorized. When they read and appraise an item in the newspaper or have a problem to solve, the students' past scientific experiences will assist them.

Like the examples in Vignette 1–1, you may also wonder about some scientific "changes of heart" or new theories. Your knowledge of the nature of science will assist you in understanding the scientific information presented to you. Remember that the products of science are constantly changing with new experimentation. Lederman (1992) asserts that "the nature of science is as tentative, if not more so, than scientific knowledge itself" (p. 352), meaning that the nature of science itself develops over time. *What does remain constant is that good science education originates with your understanding of the nature of science.*

In addition to knowledge of the nature of science, you need an understanding of scientific concepts and processes. Let's consider scientific concepts in the following section.

Scientific Concepts and Generalizations

We try to explain, predict, and control our experiences by generalizing about the patterns or regularities we observe. For example, you may generalize the following:

> *Ants are important to the environment because they help control the populations of their prey.*
>
> *Ant nests generally consist of chambers and galleries that are excavated under rocks, foliage, or underground.*
>
> *Ants contribute to the recycling of plant matter.*

Generalizations can be seen as principles or statements that have a general application.

Knowing the **generalizations** about ants may cause you to say, "Ants are impor-tant to the environment because they help recover nutrients to help other things grow" (explain) or "If we did not have ants, other animal populations would grow to uncontrol-lable population sizes" (predict). The students working with the ants also make generaliza-tions, such as the following:

> *The queen ants are bigger than the workers because their bodies are full of eggs (explain).*
>
> *The ants will put the nursery close to the surface of the mound because the sun's warmth will help the eggs develop (predict).*
>
> *I will disrupt the pheromone path so that the ants will have a harder time returning to the nest (control).*

Scientists, too, observe patterns and generalize about ants. But they do so with far more precision and reliability than your elementary students. This is the reason we study science and its methods. It is a way to sharpen your students' skills.

Scientists use an ingenious array of tools and organized methods to search for patterns in objects and events. The generalizations they invent to explain what they observe may look like these:

Many ant species secrete formic acid to use as a repellant for other animals.

Some ants inflict a sting used for defense.

The jaws of worker ants are used for defense, as well as for the care of larvae and for nest building.

Scientists know, however, that they cannot fully *explain* or understand natural events. What they do is construct *descriptions* of natural events and, when they can, predict or control events. What they may call explanations (concepts, generalizations, principles, laws, theories) are really descriptions—often brilliantly conceived and useful, but descriptions nonetheless. How well a description enables them to explain, predict, or control events is related to how it is accepted by the scientific community. That is to say, if a theory does a poor job of explaining events or has a lot of conflicting data, that theory is abandoned for one that better explains things. The changing nature of theories and their abandonment relate to the **paradigms** of science that we discuss in Chapter 2.

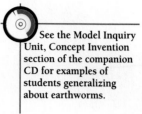

See the Model Inquiry Unit, Concept Invention section of the companion CD for examples of students generalizing about earthworms.

Paradigms are commonly accepted viewpoints within the scientific community.

Generalizations

Consider the generalization of *insects,* for example. Like other general concepts, this one stands for a class of things with similar properties, such as an animal with an adult stage characterized by a body segmented into head, thorax, and abdomen, containing three pairs of legs, and having two pairs of wings. Generalizations about scientific phenomena help us in a similar way. The statement "most matter expands when heated and contracts when cooled" interrelates several concepts. This generalization enables us to relate and explain some apparently different phenomena: a sidewalk that buckles and cracks in hot weather; telephone wires that sag in summer but not in winter; a tightly screwed jar lid that can be loosened by running hot water over it; rocks around a campfire that break apart when we douse the fire and rocks with water.

Learning key concepts and generalizations is an essential component of science education because it increases our ability to solve problems and use scientific skills. Figure 1–3 shows that a variety of animals can be classified as mammals but that only a handful need be studied to understand the general concept. Once we understand the physical

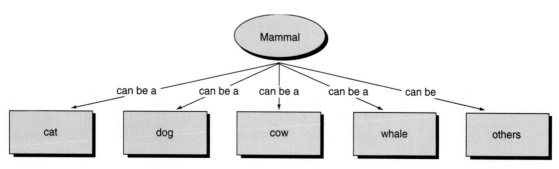

Figure 1–3
Concepts stand for a class of things with similar properties.

properties of mammals, it's easy to classify even unfamiliar animals. Even if we don't know their names, we already know a great deal about them.

Science Concepts ───────

A similar transfer of learning happens with properly learned concepts. Although few events may be studied to learn the concept (Figure 1–4), many more may be applied. Organizing thoughts into concepts, generalizations, sequences, and other patterns broadens and deepens understanding. In contrast, facts that are studied without relating them to prior knowledge can be quickly forgotten. Learning the patterns of nature allows us to continually apply, or transfer, these concepts to new objects and events. The new facts collected are connected to existing mental structures; this aids in the future retrieval of the information.

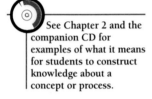

See Chapter 2 and the companion CD for examples of what it means for students to construct knowledge about a concept or process.

Cow-killers are wingless wasps, similar in structure to an ant.

Are applications of concepts possible with your students? You might test to find this out. You will want to ask questions that contain examples of objects or events that have not been studied. If a child can link unstudied examples of a studied concept or generalization, chances are that transferable learning has occurred and the child has successfully constructed knowledge of that concept. For example, knowing that ants are insects that defend themselves by stinging their prey, the child will transfer this knowledge and avoid the sting of an interesting **cow-killer.**

Application of Concepts

Scientists search for patterns, but they also look for inconsistencies in the patterns. Under certain conditions, for example, plants may not adapt and survive. The occasional deviation from the usual allows scientists to sharpen their general concepts and theories. In the same vein, we may find that, when shopping, quality does not always accompany higher prices; figuring out under what conditions this happens improves our previous notion and makes us better shoppers.

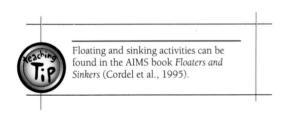

Floating and sinking activities can be found in the AIMS book *Floaters and Sinkers* (Cordel et al., 1995).

Children, too, can learn to reconstruct their concepts. A second-grade class places various small objects in water-filled pans to see which sink or float. Some children sum up what they learn by saying, "Light things float and heavy things sink." On hearing this, the teacher compares the weights of some things that floated

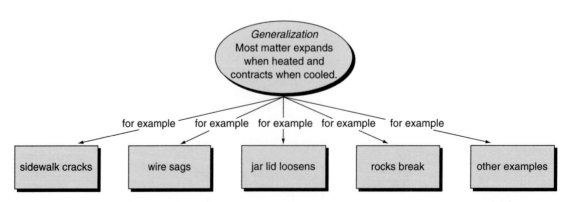

Figure 1–4
Generalizations enable us to relate and explain apparently different events.

and the weights of some things that sank. A few objects that floated are heavier than some objects that sank. This finding makes everyone look at the objects more carefully. Still, no one seems to know what to say. When the teacher calls attention to the objects' sizes, the young children soon conclude, "Things that are light for their size float. They sink when they are heavy for their size." This is a well-constructed concept based on thinking about two variables together—size and weight.

It is difficult when dealing with natural events to foresee all the conditions that might cause them to change. This is why scientists see their generalizations and theories as tentative, always subject to change with new data. It also explains why generalizations may be stated in **probabilities,** a frequent practice when dealing with living things: "Persons who eat fatty foods run a greater risk of heart attacks than those who do not eat these types of foods."

Probability refers to the possibility that a given event will occur and is often a ratio of the number of actual occurrences to the number of possible occurrences.

Parsimony ————

Scientists may offer competing explanations or theories to account for a natural phenomenon. This is likely when the phenomenon can only be observed indirectly (e.g., the makeup of the earth's core) or has happened in the distant past (e.g., extinction of the dinosaurs) and so cannot be fully tested. When competing theories account for the data equally well, scientists prefer the simplest theory that explains the data, referred to as **parsimony.** Scientists often refer to this as *Occham's Razor.* Like parsimony, this rule states that entities should not be multiplied unnecessarily and that the simplest theory is preferred. This principle helps keep the scientific enterprise more manageable and economical than it would be otherwise.

Parsimony literally means the quality of being stingy or miserly.

The Spiral Approach ————

If you switch to a higher grade level after several years of teaching, don't be surprised if a previously taught generalization shows up again in your curriculum guide. Because a science generalization consists of several concepts and accounts for many facts, students usually need more than one exposure to learn it well. So, curriculum developers often plan for children to study a science generalization several times, at increasing levels of complexity and abstraction and in different contexts, during Grades K–2, 3–5, or 6–8. This is known as the **spiral approach.** Consider an understanding of the nature of scientific investigation. This concept is studied from the early grades onward. Table 1–1 shows how the Benchmarks for Science Literacy (AAAS, 1993, pp. 6–7) are based on the spiral approach.

The **spiral approach** refers to the introduction of topics at increasing levels of complexity throughout the grade levels.

Notice the increasing complexity as the students move from kindergarten to Grade 8. In curriculum development, this is known as an *interrupted spiral approach* to teaching concepts and generalizations. The approach embodies the need to restudy ideas at higher levels of complexity while it avoids needless repetition.

The National Science Education Standards (NRC, 1996) are also based on this approach. Think back to the study of ants; the related K–4 Life Science Content Standard is as follows:

> As a result of activities in grades K–4, all students should develop understanding of the characteristics of organisms, life cycles of organisms, and organisms and environments. (p. 127)

Given this standard, students would study ants' characteristics, life cycles, and environments, as we saw in the activities described earlier. They would probably find

> **Table 1–1**

Spiral Approach of the Nature of Scientific Investigation

Grades K–2	Grades 3–5	Grades 6–8
When a science investigation is done the way it was done before, we expect to get a similar result.	Results of similar investigations are seldom exactly the same. Sometimes this is because of unexpected differences in the things being investigated, sometimes because of unrealized differences in the methods used or in the circumstances in which the investigation is carried out, and sometimes just because of uncertainties in observations. It is not always easy to tell which one.	When similar investigations give different results, the scientific challenge is to judge whether the differences are trivial or significant, and further studies are often needed to decide. Even with similar results, scientists may wait until an investigation has been repeated many times before accepting the results as being correct.
Science investigations generally work the same way in different places.		Scientific knowledge is subject to modifications as new information challenges prevailing theories and as a new theory leads to looking at old observations in a new way.

Elementary science textbook series often include planning tools that will indicate where your grade level is on the spiral approach continuum.

that the life cycle of the ant goes from egg, to larva, to pupa, to adult. They may also understand that ants are social and live in colonies. The 5–8 Life Science Standard is as follows:

> As a result of their activities in grades 5–8, all students should develop understanding of structure and function in living systems, reproduction and heredity, regulation and behavior, populations and ecosystems, and diversity and adaptations of organisms. (p. 155)

You now see that the students may look at specific structures and functions of the ant or systems within the ant. They would find that the jaws of worker ants are used for many tasks, such as defending the colony, caring for the larvae, and building the nest. Students would see that the *Solenopsis invicta* (red imported fire ant) was introduced from South America and is not native to the United States. Because it is not indigenous to the United States and has no natural enemies, it can destroy farmland, attack farm animals, and pose a hazard to humans.

The 9–12 grade-level standard is even more specialized and would look at ants from other biological levels, such as on the cellular level or how ants fit into the biosphere. Students may discover that *myrmecophiles*, or "ant lovers," may live in the ants' colony and actually benefit the ants by providing or storing food. Students may also learn that ants are omnivorous but that some species prefer one type of food. Students could also learn that ants forage in columns along chemical trails left by another ant or navigate with the use of polarized light.

As you may already know, conceptual complexity increases as students progress through the grades. You may be wondering whether process skills are developed and refined over time similar to concepts. You may even be unsure of what the process of science is all about.

Science Process and the Process Skills

Carl Sagan (1993) suggested that science is *a way of thinking*. He thought that it was more than a body of knowledge, but a *process* of finding out about the universe. Science is a way to look for regularities and is based on experimentation. What Sagan suggested is that the process of science leads to the concepts or generalizations that scientists share with each other and society.

Although the basic concepts and generalizations of science are tentative in nature, their "high quality" generally makes them last a long time. The quality is no accident. The processes and attitudes that scientists use in seeking regularities have been developed over many years to get the best results. Scientists realize the futility of trying to construct immutable laws or truths, but they also understand that the quality of their knowledge is linked to the quality of the *process* they use to generate knowledge. So, scientists continually try to sharpen their observations and their creative thinking about them.

Such an approach breeds a continuing curiosity, the willingness to listen to others' ideas, the caution to suspend judgment until enough facts are known, the readiness to try innovations, and many other qualities we collectively label *scientific attitude*. The following sections present principles that can benefit scientists, both young and old.

If the scientist's question "What do I know?" is linked to knowledge, the question "How do I know it?" reflects the habits of mind and attitude called process. At the heart of process is the nature of acceptable evidence. Science itself is often defined as a search for observable and reproducible evidence.

Evidence ————

In guiding children, help them understand that only data that can be detected by the senses are *observable evidence*. Much as a hand lens may have been required to observe the ants mentioned earlier in the chapter, sometimes instruments are used to extend the senses. The microscope allows us to see organisms too small for the unaided eye. A radio permits us to detect silent radiations from a broadcasting tower. But however aided, the senses must confirm that something tangible exists.

Most observations you will make in the elementary classroom will relate to observable evidence based on your students' use of their five senses.

Reproducible Evidence

Scientists assume that, under the same conditions, natural events are *reproducible*. That is, they will recur either naturally or in the laboratory under the same conditions. Any qualified scientist should be able to observe or reproduce the event if the necessary conditions are made available in the research literature. In the

Although they may have difficulty at times, your students should attempt to reproduce each other's data and experimental results for applicable experiments.

same way, your students should be able to reproduce each other's findings if they are recording and communicating their experiments. In either instance, questionable data will be evident. This underscores the need to follow up activities and to compare group results in your own classroom.

Interacting Objects

For a further test for evidence, envision a room where you live. Is the air temperature near the ceiling warmer or cooler than that near the floor? You probably will say warmer. Why? A common explanation we hear is that warm air rises. Think about it. Does it go up all by itself? Something is pushing it up. Cooler, heavier air displaces warmer, lighter air. In a confined space such as a room, the warm air is pushed up because there is nowhere else for it to go.

Correlation and Causation

Does breaking a mirror bring bad luck? Most children have had experiences with common superstitions, claims of magic, or astrology. These practices offer many chances to teach the difference between scientific cause-and-effect correlations and correlation without causation. For example, two events (e.g., breaking a mirror and then stubbing a toe) occurring one after the other does not provide a scientific reason to assume that one event caused the other.

One reason that people outside the scientific community adopt seemingly plausible but untrue ideas comes from their concept of authority. To the nonscientist, an "authority" may simply be someone who—by personality, position, or unsubstantiated eloquence—attracts much attention. But in science, what counts is tested evidence. For the scientist, untested scientific ideas receive scrutiny whether they come from a distinguished scientific veteran or a novice in the field.

Students have a natural tendency to seek "right" answers. You can overcome this through questioning strategies.

The Nature of Proof

It is better to refer to *testing a hypothesis* than to *proving a hypothesis* in elementary science. Seldom can we experimentally prove anything in an elementary classroom. We can perform well-designed experiments and observations that yield data that lend power to the ideas behind them. It is also wise to avoid saying to children that they are *right* or *wrong* when they give their ideas and explanations. Such behavior sets us up as arbitrary authorities who accept or reject proposals. Instead, we can simply ask questions like "What is your evidence that ants like to eat sweet foods?" or "Why do you think this explanation of the ant's reproductive cycle is valid?" This questioning invites everyone to examine the data.

Failure as Evidence

The perseverance of scientists is well known. Many continue on fruitlessly for years to find evidence that will support a hypothesis or solve a problem. Where is the reward? Their tenacity almost seems contrary to human nature. The makeup of science as an organized discipline helps us see the reason behind this perseverance.

For the most part, science is a cooperative enterprise whose practitioners are expected to share their findings with colleagues by means of publications, the Internet, or professional meetings. Time, money, and energy are spared when results are made known to others in the profession, even when there are no major breakthroughs. This sharing narrows the search or creates methodologies that benefit all.

In your science teaching, you'll often find it useful to organize students into small groups that work as independent units to test a hypothesis or to solve a problem. At times, some groups may report that they failed to find supporting evidence for their ideas. In this situation, recognize their shared efforts as positive contributions. Commend them, when possible, on the intelligence of the methods they use, and discuss how to improve those processes. This technique builds positive attitudes and shows everyone a part of the core of values related to science. It also is representative of what happens when scientists report research at their conventions.

See the Model Inquiry Unit, Team Formation and Concept Application sections of the companion CD for examples of students forming groups and reporting findings.

Science Processes and Objectivity

The quality of the evidence we collect usually depends on the quality of the processes we use and how objectively they are applied. Performing these processes in an impersonal manner, without allowing desires and expectations to influence the process or outcome, is being *objective*. The primary way to promote objectivity is to require that all reported findings be achievable by others under the same conditions. Procedures within each process can help make such replication possible. With the ant mound activity, all materials were placed an equal distance from the mound and in equal amounts. The distance and amount control variables help each group arrive at a similar conclusion. Another example of objectivity is a **double-blind** medical experiment in which a new drug is being tested.

Double-blind experiments are tests set up so that neither the experimenters nor the patient groups being sampled know who is receiving the drug and who is being given the placebo.

Children's Experiments and Objectivity

Children will often exchange objectivity with a personal expectation; in other words, they have an answer already in mind and work toward that answer. Similarly, they may want to get results that are close to what their peers may have gotten. They will eliminate all conflicting data to make sure that their findings match others.

Anthropomorphism and Objectivity

Objectivity may be difficult for children. An example of an impediment to objectivity is viewing nonhuman objects in a subjective way, a common occurrence among primary-level students. This influence on objectivity may come about because a child's environment often portrays fantasy over reality. Children commonly read stories or see cartoons in which animals talk, the sun smiles, and steam locomotives suffer distressingly as they huff and puff up a steep mountainside. Giving human characteristics to nonhuman objects is called **anthropomorphism.** Children usually have no trouble deciding whether such events are true or fictional, but sometimes they make anthropomorphic inferences without realizing it. These inferences can take several forms.

Science educators today view anthropomorphic statements in the context of children's early attempts to explain their world. As children age, these statements decrease and become easily correctable. Anthropomorphism in all its forms can be overcome when students learn how to make proper inferences from their observations.

Anthropomorphism may take the form of personification (instilling human personality traits onto animals), teleology (ascribing a conscious purpose to nonhuman things), or animism (endowing an object with life and human feelings).

The Importance of Working with Data

Children can learn scientific concepts by reading books or from other sources, but science processes must be learned by working with data. For instance, students may be told how

Standards Link

Science Inquiry Standard

As a result of activities in grades K–8, all students should develop

• **Abilities necessary to do scientific inquiry**

• **Understandings about scientific inquiry**

(Content Standard A, National Research Council, 1996, pp. 121 & 143)

the period of a pendulum is determined, and some may understand and remember it. But students who are given a few materials and guided to figure this out for themselves soon count the number of swings per minute (measuring). They also try various ways of changing the swing rate (experimenting), taking notes of what they did (communicating), making graphs (more communicating), and drawing conclusions from their findings (inferring). These children are more likely to remember and apply the principle of pendulums throughout their lives to clocks, playground swings, and metronomes.

Perhaps what makes processing data so effective in improving children's thinking is that the children can actually observe the consequences of good and bad thinking. The objects they work with will usually "tell" them if they are on the right track: Snails will eat only what they are adapted to eat, and toy boats will sink like real boats when they are not buoyant. Science is a good subject in which to demonstrate observable consequences because it presents so many opportunities to test ideas with concrete materials.

The Interactive Nature of Process, Knowledge, and the Nature of Science

Process thinking is typically neglected in science education. One reason is that many teachers are unsure about how to facilitate hands-on learning of the process skills. In response, some curriculum writers overemphasize process teaching to the point that they neglect subject-matter content. Either extreme runs against the inseparable nature of process and knowledge that is required for scientific inquiry as suggested in the NRC Science Inquiry Standard.

Barr (1994) refers to content, processes, and attitudes that are consistent with the nature of science as "essential elements" (p. 238). In other words, scientific problems need to come from the student's own conceptual framework and be relevant to the student. The problems should help construct meaningful understandings of content and process skills. They should answer a question that can be later compared with what scientists already know. We expect elementary students to experiment with ants and determine which types of foods ants respond to as different foods are placed near the mound. This activity incorporates what students have learned about ants and involves experimentation consistent with the nature of science and scientific inquiry. What we would not encourage is that the students be provided a list of some of the 10,000 different types of ants and their food sources. Neither would we want a series of activities involving scientific skills with an absence of follow-up discussions and concept development about how ants interact with the environment.

The subject-matter background of concepts and generalizations gives purpose, meaning, and significance to what is observed. A physician's professional preparation and experience do not provide the ability to observe subtle weather signs. Likewise, a meteorologist's professional training and experience do not provide accuracy in observing subtle disease symptoms. Neither scientist is specialized enough to do the other's work effectively. Their background knowledge is inseparably mixed with the process of observation. The

Children's curiosity is enhanced through science experiences such as the exploration of ant environments.

same can be said of the students you will teach. The lessons you facilitate must be consistent with their developmental needs. Your curriculum must give children continual opportunities to learn thinking processes within a wide variety of subject-matter areas and conditions.

The trend today is to guide children to apply thinking and problem-solving strategies in all subject areas. Because process and subject-matter concepts are open ended, students can get better at constructing new concepts throughout their lives. An effective science curriculum gives chances to teach process thinking within all topics at all grade levels. Enabling you to identify and maximize these opportunities is an important objective of this book. We further explore process skills in Chapter 4.

Teaching Children

The application of concepts and processes of science to society's problems is the reason that science education is such an important subject in school. Because we are dealing with elementary-level students, however, we need to match what is to be taught with the students' interests and developmental levels.

If you have heard the expression "To a child who's discovered the hammer, all the world is a nail," you will notice that it illustrates the broad curiosity and inner need of children to try things for themselves whenever they are free to do so. Science education is of great value to children because it enhances these and other attributes that loom so large in their development. But the nature of childhood also makes us recognize several other realities.

For example, because broad generalizations and skills are so useful in science study, it is tempting to increase their scope so that they apply to more and more phenomena. This makes it difficult to know when to stop being increasingly abstract in thinking and remote from common experience. As a generalization or process approaches the most advanced scientific model, it is less likely that children can learn it or will even want to try. To persist is simply to have them bite off more than they can chew. So, teaching generalizations about molecules in the primary years, for example, or insisting that all variables be controlled in experiments is likely to be self-defeating. Our elementary students will comprehend that ants may bite and are male and female. They may have trouble understanding hymenopterans' specialized mouthparts or the concept of how males originate from unfertilized eggs and females from fertilized eggs.

It is important for children to understand and see the purpose of what they are doing. Also, they need to reach short-range goals as they progress toward goals that are farther away. Children usually learn best when working with concrete or semiconcrete materials and limited generalizations. This is a key factor when working with young students.

It is unlikely that any publisher or curriculum office can develop a program that suits every child or class. It will be your responsibility to create a suitable match between students and the curriculum. This task will require understanding how children learn science, children's developmental levels, and what is required of your science education program.

Guiding Documents for Science Education

Refer to the *http://www.prenhall.com/peters* address for links to the online versions of the standards, benchmarks, and other documents.

How can you tell what is appropriate for your students to learn? One way to see the types of processes and concepts that students at a particular grade level should be familiar with is to look at two of the guiding documents in science education. We have already referred to *National Science Education Standards* (NRC, 1996) and *Benchmarks for Science Literacy* (AAAS, 1993). The benchmarks were developed as part of Project 2061 (AAAS, 1989), which was an undertaking of the AAAS to help reform science, mathematics, and technology education. They focus on science for all Americans. The standards were a national collaborative headed by the NRC, again with the focus on scientific literacy for all. There is a high level of correlation between the two projects. Many states have adopted the benchmarks, the standards, or a state-specific variation of one of the projects as their own statewide standards for which you will be accountable in your classroom. We refer to the benchmarks and the standards throughout the text.

Are there other considerations besides process and content? The authors of Project 2061 and the standards both discuss societal perspectives as they relate to science education.

Societal Considerations

We began this chapter with a discussion of the nature of science and how students observed ant mounds in the schoolyard. These observations provided the basis for deeper exploration into ants—allowing students to further construct concepts of ants and their behaviors, as well as scientific process skills. A well-planned curriculum usually contains many of these everyday applications.

It is important to educate people and to change people's attitudes in order to cope with today's challenges. Naturally, the education system plays a major role in this process. For example, science education is focusing on such topics as AIDS, endangered species, wetlands, environmentally safe food, uncontaminated drinking water, multicultural career opportunities, and gender equity in science-related careers.

Every society wants its contributing members to be literate—that is, to have enough background knowledge and ability to make informed decisions, communicate, produce, and improve the general welfare. In a society as advanced and dynamic as the one we live in today, the amount of information increases at an accelerating rate. Under such conditions, people need a common core of knowledge. A common ground allows us to communicate more efficiently with one another and facilitates public policy.

Literacy serves as the common ground for discussing and understanding diverse and complex issues. Issues such as toxic waste dumps, in vitro fertilization, AIDS, nuclear accidents, the hole in the ozone layer, the greenhouse effect, genetically altered foods, and artificial body parts are examined in our everyday encounters with the media. Knowledge of specific technical information may be considered when making purchases. For example, when buying a car, it is helpful to have some knowledge of horsepower, fuel economy, and antilock brakes. To secure a job, we are expected to know something about the nature of the position we are seeking. Our functioning and survival in our society are linked to literacy.

Science literacy is imperative in a society that leans heavily on science and technology. The AAAS (1993) views literacy in the following way:

See *http://www.prenhall.com/peters* for links to Nova Science in the News and the National Academies Science in the Headlines.

> Project 2061 promotes literacy in science, mathematics, and technology in order to help people live interesting, responsible, and productive lives. In a culture increasingly pervaded by science, mathematics, and technology, science literacy requires understandings and habits of mind that enable citizens to grasp what those enterprises are up to, to make some sense of how the natural and designed worlds work, to think critically and independently, to recognize and weigh alternative explanations of events and design trade offs, and to deal sensibly with problems that involve evidence, numbers, patterns, logical arguments, and uncertainties. (p. XI)

All children need a rich array of firsthand experiences to grow toward a full measure of science literacy. Quality science programs make it possible for advanced study, which can lead to many occupational choices and benefits to all society. An important area related to societal considerations is equity as suggested by the NRC Equity Program Standard.

Equity

Think for a moment about what the world would be like if women cultivated half of the technological developments. What advances would be made? What current problems would be minimized? What if people of color developed an equivalent proportion of scientific discoveries? How might the world be different? Estimates are that at the time of publication of this book, 85% or more of the workforce is composed of minorities, persons with disabilities, and women (Florence, 1992). How is this new workforce affecting science?

Current science education reforms promote scientific literacy for all students—or equity—as their central theme (AAAS, 1998). The belief is that science should be comprehensible, accessible, and exciting for *all* students from kindergarten through Grade 12. In reality, these goals are rarely achieved, *especially for underrepresented populations.* The National Science Foundation (NSF, 1996) reports that we see a typical pattern of males scoring higher than females and white students scoring higher than black or Hispanic students on national assessments.

Science has long been studied in the traditions of the white, Anglo male. This focus makes it difficult for females or minorities to place science in an understandable social context. Think about a living scientist. Is this person male or female? Is this a person of color or white? What does this person look like? Stop for a moment and consider your image of a scientist. Is your image stereotypical?

Children often view a scientist as a white male with a lab coat, a pocket protector full of pencils, and unkempt hair—a nerd with glasses. This view furthers the problem of equity. Not only do most boys not want to be this "scientist," but what woman or minority would want to be perceived as this image? As a teacher, you will probably pass your views of a scientist on to your students.

You can begin to remediate stereotypical images by bringing local minority and female scientists into the classroom.

The Language of Science

Another way to help correct the imbalance of science achievement is to think about how science is taught at the elementary level. If science is just rote learning of disjointed facts, it becomes an especially difficult enterprise for minorities who do not have a strong command of the language. It is no wonder that these students do not elect to take more than the required minimum of science courses as they go on to high school. It's surprising that every student is not eventually turned off by this language-intensive, fact-only approach.

In an attempt to help students understand the "language" of the scientist, the National Science Teachers Association (NSTA) published *The Language of Science* (Mandell, 1974, p. 1). The author of this book equates the language of science to a foreign language and stresses the importance of *knowing the language* in order to be a participant in the science classroom. Along these lines, Karen Gallas (1995) discusses why "science talk" is so important for children and why teachers need to help them develop the language of science. As Jay Lemke (1990) puts it,

> It is not surprising that those who succeed in science tend to be like those who define the "appropriate" way to talk science: male rather than female, white rather than black, middle- and upper-middle-class, native English speakers, standard dialect speakers, committed to the values of Northern European middle-class culture. (p. 138)

What these three authors, and many others, are saying is that teachers need to understand that the language of science is often a barrier to equity in the classroom.

Another major consideration in the development of a quality elementary science program is the matter of gender equity. As an educator, it will be your responsibility to select science textbooks, teaching materials, and methodologies that present realistic role models for men and women in all walks of life. In addition to arranging for female role models to visit your classroom, you may want to try assigning student biographies of famous female scientists. The importance of this issue cannot be understated as we go into an era where we will need a growing number of science and technology professionals that are women.

The current science literacy problem that exists in many minority populations may really just be a forewarning of an increasing science literacy problem with all students. Your contribution in the classroom will have a major impact on the types of career decisions your students make.

Teacher as Researcher

One way you can grow as a professional is to research your own teaching. This is an especially important concept in science, where the curriculum is not as defined as in the basal reading program, for example. Science and teaching both involve inquiry and experimentation. As you are aware, most of us were not exposed to these two types of activities in elementary school. Therefore, we need to study how we as teachers are effecting positive changes in our classrooms where science teaching is concerned. This is not to say that we should be doing dissertation-level educational research. The teacher as a researcher is a professional who analyzes his or her teaching practices and attempts to make the classroom a better learning environment.

One way to begin is to relate your classroom teaching to a science endeavor. You begin with an observation. In this case, let's say it is an observation of a teaching method that is not working or a student behavior that is not what you had hoped for in your classroom. Then, you research the problem and collect information on which to base a hypothesis. Like other scientists, you review journals for ideas and information regarding your observations. Next, you set up an experimental design to test your hypothesis. Most of the time, this is a modified version of what you found while reviewing the professional publications. You then carry out the experiment and collect data. The data may be student interviews about the experiment, personal observations, audio- or videotapes, or a personal journal of observations. Once the data are collected, you analyze them in terms of your original hypothesis. Did the experiment work out? The final step is to share the information with colleagues. This is an important step, whether the experiment was successful or not. If you were successful, other teachers may want to try your approach. If you were unsuccessful, it may indicate that the other teachers will have to modify the experiment or try it with their classes to see if it works for them.

See *http://www.prenhall.com/peters* for links to information related to teachers as researchers.

Metaphors

One way to analyze your role in the classroom is to characterize your role as a teacher through a metaphor. For example, if you characterize yourself as a "coach," then this contrasts sharply with the metaphor of a "king." A coach would assist children in development of skills, whereas a king would clearly be the ruler of subjects. Other examples of metaphors are the teacher as a "grandmother," a "ship's captain," a "military officer," a "policewoman," a "psychologist," or a "resource manager" (see Lorsbach [1995] for an example of metaphors as applied to elementary science education or Briscoe [1991] for a study of a specific teacher who used metaphors to assist in teacher change).

No matter which metaphor you choose, reflective teaching through the use of teacher research is important to your ongoing professional development and the success of your students. Thinking about metaphors can help you explore your role as a teacher. For instance, thinking about changes to your current teaching practices in the light of a "new metaphor" can help a teacher develop new teaching methodologies consistent with the desired changes. If you change from being a "dictator" to a "speaker of the house," this would have some obvious effects on your teaching routines. Students would be able to have a say in their education instead of you deciding everything for them.

It is important to consider metaphors as a means to conceptualize your teaching and beliefs. If you find that your metaphor is like the "teacher as a comic" or "teacher as a drill sergeant," then careful selection of a new metaphor (or multiple metaphors) may be warranted.

See *http://www.prenhall.com/peters* **for examples of metaphors for teachers.**

Summary

1. The nature of science suggests that (a) there is no single set or sequence of steps in a scientific investigation, (b) scientific knowledge is subject to change, (c) scientific knowledge must be at least partially supported by empirical evidence, (d) scientific knowledge is partially the product of the creative imagination of the scientist, (e) given the importance of scientists' individual creativity, scientific knowledge is necessarily subjective to some degree, and (f) scientific knowledge is a product of both observation and inference.
2. Scientists use tools and organized ways to search for patterns in objects and events. They generalize the data they collect and form explanations in the form of principles, theories, and laws. Elementary students can construct and refine their own concepts by using similar methods.
3. Children need to experience the processes of science, including making observations, interacting with objects, testing hypotheses, working with data, and experimenting.
4. An interrelationship exists between science and society. It is important to understand the roles of women and minorities in the scientific enterprise as you plan and facilitate science lessons.

Reflection

1. One way to begin exploring how you will teach elementary science is to investigate your attitudes toward science. Fill in the information in Figure 1–5 and be ready to share it with your classmates. If you have time, compare your attitudes with those of your parents, friends, or study partner.
2. Write down your memory of elementary science experiences. Which of these experiences are hands-on activities that promote the nature of science and scientific understanding? Which are entertainment, show-and-tell, or memorization activities? Be ready to share with others the implications of why you would remember one experience more than another experience, or which have helped more with later science experiences.
3. Observe an elementary science class at your practicum site and note how the teacher provides equity in terms of gender. Does the teacher call on boys more than girls? Are the boys dominating the experiments? Are the girls afraid to answer questions or provide explanations? Think of ways to promote equity in your classroom, and share these with the class.
4. Use the resource *Multicultural Women of Science: Three Centuries of Contributions* (Harris-Stewart, 1996, Maywood, NJ: The Peoples Publishing Group) to enhance your own understanding of the contributions of multicultural women to the field of science. This book contains many hands-on activities. An increasing number of other

Positive	Better	Average	Poor	Negative
Inclusive				Exclusive
Popular				Weird
Invigorating				Exhausting
Safe				Dangerous
Fun				Boring
Beneficial				Harmful
Rewarding				Punishment
Involving				Lethargic
Important				Trivial
Innovative				Ancestral
Enjoyable				Mundane
Influential				Worthless
Powerful				Ineffective
Exciting				Monotonous

Figure 1–5
Attitudes toward science and science teaching. Place a check in the box that best describes your attitude.

related resources are available for use with your students. The books *From Sorceress to Scientist: Biographies of Women Physical Scientists* (Nies, 1990, Tarzana, CA: California Video Institute) and *From Priestess to Physician: Biographies of Women Life Scientists* (Nies, 1996, Tarzana, CA: California Video Institute) both include biographies, demonstrations, and lab activities. Use activities and stories from these two books to help promote positive female role models with your practicum class and future elementary students.

5. *Teaching About Evolution and the Nature of Science* (National Academy of Sciences, 1998, Washington, DC: National Academy Press) is available online (*http://books.nap.edu/html/evolution98/*) and includes activities that relate to the nature of science. Try some of these activities and share them with your classmates.

References

American Association for the Advancement of Science (AAAS). (1989). *Science for all Americans.* Washington, DC: Author.

American Association for the Advancement of Science (AAAS). (1993). *Benchmarks for science literacy.* New York: Oxford University Press.

American Association for the Advancement of Science (AAAS). (1998). *Blueprints for reform.* New York: Oxford University Press.

Barr, B. B. (1994). Research on problem solving: Elementary school. In D. L. Gable (Ed.), *Handbook of research on science teaching and learning* (pp. 237–247). New York: Macmillan.

Briscoe, C. (1991). The dynamic interactions among beliefs, role metaphors, and teaching practices: A case study of teacher change. *Science Education, 75,* 186–199.

Chinery, M. (1991). *Life story: Ant.* New York: Troll Associates.

Climo, S. (1995). *The little red ant and the great big crumb: A Mexican fable.* New York: Clarion Books.

Cole, J. (1996). *The magic school bus gets ants in its pants.* New York: Scholastic.

Cordel, B., Lile, D., McKibban, M., West, G., Laidlaw, W., Landon, K., Youngs, D., & Wiebe, A. (1995). *Floaters and sinkers.* Fresno, CA: AIMS Education Foundation.

Council for Environmental Education. (1992). *Project WILD.* Bethesda, MD: Author.

Demuth, P. D. (1994). *Those amazing ants.* New York: Simon & Schuster.

Dorros, A. (1987). *Ant cities.* New York: HarperCollins.

Florence, P. (1992). *Northwest women in science: Women making a difference—A role model guide.* Richland, WA: Northwest College and University Association for Science, Northwest Women in Science.

Gallas, K. (1995). *Talking their way into science: Hearing children's questions and theories, responding with curricula.* New York: Teachers College Press.

Gazlay, S. (1998). *Field detectives: Investigating playground habitats.* Fresno, CA: AIMS Education Foundation.

Hepworth, C. (1992). *Antics!* Los Angeles: Putnam & Grosset.

Hoose, P. M., Tilley, D., & Hoose, H. (1998). *Hey little ant.* Berkeley, CA: Tricycle Press.

Imes, R. (1992). *The practical entomologist.* New York: Simon & Schuster.

Lawrence Hall of Science. (1996). *Ant homes under the ground.* Berkeley, CA: Author.

Lederman, N. G. (1992). Students' and teachers' conceptions of the nature of science: A review of research. *Journal of Research in Science Teaching, 29,* 331–359.

Lemke, J. L. (1990). *Talking science: Language learning and values.* Norwood, NJ: Ablex.

Lorsbach, A. W. (1995). The use of metaphor by prospective elementary teachers to understand learning environments. *Journal of Elementary Science Education, 7*(2), 1–26.

Losi, C. A. (1997). *The 512 ants on Sullivan Street.* New York: Scholastic.

Mandell, A. (1974). *The language of science.* Arlington, VA: National Science Teachers Association.

Most, B. (1980). *There's an ant in Anthony.* New York: Mulberry Books.

National Research Council (NRC). (1996). *National science education standards.* Washington, DC: National Academy Press.

National Science Foundation (NSF). (1996). *The learning curve.* Washington, DC: Author.

Parker, S. (1999). *It's an ant's life.* Pleasantville, NY: Reader's Digest.

Pinczes, E. (1993). *One hundred hungry ants.* Boston: Houghton Mifflin.

Pinczes, E. (1995). *A remainder of one.* Boston: Houghton Mifflin.

Sagan, C. (1993). *Broca's brain: Reflections on the romance of science.* New York: Random House.

Steiner, T. J. (1998). *A bug's life.* Burbank, CA: Mouse Works.

Teacher Created Materials. (1997). *Thematic unit: Ants.* Huntington, CA: Author.

http://www.prenhall.com/peters   29

Suggested Readings

Alcoze, T., Bradley, C., Hernandez, J., Kashima, T., Kane, I. M., & Madrazo, G. (1993). *Multiculturalism in mathematics, science, and technology: Readings and activities*. Menlo Park, CA: Addison-Wesley. (A teacher resource for exploring many cultures and global perspectives.)

American Association for the Advancement of Science (AAAS). (1993). The nature of science. In *Benchmarks for science literacy* (pp. 3–21). New York: Oxford University Press. (Explores the nature of science in the context of various grade levels.)

Dunbar, R. (1995). *The trouble with science*. Cambridge, MA: Harvard University Press. (A history of science and the nature of science.)

Hatton, J., & Plouffe, P. B. (1997). *Science and its ways of knowing*. Upper Saddle River, NJ: Prentice-Hall. (A collection of essays showing the relationships between fact and theory and the nature of science.)

National Research Council (NRC). (1998). *Every child a scientist: Achieving scientific literacy for all*. Washington, DC: National Academy Press.

National Research Council (NRC). (1999). *Selecting instructional materials: A guide for K–12 science*. Washington, DC: National Academy Press.

National Research Council (NRC). (2000). *Inquiry and the national science education standards*. Washington, DC: National Academy Press.

National Science Resources Center, National Academy of Sciences, Smithsonian Institution. (1997). *Science for all children: A guide to improving science education in your school district*. Washington, DC: National Academy Press. (A comprehensive book on how science education can be changed at the elementary level.)

Chapter 2

Constructing Science Experiences

Children's Learning

Dr. Ken Tobin
University of Pennsylvania

"Hold it! Hold it! Oh, no! Ana, you've got to hold it while I connect the roof on." Michael is agitated with Ana. They have been working on building a castle for 3 days now, and still the walls will not stay up. They planned a good castle, and the drawings looked very good, but the materials Ms. Roberts had given them to build with were not working.

Ana is feeling grumpy about this whole activity. It is not her fault that the walls will not stay up. Every time she holds them up, the pins come loose. Why can't they use glue anyway? "Castles are not made out of pins and straws!" she asserts.

Ms. Roberts is pleased with the activities. The students are busy, and they are doing science. Furthermore, the activities in which they are engaged involve manipulatives and an opportunity to exchange ideas orally. Further, they integrate drawing, writing, social studies, and literature. The idea of building castles arose from their studies of Germany. Importantly, they allow the students to engage in problem solving. Ms. Roberts perceives her role to be that of a facilitator: closely observing her students, learning from listening to them, and helping them meet their goal of building a castle.

Teachers like Ms. Roberts have long accepted that a hands-on approach is an appropriate way to teach science. Recently the term *hands-on/minds-on* has become a popular way to describe school science. Ms. Roberts's Grade 3 science lesson is typical of what can be observed in many elementary classrooms. The activity is consistent with a hands-on/minds-on metaphor and the teacher's role as facilitator. However, even though Ms. Roberts's students are involved in an extensive hands-on activity that promotes communication and problem solving, the development of scientific ideas is absent. Scientific knowledge does not reside in the materials the students use. Rather, scientific knowledge needs to be co-constructed in interactions in which students and teacher interact verbally by using a shared language during the activity. For example, the realization that a structure can be made rigid through the use of triangular braces is a reasonable goal for the activity described. But in this case, it is unlikely that the students will construct that understanding.

And even if they do include triangular braces in their structures, it is unlikely that they will associate that inclusion with increased rigidity of the structure. Manipulations of materials are a context for rich conversations in which those who know science can facilitate the learning of those who do not know. It is essential to student understanding that the teacher mediate the language of the child and the language of science. This does not imply a return to the days when teachers transmitted facts in lectures or when the principal learning resource was a textbook. But it does require students to talk science—in ways that connect their experiences in other subject areas and the relevant contexts to their lives outside school.

How are the children in Vignette 2–1 learning?

As their teacher, what would you do to increase the students' scientific concept of structures?

Teaching is seen as the actions or methods used by an educator to create an environment that will promote learning by students.

Learning is a process by which students' knowledge, attitudes, behaviors, and beliefs are formulated or modified.

These questions relate to the **teaching** and **learning** of elementary science. Think back to your elementary school experiences. How did you learn about scientific ideas and concepts of strength as discussed in the vignette? Was the "body of knowledge" you learned handed down from the teacher through worksheets, class reading of the textbook, activities, or lectures? As you learned, were you actively engaged in seeking new knowledge? Did you team up with others to help one another learn? Did the teacher emphasize scientific understanding? Were these understandings useful in other situations, both in school and outside school? Answering these questions provides you an indication of a teaching perspective and a perspective of how children can learn science more effectively.

Effective science learning is crucial for your future elementary students. Today's global society is experiencing rapid changes in scientific knowledge and the application of scientific knowledge in the form of technology. Current predictions indicate that the total amount of knowledge doubles every 18 months or less and that 80% of the scientists who have ever lived are alive right now (Petersen, 1994, 1997). The science experiences you provide will develop the foundation your students need to continue meaningful learning experiences throughout their lives. Thus, a first step to successful science teaching is to consider your own views of science and science learning.

Paradigms

Teachers should be aware that science is not just a body of knowledge but a paradigm through which to see the world. (American Association for the Advancement of Science [AAAS], 1998, p. 202)

Take a moment to think about how you currently view the nature of science and science learning. Is it different now from when you were in elementary school? If so, what changed your viewpoint? Maybe you are science phobic because of past experiences. If you are, then what could have been done differently to dispel your fear of science? What influences how science is currently taught and how you will teach science? The current paradigm for teaching and learning science is seen as integral to educational reform.

Understanding Paradigms ────────

Where did the idea of paradigms begin? Thomas Kuhn (1962) first defined a **paradigm** as a commonly accepted viewpoint. He defined a *paradigm shift* as a radical change in this viewpoint. For example, the paradigm of a sun-centered solar system replaced the paradigm of the earth-centered solar system. Paradigm shifts occur because scientists use experimentation and new technologies to better explain observed scientific phenomena.

> A **paradigm** is a typical viewpoint or ideal example that provides a model for all related processes or systems.

Scientific discussion, experimentation, and publication generally center on current paradigms. Deviating from the paradigm is apt to place a scientist's research funding and acceptance of publications in jeopardy. Ideas that are inconsistent with current paradigms are generally dismissed. Occasionally, however, because of advances in technology or because of new research, a paradigm shift and an accompanying revolution in the scientific community occur. Old ideas are discarded as a new theory emerges and becomes the dominant paradigm. An example is the presentation of the plate tectonics theory in 1956. The plate tectonics theory changed how scientists viewed the movement of continents and seafloor spreading. Even as paradigms in science change our perspectives and understanding of how the world works, they also transcend science education and our understanding of how to better teach science.

Standards Link

Science Teaching and Learning Standard

Teachers of science guide and facilitate learning. In doing this, teachers

- **Focus and support inquiries while interacting with students.**
- **Orchestrate discourse among students about scientific ideas.**
- **Challenge students to accept and share responsibility for their own learning.**
- **Recognize and respond to student diversity and encourage all students to participate fully in science learning.**
- **Encourage and model the skills of scientific inquiry, as well as the curiosity, openness to new ideas and data, and skepticism that characterize science.**

(Teaching Standard B, National Research Council, 1996, p. 3)

Paradigms of Science Education ────────

Looking at the research related to the national science education standards of the National Research Council (NRC, 1996) and Project 2061 of the American Association for the Advancement of Science (AAAS, 1993), we find that **constructivism** is the current paradigm in science education. This paradigm is reflected in the Science Teaching and Learning Standard in the Standards Link.

> **Constructivism** is seen as constructing personal knowledge from your experiences.

The authors of this standard provide a research-based explanation of how children engage in inquiry to learn science. They underscore the need for teachers to guide and facilitate learning in science and to provide inquiry experiences for their students. They also emphasize the importance of student discourse.

You will notice that **inquiry** is a strand throughout the Science Teaching and Learning Standard as it is throughout the standards document. Figure 2–1 contains some characteristics of classroom inquiry.

As you read about different perspectives of teaching and learning science in this chapter, consider the ability of each perspective to support scientific inquiry as outlined in Figure 2–1.

> **Inquiry** is a term used to describe the activities that students engage in to help them construct knowledge and understanding of scientific ideas.

- Learners are engaged by scientifically oriented questions.
- Learners give priority to evidence, which allows them to develop and evaluate explanations that address scientifically oriented questions.
- Learners formulate explanations from evidence to address scientifically oriented questions.
- Learners evaluate their explanations in light of alternative explanations, particularly those reflecting scientific understanding.
- Learners communicate and justify their proposed explanations.

Figure 2–1
Essential features of classroom inquiry.
Source: From *Inquiry and the National Science Education Standards: A Guide For Teaching and Learning* (p. 25). Copyright © 2000 by the National Academy of Sciences. Courtesy of the National Academy Press, Washington, DC.

Children's Learning and Your Classroom ────────

Again pause for a moment and contemplate yourself teaching science in the elementary classroom. What methods will you employ to be consistent with the standards? Will the continuous changes in science and technology make it impossible for you to teach science as you learned it in elementary school? Will you be able to engage students effectively in understanding science?

Thinking about and sharing your viewpoints related to the questions and statements above may bring about many new questions. As you continue to read and reflect on this chapter, you will come to understand constructivism. You will see why it has emerged as the paradigm for knowledge construction in science.

Constructivism

What does it mean to know?

What does it mean to be a knower?

Is there a relationship between the knower and the known?

See the Model Inquiry Unit section of the companion CD for examples of inquiry and the constructivist approach to teaching.

These questions may be too philosophical for you at first glance. They are, however, at the heart of the constructivist-learning paradigm. The knower–known relationship is also the basis for the current reform movement in education. This movement emphasizes the *active role of the learner* as constructing her or his own knowledge. It also places the teacher in a more facilitative role in the learning process.

Constructivism is the belief that all knowledge is constructed by an individual, not passed on from the teacher to the student (Tobin & Tippins, 1993). When using constructivism as a referent for science teaching, student learning is maximized. This occurs because the teacher's role is to facilitate the learning process, as opposed to transferring knowledge. The teacher's purpose is to provide the best materials and learning situations to make learning individually meaningful for each student. Students change in some way as a result of the learning. They may replace a prior belief about a science concept, add to their existing knowledge, or modify something they already know. The learning, or construction, takes place in a context of what each learner already has in her or his mental store.

Cobern (1993) likens the constructivist approach to a construction site where existing structures are the foundation upon which to build new knowledge. To get a better idea of constructivism in general, look at the following teaching example. Ask yourself questions such as Will this activity provide a meaningful learning experience for the students? or How will the children learn?

A General Constructivist Approach to Teaching

Ms. Terrell, referring to the K–4 Earth and Space Standard D, has developed this objective: "The students will discover the observable changes in the moon as it travels across the sky over the coming months" (NRC, 1996, pp. 130, 134). As she prepares for the phases of the moon activity, she asks the students what they have observed in relation to the moon as it appears in the sky.

Ms. Terrell then asks the students to put together a science journal with blank pages. Today there's a new moon, and she instructs students to look at the moon each day or night, As it becomes visible, students should date each journal page and draw and describe the moon they observe in the sky. Each day, they will compare their pictures with each other's and to predictions they find on the Internet and in the newspaper. They will also explore children's books such as *The Moon Seems to Change* (Branley, 1987) and *Day Light, Night Light* (Branley, 1975). At the end of this exploration period, Ms. Terrell will have the students discuss what they found out and generate ideas about this phenomenon.

To test their ideas, Ms. Terrell brings in a homemade **astronomy dome.** She instructs the class from inside the dome. There, she has one student hold up a spotlight to indicate the sun. Other students hold up a model earth and moon. Together, they replicate the motions of the earth, the sun, and the moon. They demonstrate what happened throughout the month as the moon circled the earth. Ms. Terrell asks the students to explain what is going on and whether this matches with their moon drawings. As an informal assessment, students shade in a series of blank circles that represent moon images as the sun would light them. Finally, the class discusses the vocabulary associated with the phases of the moon.

> An **astronomy dome** is made from two sheets of black painter's plastic taped side by side with box tape to form a "dome." A box fan is taped to one end to inflate the dome, and the other end is sealed shut.

As you may infer from this constructivist-based lesson, students have learned the material in a context that they can understand. They will readily recall the information in the future and apply the processes they learned in this and other situations.

Students have observed the **waxing** and **waning** of the moon and recorded it in illustrations. The terms and processes make sense because this relevant context is provided. The learners are engaging in activities that relate to their own previous experiences. To better understand constructivism, let's look at an early influence on the constructivist approach to teaching and learning.

> **Waxing** refers to increasing in size; **waning** refers to decreasing in size.

Piaget and Constructivism

Often viewed as an early constructivist, Jean Piaget focused his research on children's construction of knowledge through **equilibration** (Bettencourt, 1993; Bybee & Sund, 1990). Piaget's theory involves mediating mental processes (Labinowicz, 1980). To understand these processes, it is important to understand the notion of a schema. A **schema** is viewed as a concept, pattern of action, theory, model, or idea that is part of our

> **Equilibration** is a process by which a learner compensates for a mental dilemma and constructs new knowledge.

> A **schema** is a cognitive framework used to store and organize information such as knowledge and experiences.

cognitive repertoire. *Schemata* (the plural of *schema*) are "meaningful units" that are used over and over again (Henriques, 1990, p. 143). Schemata become relevant as we need them. They help us function on a daily basis and deal with new experiences. For schemata to be effective, they need the capability to be modified to fit new experiences through the processes of **assimilation** and **accommodation.** We assimilate when we adjust our schemata to include new details; we try to transform incoming information so that it fits with our existing way of thinking (Siegler, 1986). Accommodation means restructuring our schemata so that we can make sense of situations.

An example of assimilation is when a child has a schema that involves birds such as robins, sparrows, and pigeons. When the child sees a new type of bird, like an osprey or hawk, she or he may need to adjust the schema to assimilate the new information of a much larger bird that is flying overhead. Later, if the child sees a penguin or an ostrich at the zoo, assimilation may not be as useful. This new information includes birds that do not fly. The child may not be able to simply assimilate the new information. Now the child must adapt her or his ways of thinking to new experiences (Siegler, 1986). This process is called accommodation because the schema can now accommodate the new information.

The result of the accommodation is that the child's schema can now accept birds that fly and birds that do not fly. Equilibration is primary to children's construction of reality. Equilibration involves both assimilation and accommodation. It is the overall interaction between existing ways of thinking and a new experience (Siegler, 1986). For example, with the phases of the moon activity, the students may not have known that the moon *reflects* light. Their schema may have been that objects in the night sky all *give off* light. Certainly assimilation and accommodation are useful in resolving this **disequilibrium.**

In general, Piaget sees cognitive development as resolving the disequilibrium that may exist in the child's mind. In his theory of development, equilibration, through assimilation and accommodation, is the foundation for significant developmental changes in the child. What does this say to us as future teachers? We can assist children in building their neural connections. To better understand how, it is helpful to take into consideration Piaget's stages of development.

Piaget's Stages of Development

Piaget developed his theory based on his observations and studies regarding scientific conceptions of children. With this, Piaget proposed stages in the development of thought at different ages. The three stages that elementary teachers are most concerned with are the preoperational stage, from about 2 to 7 years old; concrete operational stage, from about 7 to 12 years old; and the formal operational stage, from about 12 years old and beyond (see Appendix E).

Children who are *preoperational* are not yet able to do a certain kind of thinking. Piaget calls this kind of thinking **operations,** or mental tasks. The latter part of the stage, which lasts from about ages 4 to 7, is known as the *intuitive thought substage.* Because this is the time when most children begin school, we'll start our study of children's thinking at the intuitive period of their mental development.

"Intuitive thought" explicates well how 4- to 7-year-olds think. They typically use their sense impressions or intuition rather than logic in forming judgments. They also tend to remember only one thing at a time. A common activity to demonstrate intuitive thought is to have a child roll out a ball of clay and then to ask the child about what happened. Children at this stage will suggest that there is "more clay" because it is rolled out and appears longer.

Children who are *concrete operational,* in contrast, are logical thinkers, but the ideas they consider must be tied to concrete materials they can manipulate. They must

---

Assimilation can be seen as the way we adapt new information into existing mental structures so that our minds can seek equilibrium.

Accommodation is a circumstance where no preexisting mental structures are available for assimilation and the child must adapt her or his mental structures to accommodate new information.

Disequilibrium is when a child's conception of a thing or event is no longer adequate and the child seeks to establish a balance through assimilation and accommodation.

Used in this text, an **operation** is a mental action such as adding numbers or classifying objects.

have some firsthand experience with the materials to think about them. Specific examples, models, and detailed explanations are needed with concrete operational children.

In the stage of formal operations, children are able to think much more abstractly. They have far less need to refer to concrete objects. This stage generally occurs after elementary school or middle school. It is considered the summit of cognitive development because students can now handle formal logic and abstract reasoning.

To better understand the preoperations and concrete operations stages, see the related activities for Chapter 2 at the *http://www.prenhall.com/peters* Web site.

A Piagetian Approach to Teaching

Returning back to Ms. Terrell's students, we can see that they are not yet at the formal operations stage. Their teacher is engaging them in concrete activities during which they are actually manipulating materials versus thinking about them abstractly as they will later do in the formal operations stage. In class, the children are building a "moon phaser" with a paper dial, downloaded from the Internet. They will use the moon phaser to predict when the next full and new moons will occur and to study related terms. Ms. Terrell's objectives for the students are as follows:

1. Locate the horizon and zenith with their moon phaser.

2. Determine the current moon phase.

3. Find the moon's approximate position in the sky for a given date and time.

4. Determine the approximate time of moonrise and moonset for eight moon phases.

This activity meets all of these objectives and appears to be at an appropriate developmental level for her students. Because her students have never used this type of device, Ms. Terrell anticipates that they will be very active assimilating and accommodating new information. Later, the students will apply the information from this activity as they work with balls and flashlights to re-create the phases of the moon in a different way.

Formal operational students can explore a question such as "If you were on the moon, which phase would the earth be in when the moon is in the waning gibbous phase as seen from the earth?"

Throughout the stages of development, concrete activities play an important role in the process of cognitive growth. Assimilation, accommodation, and equilibration all require thought processes. As teachers, we must facilitate learning that keeps the mind active, as we see done with the moon activity (particularly when students are unable—such as in space science activities—to manipulate "real" space objects). We also need to keep in mind that reality is something children construct from their own actions. It is not something waiting to be found or discovered (Piaget, 1954; Piaget & Inhelder, 1969).

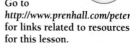

Go to *http://www.prenhall.com/peters* for links related to resources for this lesson.

But is it solely a teacher's activities that cause children's development and construction of meaning? What other factors or influences may come into play in children's development? Is a social or cultural influence involved? Some theorists believe that culture and social exchange are important in the knowledge development process.

Vygotsky and Social Constructivism

Is the role of others important to our learning? L. S. Vygotsky's theory of constructivism includes the role of culture and society. Vygotsky thought that behavior must be studied in a social and historical context, giving rise to the term *sociohistorical*. Vygotsky theorized that children do not simply reproduce what is said or shown to them but that instead they undergo socially mediated cognitive constructions.

See *http://www.prenhall.com/peters* for additional information on Vygotsky.

Children look at the moon as it appears in space to help construct understandings of the phases of the moon.

Lev Vygotsky was born in the same year as Piaget. Although he died at the age of 38 and was not well known in our country, English translations of his more than 180 written works indicate that Vygotsky understood an important facet of cognitive development. For Vygotsky, cognitive development is a matter of an individual's social interaction within the environment. The mechanism of social behavior and the mechanism of consciousness are the same according to his theory (Vygotsky, 1978). That is to say, we know ourselves because of our interactions with others. Consciousness can only be explained in terms of socially-meaningful activity.

How does Vygotsky compare to Piaget? Like Piaget, he believed that learners construct their own knowledge and that a deeper meaning goes beyond perception. A major difference does exist between the two theories, though. Piaget was a developmental constructivist and saw *development as leading learning,* which he described in his stages of development. Piaget placed an emphasis on the child's internal processes. Vygotsky, however, *saw learning as leading development.* Students engaged in learning **spontaneous concepts** with their peers will later restructure these same concepts into **scientific concepts** within their own cognitive structures. In other words, a concept such as "light" begins in an informal social setting as children talk about light and darkness (e.g., a child telling her father that she needs a nightlight because her bedroom is dark). Later, through time and repeated use, this concept and related spontaneous concepts will become better organized into one's cognitive structure as a more systematic "scientific concept." The child will better understand the nature of light and be able to apply this concept as needed to make sense of her world (e.g., the light from the sun provides energy to the earth).

Spontaneous concepts are the concepts acquired informally from everyday life experi-

Scientific concepts are those concepts represented by a systematically organized body of knowledge and are usually learned through formal instruction.

Scientific Concepts

As a child grows, words begin to take on meaning and communication begins to develop (Vygotsky, 1986). The child finds names for objects, and informal, spontaneous concepts begin to develop as a result of the verbal exchange with others. These concepts are often vague and tend to be illogical and unsystematic, but they are further developed through the use of **psychological tools** or signs.

     Psychological tools are used like the tools that any craftsperson uses to perform tasks better. Psychological tools, as mental tools, allow us to improve our communication and to adapt to our environment. They can be either external or internal. Writing notes in a notebook is an example of external psychological tools; these notes help us augment the mind's capacity. Internal psychological tools, such as the formulas and rhymes we call mnemonic devices, also assist us in mental development.

     Signs, as a kind of mental tool, assist us in regulating our thinking and are part of Vygotsky's theory. For instance, if we write a note and stick it to the refrigerator or if we place a name in an appointment book, we are creating a sign. These activities help us remember important dates or information. Vygotsky's term **semantic mediation** refers to how we, as humans, use tools and signs to assist us in remembering. Mental tools, such as signs, are representative of our culture and are unique to humans. All animals share mental behaviors such as attention and perception (lower or biological forms); however, semantic mediation provides a level of understanding that separates human thoughts from those of other animals. This higher order thought process is known as *cultural mental behavior,* as opposed to the *natural mental behavior* common to all animals (Vygotsky, 1981).

     The main difference between lower biological forms and higher social forms is the shift that occurs from outside control (teacher and peer-supported activity) to self-directed (autonomous) control. Social collaboration is gradually lessened as a child takes on more responsibility for her own learning. To put it another way, the development of higher forms of mental processes occurs through a child's enculturation into society as a result of the educational process. Instruction is a principle source of the child's concepts. For Vygotsky, as for Piaget, the stages of concept development reflect a maturation process. Figure 2–2 illustrates the stages of concept development from simple labeling of objects to abstract and systemized knowledge of scientific concepts (Dixon-Krauss, 1996).

     Note the similarities and differences between the stages proposed by Vygotsky and those proposed by Piaget. You can see that Piaget focused on the children's mental development as they went through the stages (development leading learning). For Piaget, higher development levels lead to the ability for more advanced learning. Vygotsky, conversely, emphasized learning (learning leading development). He saw learning on a continuum of simply naming things, to spontaneous concepts, to scientific concepts. Learning leads to higher developmental levels.

Psychological tools are the culturally developed signs used in mental and social activities; examples are letters, words, numbers, speech, and pictures.

Semantic mediation is the transformation of lower forms of mental behavior to higher forms of mental behavior through the use of signs.

Heaps	Child groups objects into random categories.
Complexes	Traits of objects are analyzed and concrete factual relationships among diverse objects are established.
Potential Concepts	Transition from the concrete and spontaneous to the abstract and scientific concept.
Genuine Concepts	Abstract and systematic concepts that are common to a culture.

Figure 2–2
Vygotsky's stages of concept development.
Source: From Table 1.1, p. 12, *Vygotsky in the Classroom* by Lisbeth Dixon-Krauss. Copyright © 1996 by Longman Publishers USA. Reprinted by permission of Addison-Wesley Educational Publishers Inc.

The Zone of Proximal Development and Scaffolding

The importance of working with others supports the use of cooperative learning in the classroom.

Can we as elementary science teachers maximize learning by taking advantage of social collaboration? Is group work important in the classroom?

Vygotsky noted that when children were placed in groups that were under the guidance of an adult or when they collaborated with a more experienced peer, they could perform at levels higher than were possible when working on their own. Furthermore, what was possible in the group situation now would be possible on an individual basis later. For instance, if a child was able to complete a classification of leaves based on common properties with the assistance of a more knowledgeable classmate, this same child could later complete this classification task independently.

Social constructivists would argue that the only good kind of instruction is that which marches ahead of and leads development. Instruction must be aimed not so much at the ripe as at the ripening functions (Vygotsky, 1962). So with group or teacher assistance, a child's instruction should always be slightly ahead of what was possible for that child on her own level. If the student can already complete a classification based on two properties but not on three, instruction should be directed at classifying with three properties under the guidance of the teacher or learning group. For example, a student may be able to perform a dichotomous classification of objects that are either animals or plants. This same child may not be able to classify objects that are plants, mammal animals, or non-mammal animals.

The **zone of proximal development** is the gap between a child's current level of development and the child's potential level of development when supported by collaboration with a more capable peer.

Scaffolding is when an adult first structures a learning task and then provides the dialogue needed to guide a child's successful participation in that task.

The term **zone of proximal development** is used to indicate the difference between what a child can do with the help of a more knowledgeable person and what the child can do independently. The goal of instruction is to actively engage the student in solving problems within the zone of proximal development. The teacher's role is that of a facilitator or mediator. The teacher provides an environment where learning in the zone of proximal development is maximized. The teacher acts as a **scaffold** and provides just the right amount of support to accomplish the developmental goal. Alternatively, the teacher can arrange a cooperative learning group in which another student will be the knowledgeable other.

The "scaffolding" support that a teacher provides is analogous to the scaffolding that painters use. They may reach many areas independently, but when they cannot reach an area on their own, they require a scaffold to assist them in performing the task. Correspondingly, painters would not use high scaffolding to paint a baseboard or normal wall. The implication here is that the teacher should not provide more guidance than is needed for developmental support; too much support will not promote the development of independent thought in children.

See the Constructivist Pedagogy section of the companion CD for examples of scaffolding and the zone of proximal development.

A Vygotskian Approach to Teaching

As an extension to their moon activities, Joshua's class had been discussing the principles of light, mirrors, and reflection. As Joshua shared this new information with his sister Melanie, she thought it would be interesting to aim their new laser pointer near the cat and see if the cat would chase the light beam. Joshua instructed Melanie not to look at the light beam directly and not to let the cat see her pointing the laser. He also described for her how light travels in a straight line and how light is reflected by a mirror.

Melanie tried out many different ideas but is now using a large mirror in the hallway and some hand mirrors borrowed from her parents' bathroom. She got the idea to try the mirrors from her brother talking about reflections. She also saw how the light reflected from her own vanity mirror as she tried different ways to make the light shine into another room.

Melanie is involved in experimentation here. She is looking at the relationship among mirrors, reflections, and pathways of light. She is also engaged in dialog with her older brother. She is asking questions and trying out some new ways of doing things to answer her question about the light beam and the cat. She is absorbed with the activity and curious about how the light beam can be redirected to reach her goal. Together, the children are engaged in an interactive learning situation.

Think about how scientists, engineers, physicians, computer technicians, and other professionals carry on activities within the workplace. Do they work independently or as a team? Do physicians imply that, to be effective, they must know the answer to every question and not rely on others? It is the same with the laser activity. For example, a child's concept of a mirror tends to be that of an object used to see themselves and not that of an instrument to reflect light. Melanie relies on her brother for guidance. He leads her into thinking about mirrors in new ways.

Has Melanie changed in her knowledge of mirrors? As Melanie communicates, she begins to have a more logical and systematically structured verbal definition for the mirror. She uses psychological tools and signs to assist her in controlling her mental behavior. It is now more in keeping with culture's accepted body of knowledge related to mirrors. Melanie now has the beginning of a scientific concept. Her previous spontaneous concept becomes a part of this new scientific concept, making the new concept more meaningful. Melanie is eventually able to complete the task with the laser pointer because she received some assistance from her older brother. Her brother became the scaffold for her learning in this situation.

See the Constructivist Pedagogy section of the companion CD for examples of social learning.

Our role as teachers is to assist students in developing tools and signs, as well as in maximizing the integration of spontaneous concepts and their related concrete experiences into scientific concepts. When this happens, spontaneous concepts can be logically defined, retrieved, and used by the child.

Collaborative learning and thinking as seen with the laser activity is the foundation of Vygotsky's theory. It is the very means by which a child learns the fundamentals of society. It is the method of moving from lower learning to higher learning and is the system by which activities within a child's zone of proximal development are successful. Scientific experimentation and problem-centered activities, or those that have multiple solution paths, provide the framework for successful science experiences. Much like scientists and engineers engaged in collaborative research, your interactions with students will promote learning.

Your role as a teacher will be to facilitate this type of activity and to adapt the curriculum to meet your students' needs. Like the physician who must consult on many cases, you will not be an expert in all areas and will rely on others, including students, to assist you in knowledge acquisition. Neither will you be available at all times for every patient. You will need to employ the help of nurses, technicians, and others in the form of students. These knowledgeable others will assist in the scaffolding process, communicating the terminology and processes to their peers.

Peer tutoring, when a high-achieving student tutors a lower achieving student, is an excellent application of Vygotsky's theory.

The Role of Language

Because language is central to Vygotsky's theory, it is important that students understand and use the language of science (Gallas, 1995; Lemke, 1993). Science is a foreign language for them—one with comparatively more new terms than found in a foreign language text. Social constructivist theory suggests that a child constructs an understanding of language from the whole to its parts. If this is the case, then the elementary classroom should surround children with stories and trade books on science topics so that the children are exposed to the content of science through a whole language or integrated approach to learning. Vocabulary should remain in the context of what is read, not be encountered as a separate, out-of-context, memorization drill. Science instruction should be a model of how

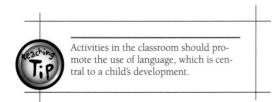

Activities in the classroom should promote the use of language, which is central to a child's development.

science is performed by scientists. Figure 2–3 presents further suggestions for teaching within a social constructivist framework.

Driver, Asoko, Leach, Mortimer, and Scott (1994) sum up the learning of science as follows:

[Science learning] involves being initiated into scientific ways of knowing. Science entities and ideas, which are constructed, validated, and communicated through cultural institutions of science, are unlikely to be discovered by their own empirical enquiry; learning science thus involves being initiated into the ideas and practices of the scientific community and making these ideas and practices meaningful at the individual level. The role of the science educator is to mediate scientific knowledge for learners, to help them to make personal sense of the ways in which knowledge claims are generalized and validated. (p. 6)

Planning the Curriculum	Plan to assess students' preconceptions through class and individual discussions, drawings, writing activities, and other assessment procedures.
	Plan to build on students' prior knowledge to take advantage of spontaneous concepts.
	Plan to keep students involved in the lesson through the use of challenging and open-ended activities.
Opportunities to Develop Scientific Concepts	Provide as many chances as possible for students to explore phenomena and communicate with each other.
	Use concrete examples whenever possible.
	Organize many opportunities for oral and written language so that students share meanings and construct concepts.
Time and Classroom Management	Provide ample time for small-group activities.
	Leave plenty of time after instruction for reflection and questions by the students.
	Arrange the classroom to maximize peer interaction and small-group activities
	Use reading, writing, and science centers effectively and not just as a management tool for those who get their work done early.
Listening and Questioning Skills	Ask questions before the lesson to evaluate students' prior knowledge and to assist students in recalling the information.
	Listen carefully to students as they are talking to you and others so that you can adjust their lessons to fit their zone of proximal development.
	Ask open-ended questions and encourage elaboration of students' answers.
Planning and Facilitating Classroom Activities	Develop lessons that offer multiple pathways for learning, such as reading, writing, listening, and small-group activity.
	Plan activities that connect in-school learning to out-of-school learning.
	Construct lessons that are culturally diverse.
	Use creative writing and subject-matter specific journals.
	Use assessment procedures that can show where a student is on the continuum of learning.
	Vary assessment procedures to check for student understanding.

Figure 2–3
Social constructivist teaching suggestions.

As you can see, social constructivism has important implications for the teacher. Students construct new knowledge within a sociohistorical framework, where language is an important component.

A Constructivist Model

A constructivist model describes the learning process in terms of the student, not the teacher. We cannot prescribe a curriculum for everyone. Notwithstanding, when students are actively engaged, they are constructing knowledge. Learning is taking place, not as a result of the teacher transferring the knowledge from a text or a personal knowledge base, but as the students interpret and make sense of their surroundings.

A constructivist approach implies that the use of a variety of activities in the classroom promotes a child's making sense of the world and developing scientific concepts.

Similar to the social constructivist theories, as the students interpret their surroundings, the new interpretation is influenced by their prior knowledge. It is therefore the teacher's role to facilitate activities that will guide the learner into developing meaningful concepts. Constructivists generally agree that discourse is especially important in negotiating meaning and developing socially agreeable constructs. Therefore, open-ended questioning is important before, during, and after activity periods.

See the Constructivist Pedagogy, Private Speech section of the companion CD for examples of students interpreting their surroundings and developing meaning from their observations.

A Constructivist Approach to Teaching

As they continue their moon studies, Ms. Terrell's class looks at the question "What kind of information can we collect in order to predict when the moon will rise tomorrow evening?" from a page in the *Out of This World* activity guide shown on the following page. The students document the angle of elevation of the moon every 30 minutes for a total of 5 hours. They build "lunometers" with rulers and protractors to measure the moon's angle as it rises. They also graph the results of their observations and actively engage in making sense of the data.

If knowledge is the result of constructive activity, then it cannot be transferred effectively to a passive receiver. The construction of knowledge must be an active process by the individual learner. The role of the teacher is to orient the learner in a general direction and then attempt to prevent the learner from going in directions that would be inappropriate. This is exactly what we find with the lunometer activity.

How can we make today's science classrooms different from those in the past? One way is to change our perception of teaching from promoting rote learning proposed by behaviorists to engaging students in a series of well-thought-out logical steps. Teachers should scaffold a child's growth in building conceptual knowledge from the child's prior knowledge to knowledge that is the cultural development of society.

The teacher's role as a facilitator of the curriculum is to provide the resources for learning, to engage students actively, and to refocus students' activity when appropriate so that they remain productive in the learning process. For example, Ms. Terrell provided the lunometer template and then guided students in making sense of the data as they were collected. Her role in the activity was to pose a problem to solve and invite students to make observations that accomplish the task. She then steps aside and allows the students to interact with the environment and each other. Ms. Terrell only intervenes when necessary. Intervention is used to refocus student discussion in a more productive way, initiate a new pattern of activity, or begin an assessment activity for the students to express their personal understanding.

The 🌙 Shines Bright

In the investigation, you will chart the movement of the moon for 5 hours beginning at moonrise. The best time of month is just before full moon. At full moon, the moon rises at the time the sun sets.

Carefully record the time the moon rises and make a measurement of its angle of elevation with your luneometer. This will be zero unless the moon rises behind hills or mountains. Repeat the measurement in every 30 minutes. Observe the timing with care. Enter the information into the table.

One person needs to point the lunometer at the moon and the other take the reading on the scale.

Time	Angle of Elevation	Amount of Change in 30 minutes
Moonrise:		

Total of Change: _____

Average Change: _____

Children determine the angle of elevation of the moon as part of their exploration of the phases of the moon.

Source: M. Lind, P. Knecht, B. Dodge, A. Williams, & A. Wiebe, *Out of This World* (Fresno, CA: AIMS Education Foundation, 1994), p. 73. Used by permission from the AIMS Education Foundation, 1-888-733-2467.

The Constructivist Learning Model ———

Robert Yager (1991) described the constructivist learning model (CLM) as a promising new model in learning. It focuses on the learner instead of the teacher. Building on the work of researchers at the National Center for Improving Science Education, Yager introduced a set of constructivist strategies for teaching, which are provided in Figure 2–4.

Try using the constructivist learning model in planning your next lesson.

As you can see, the CLM is an ongoing four-part process. First, you get the students to think about a phenomenon in a new way (invitation part). Then, they explore the phenomenon (exploration part) and develop explanations or solutions (constructs; proposing explanations and solutions part). Finally, they share their new ideas with others or reexplore the phenomenon in a new way (taking action part).

When constructivist theories such as the CLM are used, the focus is on the learner and the learning environment. This makes your job as a teacher–facilitator different from what you may have experienced from your teachers in elementary school. As you read through the remaining chapters of this text, think about how you can use the tenets of constructivism to enhance the learning environment of your students.

Invitation
- Observe surroundings for points of curiosity
- Ask questions
- Consider possible responses to questions
- Note unexpected phenomena
- Identify situations where student perceptions vary

Exploration
- Engage in focused play
- Brainstorm possible alternatives
- Look for information
- Experiment with materials
- Observe specific phenomena
- Design a model
- Collect and organize data
- Employ problem-solving strategies
- Select appropriate resources
- Discuss solutions with others
- Design and conduct experiments
- Evaluate choices
- Engage in debate
- Identify risks and consequences
- Develop parameters of an investigation
- Analyze data

Proposing Explanations and Solutions
- Communicate information and ideas
- Construct and explain a model
- Construct a new explanation
- Review and critique solutions
- Utilize peer evaluation
- Assemble multiple answers/solutions
- Determine appropriate closure
- Integrate a solution with existing knowledge and experiences

Taking Action
- Make decisions
- Apply knowledge and skills
- Transfer knowledge and skills
- Share information and ideas
- Ask new questions
- Develop products and promote ideas
- Use models and ideas to elicit discussions and acceptance by others

---

Figure 2–4

Constructivist strategies for teaching.

Source: R. Yager, "The Constructivist Learning Model." Reprinted with permission from NSTA Publications, September 1991, from *The Science Teacher,* National Science Teachers Association, 1840 Wilson Blvd., Arlington, VA 22201-3000.

Summary

1. Piaget's works help provide insight into how children grow intellectually. He defined the stages that children go through as they develop and the characteristics of these stages. Piaget also explained the learning process as a dynamic balance between assimilation and accommodation and a result of seeking equilibration as a result of new experiences. Piaget was a developmental constructivist who viewed development as leading learning.
2. Vygotsky's constructivism is a sociohistorical theory in which behavior is studied in a social and historical context. In this theory, children undergo socially mediated cognitive constructions. Psychological tools and signs assist us in semantic mediation and the development of scientific concepts. The zone of proximal development allows a child's instruction to be slightly ahead of her development. Later, what she could do with the assistance of another, she can now do on her own. Vygotsky was a sociohistorical constructivist who saw learning as leading development.
3. In either constructivist theory, the curriculum is not a set of right answers and truths to be taught, but rather a set of culturally accepted ideals used to guide learning. Elementary science teachers must understand the goals of the curriculum, the individual children in their classrooms, and how to structure the learning environment to meet these individual needs in the elementary science classroom.

Reflection

1. Discuss with your classmates the following common ideas related to scientific knowledge, teaching, and learning:

    *   Elementary students already have conceptions of science when they arrive at the elementary classroom.

    *   Every child is a scientist.

    *   Teachers and students can learn science together.

2. Try some Piagetian tests on children at your practicum site (see the companion Web site). What observations can you make? Compare these observations with those made by other students in your methods class. What do you note?
3. Discuss constructivism with a teacher at your practicum site. What is her or his viewpoint? Discuss it with your educational psychology professor. What is her or his viewpoint? The current science education research trend, or paradigm, is toward a constructivist perspective. Why do you think this is so? Mathematics educators also operate under a constructivist paradigm. What does your mathematics methods instructor have to say about constructivism? What are some views of your other methods instructors?
4. Observe students in a classroom working together to solve a problem. Does it become clear that some students could not have completed the problem on their own? What is the teacher's role as students engage in the collaborative activity? How can you, as an outside observer, tell whether the students are learning? How will the teacher know whether learning has occurred? Share your findings with classmates.

References

American Association for the Advancement of Science (AAAS). (1993). *Benchmarks for science literacy.* New York: Oxford University Press.

American Association for the Advancement of Science (AAAS). (1998). *Blueprints for reform.* New York: Oxford University Press.

Bettencourt, A. (1993). The construction of knowledge: A radical constructivist view. In K. Tobin (Ed.), *The practice of constructivism in science education* (pp. 39–50). Washington, DC: AAAS Press.

Branley, F. (1975). *Day light, night light.* New York: HarperCollins.

Branley, F. (1987). *The moon seems to change.* New York: HarperCollins.

Bybee, R. W., & Sund, R. B. (1990). *Piaget for educators* (2nd ed.). Prospect Heights, IL: Wavelend Press.

Cobern, W. W. (1993). Contextual constructivism: The impact of culture on the learning and teaching of science. In K. Tobin (Ed.), *The practice of constructivism in science education* (pp. 51–69). Washington, DC: AAAS Press.

Dixon-Krauss, L. (1996). Vygotsky's sociohistorical perspective on learning and its application to Western literacy instruction. In L. Dixon-Krauss (Ed.), *Vygotsky in the classroom: Mediated literacy instruction and assessment* (pp. 7–24). White Plains, NY: Longman.

Driver, R., Asoko, H., Leach, J., Mortimer, E., & Scott, P. (1994). Constructing scientific knowledge in the classroom. *Educational Researcher, 23*(7), 5–12.

Gallas, K. (1995). *Talking their way into science: Hearing children's questions and theories, responding with curricula.* New York: Teachers College Press.

Henriques, A. (1990). Experiments in teaching. In E. Duckworth, J. Easley, D. Hawkins, & A. Henriques (Eds.), *Science education: A minds-on approach for the elementary years.* Mahwah, NJ: Lawrence Erlbaum.

Kuhn, T. (1962). *The structure of scientific revolutions* (2nd ed.). Chicago: University of Chicago Press.

Labinowicz, E. (1980). *The Piaget primer: Thinking. Learning. Teaching.* Menlo Park, CA: Addison-Wesley.

Lemke, J. L. (1993). *Talking science: Language, learning, and values.* Norwood, NJ: Ablex.

Lind, M., Knecht, P., Dodge, B., Williams, A., & Wiebe, A. (1994). *Out of this world.* Fresno, CA: AIMS Education Foundation.

National Research Council (NRC). (1996). *National science education standards.* Washington, DC: National Academy Press.

National Research Council (NRC). (2000). *Inquiry in the national science education standards.* Washington, DC: National Academy Press.

Petersen, J. (1994). *The road to 2015.* Corte Madera, CA: Waite Group Press.

Petersen, J. (1997). *Out of the blue: Wild cards and other big future surprises—How to anticipate and respond to profound change.* Arlington, VA: Arlington Institute.

Piaget, J. (1954). *The construction of reality in the child.* New York: Basic Books.

Piaget, J., & Inhelder, B. (1969). *The psychology of the child.* New York: Basic Books.

Siegler, R. S. (1986). *Children's thinking.* Upper Saddle River, NJ: Prentice Hall.

Tobin, K., & Tippins, D. (1993). Constructivism as a referent for teaching and learning. In K. Tobin (Ed.), *The practice of constructivism in science education* (pp. 3–21). Washington, DC: AAAS Press.

Vygotsky, L. (1962). *Thought and language* (E. Hanfmann & G. Vakar, Eds.). Cambridge: MIT Press.

Vygotsky, L. (1978). *Mind in society: The development of higher psychological processes.* (M. Cole, V. John-Steiner, S. Scribner, & E. Souberman, Eds.). Cambridge, MA: Harvard University Press.

Vygotsky, L. (1981). The genesis of higher mental functions. In J. V. Wertsch (Ed.), *The concept of activity in Soviet psychology* (pp. 144–188). Armonk, NY: Sharpe.

Vygotsky, L. S. (1986). *Thought and language* (A. Kuzulin, Ed.). Cambridge: MIT Press.

Yager, R. (1991). The constructivist learning model. *The Science Teacher, 58*(6), 52–57.

Suggested Readings

Bodrova, E., & Leong, D. J. (1996). *Tools of the mind: The Vygotskian approach to early childhood education.* Upper Saddle River, NJ: Merrill/Prentice Hall. (A guide to incorporating Vygotsky's ideas into teaching.)

Brooks, J. G., & Brooks, M. G. (1993). *In search of understanding: The case for constructivist classrooms.* Alexandria, VA: Association for Supervision and Curriculum Development. (A guide to developing classrooms that encourage understanding of concepts.)

Chaille, C., & Britain, L. (1991). *The young child as scientist: A constructivist approach to early childhood education.* New York: HarperCollins. (An overview of how children construct knowledge.)

Dixon-Krauss, L. (Ed.). (1996). *Vygotsky in the classroom: Mediated literacy instruction and assessment.* White Plains, NY: Longman. (An overview of Vygotsky's theory, including the zone of proximal development and scaffolding.)

Duckworth, E. (1987). *"The having of wonderful ideas" and other essays on teaching and learning.* New York: Teachers College Press. (A Piagetian view of education.)

Tobin, K. (Ed.). (1993). *The practice of constructivism in science education.* Washington, DC: AAAS Press. (An edited compilation of the nature of constructivism and what it means for teachers.)

von Glasersfeld, E. (1995). *Radical constructivism: A way of knowing and learning.* Washington, DC: Falmer Press. (A comprehensive work on radical constructivism.)

Chapter 3

Planning for Inquiry

VIGNETTE 3-1

Open-Ended Divergent Thinking Unit

Jerry Mayernik
Northway Elementary School, North Hills School District, Pennsylvania

Comeback Cans

A thin stripe of yellow tape in the school hallway marks the starting line for the test track. In a few minutes, colorful cans of many sizes will clink, clank, and thump their way down the long, narrow test course, with students whispering encouragement to their carefully constructed devices as the cans slow down, wiggle, and begin the trip back to the starting line. At no time are science terminology, textbook pages, or vocabulary words referred to as the children test, refine, and retest their "comeback cans."

In my science class, the school year begins with a demonstration of "Herbie, the Wonder Can," a 3-pound coffee can rigged with a rubber band and a large fishing sinker inside. When Herbie is carefully rolled across the classroom, it magically slows, stops, and returns to its starting point. After students are shown how to construct a similar device, they are challenged to build their own comeback cans and test them against the best efforts of Herbie. The next day, cans of all sizes and construction litter the windowsill, ready to challenge Herbie in a test of endurance.

Which can will roll the longest distance and return to the yellow stripe? After several cans traverse the track, students begin to realize that variations exist in their methods of construction. Some cans have thicker rubber bands, some thinner. Some devices are larger, some fatter, some longer. The masses inside are small, huge, and everywhere in between. Which of these variables are critical to can performance? What are the optimal can size, rubber band width, and mass? Students are encouraged to study the construction of the leading cans and to modify or refine their cans, as they like. Finally, after weeks of testing and retesting, trial and error, and elation and frustration, the top cans compete in the Comeback Can Derby. The five winning can-builders are awarded small trophies in honor of their efforts.

This activity promotes divergent thinking. Although the comeback cans have a common construction, the task encourages a wide variety of responses. The winning cans have never been constructed in quite the same way. This activity allows students to explore, analyze, and adapt. It encourages children to attempt a novel approach (like a "Bigfoot" can, with Plexiglas "wheels" twice the diameter of other competitors'). The experience provides the "mental hooks" upon which learners will hang physics concepts in high school.

See *http://www.prenhall.com/peters* for links to the comeback can and similar activities.

Before the "comeback can" activity, you may want to use the "rolling cans" activity: Try rolling a full can of sand, an empty can, and a half-full can of sand down a ramp.

In the vignette, we find Mr. Mayernik's class involved in a challenging inquiry activity. How will you plan for inquiry activities in your own classroom? What considerations did Mr. Mayernik make as he prepared for this activity?

To help you think about planning and your classroom activities in a different way, envision yourself working in a manufacturing company that makes sport utility vehicles (SUVs). Your job is to assist in developing a new SUV. As you think about your new job, consider that you cannot talk with any other employees throughout the day. More experienced employees do not help you in any way. You also have to separate the workday into time periods. First, you will complete all the scientific undertakings, then the mathematical duties, some people-related responsibilities, and finally the language-type assignments. You spend the same amount of time each day on the four categories of tasks, regardless of how successful you are with any one type of task. You never spend very much time on reflection. You do not consider why the new vehicle needs to be built, whom it is being built for, or how it can be made differently. Nor do you spend any time trying to make the process or product better. You just want to meet a minimal standard for the construction of a new vehicle.

How successful will you be in your job with the above constraints? Now, think how successful elementary students will be with similar constraints. As a teacher, you are assisting children in constructing new knowledge. A big part of this process is planning. Good planning will produce a better automotive product just as it worked to promote inquiry with the students in the Vignette 3–1.

National Standards and Planning

See *http://www.prenhall.com/peters* for links to all the National Science Education Standards.

See *http://www.prenhall.com/peters* for a link to the document *Inquiry and the National Science Education Standards: A Guide for Teaching and Learning.*

The authors of the *National Science Education Standards* (National Research Council [NRC], 1996) provide specific guidelines for how you can plan a science program. These are illustrated in the Inquiry Planning Standard shown in the Standards Link box.

Think about the components of this standard as you read this chapter. Remember that inquiry teaching and learning is a dynamic process. Students are naturally curious and enjoy inquiry. Your job is to further develop their ability to solve problems, transform information into meaningful knowledge, and become lifelong learners. You, as an elementary teacher, can convert your classroom into a better learning environment through a variety of inquiry activities. Table 3–1 shows the diversity of inquiry tasks available to you as you plan your activities.

Inquiry Planning Standard

Teachers of science plan an inquiry-based science program for their students. In doing this, teachers:

- Develop a framework of yearlong and short-term goals for students.

- Select science content and adapt and design curricula to meet the interests, knowledge, understanding, abilities, and experiences of students.

- Select teaching and assessment strategies that support the development of student understanding and nurture a community of science learners.

- Work together as colleagues within and across disciplines and grade levels.

(Teaching Standard A, National Research Council, 1996, p. 30)

Table 3-1

Essential Features of Classroom Inquiry and Their Variations

Essential Feature	Variations			
Learner engages in scientifically oriented questions	Learner poses a question	Learner selects among questions, poses new questions	Learner sharpens or clarifies question provided by teacher, materials, or other source	Learner engages in question provided by teacher, materials, or other source
Learner gives priority to evidence in responding to questions	Learner determines what constitutes evidence and collects it	Learner directed to collect certain data	Learner given data and asked to analyze	Learner given data and told how to analyze
Learner formulates explanations from evidence	Learner formulates explanation after summarizing evidence	Learner guided in process of formulating explanations from evidence	Learner given possible ways to use evidence to formulate explanation	Learner provided wih evidence
Learner connects explanations to scientific knowledge	Learner independently examines other resources and forms the links to explanations	Learner directed toward areas and sources of scientific knowledge	Learner given possible connections	
Learner communicates and justifies explanations	Learner forms reasonable and logical argument to communicate explanations	Learner coached in development of communication	Learner given broad guidelines to sharpen communication	Learner given steps and procedures for communication

More ———————————— Amount of Learner Self-Direction ———————————— Less

Less ———————————— Amount of Direction From Teacher or Material ———————————— More

Planning for Inquiry

You will find that variations in the far right column of Table 3–1 require more direction from you as a teacher. They have only one correct answer or one specific pathway to an answer. Variations to the left in Table 3–1 are less teacher directed and more student centered. These variations are increasingly divergent. They will have more than one answer or pathway to an answer. Let's look at an example. In the illustrations below, both teachers are planning to teach about **food chains.** See whether you notice any differences.

Teacher-Directed Example ————

Mrs. Steen plans her activities to begin with reading *The Magic School Bus Gets Eaten* (Cole, 1996). This story gains student interest and initiates discussion. Next, she asks her students to list the plants and animals found in the story. The students list these in their notebooks. Now, she directs the students to arrange the organisms according to a food chain illustrated on the chalkboard. The students list phytoplankton, zooplankton, anchovies, tuna, and people as a food chain. Mrs. Steen then asks about the source of energy for the food chain.

     In this example, students are engaging in questions and activities directed by the teacher. Learner self-direction is low, and teacher direction is high (see Table 3–1).

Learner-Directed Example ————

Mr. Mitchell plans his lesson to start with reading *What Do You Do When Something Wants to Eat You?* (Jenkins, 1997). The students read about how certain fish, reptiles, amphibians, and other animals escape danger. Mr. Mitchell asks why the animals need to defend themselves in the examples provided in the book. The students respond in a variety of ways, and Mr. Mitchell allows them to ask about examples of animal defenses not found in this story. Soon, students are posing questions about why animals would want to eat one another. Mr. Mitchell continues the lesson by reading *Who Eats What?* (Lauber, 1995). Various food chains are provided in the book. The students give other possible examples when prompted by Mr. Mitchell about what food chains may have been a part of their dinners last night.

     As the discussion continues, the students come to realize that there are many kinds of food chains, that food chains are part of food webs, that plants are the basis of a food chain, and that the sun is an important part of every food chain. Learners are more self-directed in this example, often asking new questions or providing a variety of answers. The teacher direction is low, as is reflected in Table 3–1.

Closed and Open Problems ————

In Mrs. Steen's teacher-directed lesson above, inquiry is generally focused on one correct answer, such as the sun being the ultimate source of energy. Students are provided specific examples and **convergent questions** related to the food chains for plants and animals. The problem that students are working on is considered *closed.* Closed-ended problems and activities foster convergent thinking. They *converge* on a common single response.

     Mr. Mitchell's example involves many answers. The correct response is considered *open* because there is more than one possibility for a correct answer. Students can answer

Food chains refer to the organisms in an ecological community that provide a continuation of food energy from one organism to the next as each one consumes a lower member in the chain and is, in turn, preyed upon by a higher member in the chain.

See the Model Inquiry Unit section of the companion CD for examples of learner-centered teaching.

Convergent questions are asked with predetermined answers in mind.

divergent questions based on a variety of food chains and the food chain's interaction within the ecosystem. Open-ended problems and activities lead to a wide variety of responses and produce divergent thinking. With open-ended problems, answers and other possible experiences *diverge* out from a single beginning experience, question, or problem. A balance of both open-ended and closed-ended problems and activities are needed for scientific inquiry during the elementary years.

Divergent questions do not have single answers, are used to promote discussion, and allow for creative thinking.

Closed- and Open-Ended Activities

Closed-ended activities tend to be short and tightly focused. Open-ended activities are usually longer and branch out into many related questions. Closed- and open-ended activities also differ in other ways. To see how, let's consider each type. We begin with some common closed-ended examples involving children 5 to 12 years old. In each case, the children are active; they do things.

Closed-Ended Activities ─────────

In Mrs. Imat's class, children work on the "Mouth Map" activity from the book *Gobble Up Science* (Johmann & Rieth, 1996). Using sugar, salt, instant coffee granules, and lemon juice, they find groups of taste buds in the mouth: The tip of the tongue senses sweet, the back senses bitter, and salty and sour taste buds are predominately on the sides.

In a middle-level elementary class, some children are learning about acids and bases with the "Red-Cabbage Indicator" activity found in the book *Science Experiments You Can Eat* (Cobb, 1994). They find that cabbage juice solution is an indicator and changes color, depending on whether the substance is an acid or a base.

In an upper-level class, some children learn about variables through the "Popcorn Comparison" activity in *Fun With Foods: A Recipe for Math + Science* (Alfving et al., 1987). They are finding that the moisture content of popcorn kernels has an effect on the volume of popped popcorn produced.

The AIMS-produced *Fun With Foods* book contains many other food activities that can be adapted for use in the elementary grades.

Notice that each of these closed-ended activities illustrates some idea or procedure with concrete materials. Working with concrete materials helps the children to form realistic concepts or learn useful techniques. Once a closed-ended activity has made its point, there is no need to continue. Closed-ended activities, when taught well, help children construct a solid subject-matter background that is rooted in experience.

Direct Instruction

A common way to engage in closed-ended activities is through **direct instruction**. In direct instruction, the teacher employs lectures, worksheets, recitations, demonstrations, or specific-answer type questions in a prearranged sequence. A detailed lesson plan is generally used for a direct instruction experience. The teacher is very much in control of the lesson.

Direct instruction is a teacher-centered, well-structured approach to teaching.

One advantage to direct instruction is that the teacher can arrange the sequence of activities ahead of time and thus reduce the number of teaching decisions to be made during a lesson. This is especially helpful for inexperienced teachers who are preoccupied with management issues or who want to be sure they cover a certain curriculum. It is also helpful when introducing a new skill such as classification or learning to use a new piece of equipment. Direct instruction can also be useful when safety issues prevent student exploration.

A more important advantage is that direct instruction can be used to help students construct a knowledge base for future learning. Teachers can spend as much time as needed to think through which analogies, metaphors, activities, and questions will best support the concept they want to develop before the lesson. Instruction continues systematically until the teacher feels comfortable that most students understand the concept.

One disadvantage to direct instruction is that students construct their knowledge at different paces. Therefore, the teacher's pace may not match the students'. The students are not free to explore topics further on their own when they are interested. They are subject to what the teacher selects as themes or important concepts. Problem-solving and higher order thinking skills are better developed through a more independent learning situation.

Another disadvantage of direct, or teacher-centered, instruction is that the teacher may have gender, cultural, or other biases that will limit learning for some students. In other words, the students are subject to everything from the teacher's point of view—not their own. For example, if the teacher unconsciously believes that boys are better suited for science than girls, he may call on boys more often to answer a question or to assist in a demonstration. This behavior reinforces the cultural disadvantage girls have in the sciences (Kahle & Meece, 1994).

See
http://www.prenhall.com/peters
for links related to girls and science.

Planning a Direct Instruction Lesson

Teacher education students are exposed to lesson planning early in their professional preparation. Planning is an important component of science education, and its importance is reflected in the Program Planning Standard (see Standards Link box).

How will you plan a lesson? Will you simply write a page number from a teacher's guide? What are some ways to plan more effectively?

Many models for planning a lesson have been designed. The "objectives, materials, procedure, and evaluation of students" general format is an example of one type of lesson plan. Figure 3–1 presents an enhanced format (Briscoe, Peters, & O'Brien, 1993). It is designed to help you think about the science lesson in a new way. It challenges the teacher to look at the activities from multiple perspectives.

See
http://www.prenhall.com/peters
for a link to the science themes.

The first section is the *contextual framework*. Included here is an *overview* of the lesson in your own words. A lesson topic, a specific grade level, any curricular objectives, and applicable performance objectives can be included here too. In the contextual framework are the *science themes*. These originate in the benchmarks (American Association for the Advancement of Science [AAAS], 1993). Science themes are needed to see the "big picture" of science and how the lesson fits into the themes. Specifically, your lesson should support the development of one or more common science themes. These include systems, models, consistency, patterns of change, evolution, and scale. For each lesson, consider how you address one or more of these themes.

Contextual Framework
Overview of the Lesson
Science Themes (From *Science for All Americans,* 1989, AAAS)
[1]Science Benchmarks (From *Benchmarks for Science Literacy,* 1993, AAAS)
[1]Science Standards (From the *National Science Education Standards,* 1996, NRC)
[1]State or District Science Standards
Scientific Skills
Curricular Integrations

Materials
Supplies
Equipment

Procedure
Steps to Follow or Problem to Solve
Closed-Ended or Open-Ended Questions

Assessment
Student Assessment
Teacher Assessment

Bibliography
Sources for Content Information and Children's Literature

Figure 3–1
Lesson plan format.
[1]Use appropriate standards or benchmarks based on local requirements.
Source: Adapted from Briscoe, Peters, & O'Brien, An elementary program emphasizing teachers' pedagogical content knowledge within a constructivist epistemological rubric. In *Excellence in Educating Teachers of Science,* P. Rubba, L. Campbell and T. Dana (Eds.) Copyright 1993 by ERIC Clearinghouse, Columbus, OH.

Next, provide any applicable *standards or benchmarks.* Use the applicable *National Science Education Standards,* the *Benchmarks for Science Literacy,* your state standards, or any district standards that may apply.

Scientific skills—such as classification, observation, measurement, inference, prediction, communicating, and experimentation—should also be addressed as part of the contextual framework. If you are unsure about these skills, refer to Chapter 4. The last thing to consider as part of the contextual framework is the *curricular integrations.* Think about various ways to integrate social studies, language arts, reading, mathematics, art, music, or physical education into the lesson.

The second section in the lesson plan is a listing of *materials.* Both consumable and nonconsumable supplies and equipment should be listed here. Remember to list materials for the teacher demonstration and student participation.

The *procedure* of a direct instruction lesson plan is very specific. It has numbered steps logically arranged to meet time and curricular requirements. Write out and follow every step so that you do not forget anything. Give careful thought to what you want to say and do during the class period. Write down these thoughts in an expanded outline form. Specific teacher questions can also be placed here. This ensures that you will not forget to ask something important. A direct instruction lesson plan would look like the one provided in Figure 3–2.

See the Model Inquiry Unit, Planning section of the companion CD for examples of a teacher's planning in support of a lesson.

Contextual Framework

Overview of the Lesson

This lesson centers on the names of the nine planets and their relationship to the sun. The students will be asked to name the planets in order, give an approximation of their size, and be able to understand the concept of a satellite of a planet.

Science Themes

> *Systems*—The solar system is a common example of a system. It is a group of planets and their satellites. It also includes solid, liquid, and gaseous material in an interrelated organization.
> *Models*—The idea of a model is established as students create models of the solar system.
> *Consistency*—The planets rotate in consistent patterns in the solar system.
> *Patterns of Change*—Patterns of change are modeled as stars are formed and the visibility of planets changes throughout the year.
> *Evolution*—There is a lot of verified data on the evolution of the solar system. The launching of new spacecraft to study the solar system and beyond brings relevancy to this topic.
> *Scale*—Scale is established as the various sizes of the planets are compared.

Benchmarks for Science Literacy

By the end of fifth grade, students should know that

- Planets change their positions against the background of stars.
- Earth is one of several planets that orbit the sun, and the moon orbits Earth (AAAS, 1993, p. 63)

National Science Education Standards

As a result of their activities in Grades K–4, all students should develop an understanding of

- Objects in the sky
- Changes in Earth and the sky (NRC, 1996, p. 130)

Scientific Skills

> *Classification*—Classification activities are promoted as students develop classification systems for the planets (by composition, temperature, and size).
> *Observation*—The students will observe the night sky and record data.
> *Measurement*—The students will measure and re-create a scale model of the solar system.
> *Inference/Prediction*—The students will infer why the temperature of Venus is high, based on that planet's characteristics.

Curricular Integrations

> Measurement activities integrate *mathematics* into this lesson.
> *Art* is incorporated into this lesson as students draw planet and star models.
> *Social studies* is integrated into this lesson as students discuss ancient theories of an Earth-centered solar system.
> *Reading* is integrated into this lesson as students read *The Magic School Bus Lost in the Solar System* (Cole, 1990).

Figure 3–2
Direct teaching lesson plan for planets.

Materials

Supplies

Large sheets of paper; crayons, markers, or paints

Equipment

Inflatable planetarium (two large sheets of black painter's plastic with both sides taped together lengthwise to form a large dome). A box fan is taped to one end and turned on to inflate the dome.

Procedure

Steps to Follow

1. Introduce the vocabulary: Mercury, Venus, Earth, Mars, Jupiter, Saturn, Uranus, Neptune, Pluto, moon, satellite, orbit, asteroid, rotation, revolution (Use definitions from end of the chapter and have students repeat the words. Write the definitions on the overhead for them to copy.)
2. Read the chapter on the planets from the student's text. Discuss origins of the solar system. Read *The Magic School Bus Lost in the Solar System* book.
3. Demonstrate the relative distances between planets by creating a model with students acting as the sun, planets, and satellites (see specific measurements in the text).
4. Demonstrate the rotation of Earth and the moon and their revolution around the sun by using students to represent the sun, Earth, and the moon (see picture in supplemental materials).

Closed-Ended Questions

A. What is the center of the solar system? Describe its characteristics.
B. What is the first planet from the sun? Describe its characteristics. (Repeat for the rest of the planets.) What is the difference between the moon and a satellite? (Note: The moon is Earth's satellite. We call other "moons" by their proper name, satellite.)
C. Define an orbit.

Open-Ended Questions

A. Which planets are colder? What is a possible cause for their low temperature?
B. Give some possible reasons for Venus being so hot. (Discuss greenhouse effect.)

Steps to Follow (continued)

5. Develop three planet classifications (Monday).
6. Redraw the scale model of the planets from the text, measuring exactly from the book. (Tuesday).
7. Draw a picture of the night sky (Wednesday).
8. Find pictures of the winter and summer night sky from other books and magazines (Thursday).
9. Take students into the planetarium and demonstrate the position of the stars and planets by using the portable star projector (Friday).

(continued)

Additional Homework Activities (select one)

10. Research what causes eclipses of the sun or moon.
11. If you started today and traveled 1000 miles per hour to Jupiter, determine how old you would be when you reached your destination (see adaptation of AIMS activity from *Out of this World* (Lind et al., 1994, Fresno, CA: AIMS Educational Foundation).
12. Most people incorrectly believe that the distance from the northern or southern hemisphere of the earth from the sun causes the seasons. Research the real cause of the seasons.
13. Research the planets on NASA Internet sites.
14. Research and discuss why the International Astronomical Union, the official body for naming astronomical objects, would want to reclassify Pluto as a "trans-Neptunium asteroid" instead of a planet.

Assessment

Student Assessment

1. Design a mnemonic sentence to remember the order of planets (e.g., My Very Excellent Mother Just Served Us Nine Pizzas).
2. Describe in your journal what life would be like on Jupiter. How would it compare to life on the moon?
3. Write to NASA for more information on space exploration and present it to the class.

Teacher Assessment

Videotape lesson and review it at home.

Bibliography

Branley, F. M. (1987). *The planets in our solar system.* New York: Thomas Crowell.
Cole, J. (1990). *The magic school bus lost in the solar system.* New York: Scholastic.
Lauber, P. (1982). *Journey to the planets.* New York: Crown Publishers, Inc.
Lauber, P. (1990). *Seeing the Earth from space.* New York: Orchard Books.
National Geographic Society (Producer). (1987). *The planets* [laserdisc]. Washington, DC: National Geographic Society.
Scholastic. (1994). *The magic school bus explores the solar system* [CD-ROM]. Redmond, WA: Microsoft Corporation.

Figure 3–2   (continued)

Next, a lesson plan must address *assessment*. How will you assess your students? Chapter 5 provides an in-depth view on student assessment. Teacher self-assessment should also be considered in this section of the lesson plan, especially for beginning teachers who need to practice reflecting on their instruction. You may want to videotape or audiotape the lesson, have a peer teacher or administrator observe the lesson, seek student feedback in some way, write personal observations in a journal, or use a school-based assessment form.

The lesson plan concludes with a *bibliography*. All sources used in planning should be listed here, including audiovisual support, computer-based tools, and applicable

See
http://www.prenhall.com/peters
for links related to the use of
children's literature in science.

Internet links. Also include any fiction or nonfiction literature you will make available to students.

In review, closed-ended activities tend to be limited. Outcomes are predictable and specific. Children follow someone else's ideas or procedures. What should you do to promote children's ideas? To boost children's thinking processes, independence, and creativity, you should offer more open-ended experiences.

Open-Ended Activities

Mrs. Bell places a few food items, some balloons, and various other items such as beakers and jars out on a table and challenges her students to blow up a balloon by using the food. This activity is based on the "blowing up a balloon with a banana" activity found in *Icky, Squishy Science* (Markle, 1996). The activity is a result of informal class discussions after finishing a weather unit by reading *Cloudy With a Chance of Meatballs* (Barrett, 1978) and its sequel, *Pickles to Pittsburgh* (Barrett, 1997). Students were discussing things food could do other than be digested. Mrs. Bell challenged them to try blowing up a balloon with the food items provided. Later, the students will discover some properties of food, including the presence of bacteria.

In an upper-elementary class, Mr. Pettis allows his students to discover their own ways to cure meat, based on suggestions from the books *More Science Experiments You Can Eat* (Cobb, 1979) and *Silly Science* (Levine & Johnstone, 1995). The students complete this activity based on questions originating with the reading of *Stone Soup* (Brown, 1997), *Eating the Plates* (Penner, 1991), *Corn Is Maize* (Aliki, 1976), and other stories. Their study of the foods eaten by Pilgrims and American Indians generated possible discovery activities that could promote further inquiry.

Food activities are excellent ways to introduce diversity and multiculturalism to elementary students.

Use of Open-Ended Activities

Most exemplary teachers encourage children to try their own ideas about how to investigate and organize objects or events. This is seen in Vignette 3–1 (Mr. Mayernik's) at the beginning of the chapter. Students are allowed to discover things for themselves. When students are given some autonomy, some suggestions lead to others and there is almost no end to what may be investigated.

Open-ended activities allow students to study objects and events in two very useful ways: (a) observe similarities and differences in the properties of things and (b) discover conditions that can produce or change properties (thus the name *discovery learning*).

Note the contrast in this pair of questions:

What materials will rust?

In what ways can you get some objects to rust?

When children examine the properties of comparable things, they learn that properties usually exist in varying degrees. As students inspect these variable degrees of properties, they will observe, describe, contrast, measure, and classify them. This is why open-ended investigations of things with comparable properties are so well suited for intuitive-level students and others who lack experience with the materials being examined. A common way to facilitate open-ended activities is through the guided discovery approach.

Guided Discovery Learning

Guided discovery learning is a less teacher-oriented and more student-oriented instructional method. It would fall midpoint in the classroom inquiry continuum found in Table 3–1. In this approach, students are guided in exploration of materials. They observe phenomena, gather data on their own, make comparisons, draw inferences, and arrive at conclusions. Teachers follow up on what has been discovered and point out any misconceptions. Students are then free to explore once again. This method is especially valuable in making connections between science vocabulary and scientific concepts.

Remember the lesson plan components from Figure 3–1. The same general procedures are used here as well. Students are provided time to discover concepts based on initial information.

In guided discovery, follow-up discussion and questioning is crucial. The direct instruction approach spells out exactly what is to be learned. Guided discovery, in contrast, allows students more time to explore on their own. Sometimes students form misconceptions during this exploration. Misconceptions are ideas a person has that something is one way but it is really another.

Here's an example of a misconception. Suppose you ask a child what would happen if an astronaut "dropped" something like a pen on the moon. The child may reply that it would float away. You may then ask why the astronaut does not "float away." Students may answer that the astronaut's heavy boots weigh him down and keep him from floating away. Of course, the moon does have gravity, and this is what keeps the astronaut from floating away. The pen actually does fall toward the moon as it would on the earth. Because the moon has less mass, however, the pen falls with less force than here on the earth. In synopsis, everything on the moon is attracted to it; otherwise, the rocks and dust would also float away.

In guided discovery activities, it is crucial to follow up after student exploration and determine whether the students have made correct assumptions. Figure 3–3 presents a guided discovery lesson for electricity.

Problem-Centered Learning

Continuing with open-ended activities, we progress from the teacher-control to the student-control position of the teaching/learning continuum of Table 3–1. Now, students become more involved in the planning and implementation of lessons. Once provided an initial question, students continue an investigation until a problem is solved.

In *Science for All Americans* (AAAS, 1989), there is a message to all science teachers that good teaching starts with questions about nature or explorations of phenomena that are interesting to students and at their level. The authors go on to say that as students become familiar with the things around them, they will begin to question and find answers to these questions. This idea is at the very heart of problem solving in elementary science. Children are very inquisitive during the elementary years. Promoting and developing this inherent trait will provide lifelong skills in solving everyday problems. One way to increase problem-solving ability is through **problem-centered learning.**

Through problem-centered activities, children learn to view science as a meaningful, dynamic activity. They see science as a human endeavor in which they can participate. You will notice that the guided discovery lesson plan is very similar to the other lesson plans, except that its procedure section contains a problem for the students to solve, as opposed to a specific procedure. Generally, a problem-centered lesson will also have more open-ended questions because the teacher is not presenting specific concepts or definitions that are repeated by the students.

See *http://www.prenhall.com/peters* for links related to science misconceptions.

Problem-centered learning is a method of teaching and learning that focuses on children's ability to construct their own meaning for concepts.

Contextual Framework

Overview of the Lesson

Electricity has become very important to modern humans. The commonplace nature of electricity makes it an excellent topic of discovery in the elementary classroom.

Science Themes

> *Systems*—This activity requires the investigator to create a system that includes a power source, a power transmission, and a power consumer.
> *Models*—This activity is done on a small scale but is representative of a much larger system. Through the creation of series and parallel circuits, students will be better able to understand how/where electricity is generated, transported, and used.
> *Consistency*—Electrical systems require consistency. Dry/wet cells are designed to provide a constant voltage so that a device is not damaged by surges or suppressions in current. Likewise, the power derived at power stations requires a feedback system of substations, switching devices, transformers, and monitors to ensure that constant voltage is maintained.
> *Patterns of Change*—Power generation undergoes many changes as new technologies are created to maximize the amount of energy produced from fossil fuels while limiting harmful effects to the environment. Nuclear and solar technologies are changing the way electricity is generated. Batteries are also changing as new materials are being tried to create longer-lasting, more powerful, rechargeable, less expensive batteries.
> *Evolution*—The production and use of electricity may have important evolutionary significance. Animals, including humans, may undergo evolutionary change in response to electromagnetic fields, or may have already changed in response to the availability of light and heat from electricity.
> *Scale*—Scale is inherent to a study of electricity. Large-scale generators and transformers produce high-voltage electricity at power stations. Next, the power is transmitted through high-tension lines to substations. From the substations, electricity is scaled down and sent to neighborhoods, where it is again stepped down into a usable voltage for home use. Generally, a house has three wires coming into it. One is a common ground and two are hot wires, at 110 volts each. From there, electricity may go to electrical appliances, where it is further scaled, or transformed, into a much lower voltage, such as 9 volts.

Benchmarks for Science Literacy

By the end of fifth grade, students should be able to

- Make safe electrical connections with various plugs, sockets, and terminals (AAAS, 1993, p. 293)

National Science Education Standards

As a result of the activities in Grades K–4, all students should develop an understanding of
- Light, heat, electricity, and magnetism (NRC, 1996, p. 123)

Scientific Skills

> *Classification*—Students will be able to classify various types of circuits into series or parallel.
> *Observation*—Students will observe the various ways that light (or do not light) the bulb.
> *Measurement*—Students check individual batteries to ensure that they are producing a current.
> *Inference/Prediction*—Students will predict various ways to light the bulbs and then test the predictions. Students will infer that their house circuit is a parallel circuit as they discover the differences between the two circuits.
> *Communication*—Communication skills will be developed as students interact in small groups to solve the problem. Communication of results will also occur as groups share their findings.
> *Experimenting*—Students will have to identify the variables that cause the bulb to light up. They will also explore relationships among the batteries, wires, and bulbs. Students will construct hypotheses about the differences between series and parallel circuits. They will have to design a solution to the batteries and bulbs problem.

Figure 3–3
Guided discovery lesson plan for electricity.

(continued)

Curricular Integrations

In *language arts,* numerous stories and poems are based on electricity themes. Most children have experienced the lack of electricity in their homes at one time or another, opening up possibilities for creating short stories.

In *mathematics,* experiences can be related to meter readings/billing and electrical usage, comparisons of electrical usage among appliances, and measuring voltages.

Art can be incorporated into an electricity activity in a variety of ways. Students can draw pictures of their experiences during an electrical blackout.

Music could become part of the lesson as a discussion of how instruments have evolved through the use of electricity.

Social studies is important to the study of electricity. American communities all depend on electricity. A comparison between cultures based on the availability of electricity is important.

Safety is vital to any discussion of electricity. Local power companies are excellent sources for materials on safety topics.

Materials

Supplies

Light-bulb-shaped paper for student stories; pamphlets on safety precautions about electricity

Equipment

Class set of batteries, wires, and bulbs

Procedure

Steps to Follow

1. The introductory activity/advance organizer includes stories and poems based on electrical themes as a way to introduce the topic. A brief discussion of power outages will also be done as appropriate.
2. The first activity is to "light the bulb." Students are provided one battery, one wire, and one light bulb and are instructed to design an investigation that individually would result in lighting the bulb. Guide them in defining a complete circuit and explain the path of electricity through the bulb, if necessary. Remind them that the electrons have to go into *and back out* of the light bulb for it to function.

Closed-Ended Questions

A. What do you notice about the light bulb? (It has a base, filament, and glass enclosure.)
B. What makes the bulb light? (Electron flow through the filament.)

Open-Ended Questions

A. What were some probable ways that the light bulb was invented?
B. What are some creative ways to light a bulb?

Steps to Follow (continued)

3. The second activity is to create a circuit with two dimly lit bulbs and another circuit with two brightly lit bulbs. Students are provided two light bulbs, one battery, and four or more wires to produce a series and parallel circuit. Note that the materials only provide for one circuit to be produced at a time. Once the first one is designed, students will have to diagram the finding and then continue with the other circuit. Provide this diagram if necessary:

Figure 3–3   (continued)

Series Circuit

Parallel Circuit

Closed-End Questions

    A. How are the lights in this room wired? (parallel)
    B. What happens to the old-style Christmas tree twinkle lights when a bulb is removed? (They all go out because it is a series circuit.)

Open-Ended Questions

    A. Why do you think buildings are wired in parallel instead of series circuits?
    B. What are some ways to create a parallel circuit?

Steps to Follow (continued)

    4. Science/Technology/Society extension activity on determining appliance power consumption and reading a power meter from power company handout. Discuss how cultures rely on energy.
    5. Discuss how electricity is produced and various types of fuel. Discuss the impact on the environment (thermal pollution from steam cooling; greenhouse effect from giving off carbon dioxide; acid rain from burning sulfur; electromagnetic fields from electricity transmission).

Closed-Ended Questions

    A. What form of fuel does our local power company use?

Open-Ended Questions

    A. If we were to close down all the electrical generation plants that use fossil fuels, what impact would that have on society?
    B. What are some ways people could conserve energy?
    C. How did you feel when the power was out last time? How did it change your life?

(continued)

Assessment

Student Assessment

1. Students will complete a written story based on experiences they have had dealing with electricity.
2. Students will go to a hardware store and check types of wire and fuse boxes to determine which would be most appropriate for their house.
3. Students will actually make a series and parallel circuit (light the bulbs).
4. Students will interview family and friends to see which type of fuel (fossil, solar, nuclear) they prefer when generating electricity and why.
5. Students will record in their science notebooks the various ways they lit the bulbs.

Teacher Assessment

Invite a peer teacher to come into the room and observe questioning technique, particularly with regard to teacher dominance of questions versus students' independent inquiry.

Bibliography

Bains, R. (1982). *Discovering electricity.* Mahwah, NJ: Troll.

Berger, M. (1989). *Switch on, switch off.* New York: Franklin Watts.

Fife, J. (1996). *Watered-down electricity: Using water to explain electricity.* Huntington, WV: University Editions.

Gosnell, K. (1994). *Thematic unit: Electricity.* Huntington Beach, CA: Teacher Created Materials.

Johnston, T. (1988). *Energy: Making it work.* Milwaukee, WI: Gareth Stevens.

Markle, S. (1989). *Power up: Experiments, puzzles, and games exploring electricity.* New York: Antheneum.

Mayes, S. (1989). *Where does electricity come from?* Tulsa, OK: EDC Publishing.

Siegel, B. M., & Stone, A. H. (1970). *Turned on: A look at electricity.* Englewood Cliffs, NJ: Prentice-Hall, Inc.

Figure 3–3   (continued)

Learning with an Integrated Approach

See *http://www.prenhall.com/peters* for links related to *Blueprints for Reform.*

It may not come as a surprise to you that elementary teachers see a value in their students learning science. What you may not understand is why these same teachers do not teach more science throughout the week. One reason commonly given is increasing pressure from parents and administrators to have students score high on standardized reading and math tests. One way to satisfy both worlds is to teach more science without detracting from reading and mathematics. In other words, integrate other content areas with science as suggested in the Science Program Standard in the Standards Link.

In addition to the advantage of the time factor suggested above, integrated approaches have other benefits. One benefit of an integrated approach to science is that science becomes less of a disconnected collection of facts and more of a "coherent, meaningful body of knowledge" (Keig, 1994, p. 79). Students use their prior knowledge and new experiences to form bridges between the known and the unknown. In *Blueprints for Reform* (AAAS, 1998), the authors indicate that "providing a link to the student's own world through contextual learning can be a powerful motivating factor" (p. 126).

A second benefit of integration is that these approaches are intrinsically cooperative (Post, Ellis, Humphreys, & Buggey, 1997). Small groups of students are engaged in inquiry, and this can result in a successful learning experience for the group and for each of its members (Jones, 1990). Cooperative methods promote interaction between students. This interaction has the potential to involve students in clarifying, defending, elaborating, evaluating, and even arguing (Tobin, Tippins, & Gallard, 1994). Although cooperative learning may not always lead to the teacher's predetermined learning goal, the consensus building and negotiation are a valuable learning tool.

A third benefit of an integrated approach is that this method is a direct application of the multiple intelligences theory provided by Howard Gardner (Charbonneau & Reider, 1995; Sunal et al., 2000). Because children learn in different ways, an integrated curriculum that promotes various approaches to learning will support the various learning styles. Students can benefit from the "multilevel instruction" and "multitasking" inherent in integrated approaches to the curriculum (Roberts & Kellough, 2000, p. 3).

A fourth benefit of an integrated approach is that it generally includes a variety of children's books. Children's literature is captivating to young people and useful in developing emerging concepts. Children's books help place new vocabulary in a context that makes constructing meaning easier. For example, if a student looks at a selection of dinosaur books, he will begin to develop the concept or scheme of "dinosaurness." He will relate the pictures he sees to the story he is reading to determine what characteristics belong to the dinosaur. Books allow children to learn from a whole language approach.

The notion of the whole language movement is to use real books to teach reading literacy in a natural context. It is a method in which meaning is constructed from an entire passage (top down) instead of individual words (bottom up). That is to say, we construct the essence of the passage by reading the passage and looking at the meaning of all the words together. This is in contrast to finding the meaning of each word and then trying to develop a general idea by building the individual word meanings together.

Educators have taken whole language a step further and developed the concept of whole learning, in which all content areas are integrated and often based on story themes. Rote, or repetitive, memorization of science facts does not lead to an understanding of science any more than learning disjointed words in language class would lead to an understanding of poetry or literature.

Whole learning as applied to science can be thought of as a synergy of scientific knowledge, process skills, and attitudes. Children begin to value science because they

---

> ### Standards Link
>
> #### Science Program Standard
>
> The program of study in science for all students should be developmentally appropriate, interesting, and relevant to student's lives; emphasize student understanding through inquiry; and be connected with other school subjects.
>
> - **The program of study should include all of the content standards.**
>
> - **Science content must be embedded in a variety of curriculum patterns that are developmentally appropriate, interesting, and relevant to students' lives.**
>
> - **The program of study must emphasize student understanding through inquiry.**
>
> - **The program of study in science should connect to other school subjects.**
>
> (Program Standard B, National Research Council, 1996, p. 212)

See *http://www.prenhall.com/peters* **for International Reading Association and other links related to the use of children's literature.**

enjoy reading about it in an interesting context. Mathematics, language, social studies, and science activities based on literature build on familiar contexts and further reinforce a positive attitude toward science and other subjects (see Tchudi & Lafer, 1996, for examples). The advantages of whole learning are that it allows the child to

- Learn in a social environment that fosters rich language activities
- Put scientific concepts into a meaningful context by connecting them with literature and other content areas
- Spend more time on learning science because it becomes a part of the normal reading and mathematics curriculum

Planning Integrated Lessons with Children's Literature

Remember some of the food-related science activities found earlier in this chapter? These activities incorporated the food theme in children's books as an integral part of the lesson. The food topic could have been extended into other content areas to further integrate the lessons.

See the Planning and Management section of the companion CD for examples related to planning thematic or integrated science experiences for children.

For mathematics, the teacher could have used the book *Spaghetti and Meatballs for All!* (Burns, 1997) as a way to introduce geometry, *Each Orange Had 8 Slices* (Giganti, 1992) to promote counting skills, or *Gator Pie* (Mathews, 1979) to study fractions. Language skills and poetry could have been introduced through the story *Never Take a Pig to Lunch and Other Poems About the Fun of Eating* (Westcott, 1994). Social Studies could have been brought in through *Everybody Cooks Rice* (Dooley, 1991) or *The Tortilla Factory* (Paulsen, 1995). Other activities may have originated from the *Food* (Willrich, 1993) or *Food and Nutrition* (Sterling, 2000) thematic unit books and the countless other children's books related to the food theme. Although each of the above-mentioned books is associated with other content areas, they all support science concepts in one way or another.

When choosing books to use in a whole language lesson, keep the following points in mind:

- *Is the book appropriate for your students' developmental level?* Do not use a book just because it has the same title as the unit you are currently studying. Check that it is written at an appropriate reading level. If you are not going to read it to the class, make sure that your advanced readers can read it to other students.
- *Is the content appropriate?* Before placing a book out for students to read, be sure that the content will not develop further misconceptions about the topic under study. Students have many false notions about scientific phenomena, and you do not want to reinforce these or add to them. Preread each book and note any inconsistencies; eliminate nonsupportive books.
- *Will the book be interesting to your students?* Select a wide variety of books if possible. This will ensure that you meet the individual needs of your students. Consider gender and cultural diversity when selecting books. Look for colorful illustrations and a good story line.
- *Does the book encourage scientific investigation?* Your purpose for starting with children's literature is to provide a baseline for further knowledge and process skill development. Select books that are good springboards to further learning.

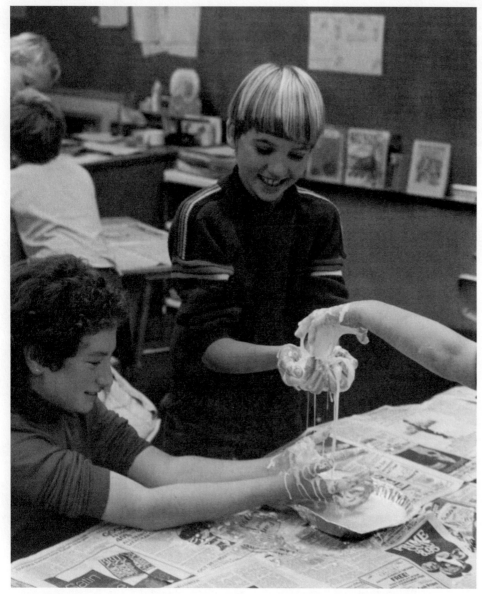

Children interact with a cornstarch and water mixture as part of an integrated, problem-centered lesson.

Reprinted from the Great Explorations in Math and Science (GEMS) teacher's guide entitled *Oobleck: What Do Scientists Do?*, copyright by The Regents of the University of California, and used with permission. The GEMS series includes more than 70 teacher's guides and handbooks for preschool through eighth grade, available from LHS GEMS, Lawrence Hall of Science, University of California, Berkeley, CA 94720-5200. (510) 642-7771.

For teaching ideas by using children's literature, see Figure 3–4.

Green Goo as an Example

A good example of an integrated, problem-centered lesson is one on green goo. The teacher can begin by reading the story *Bartholomew and the Oobleck* (Geisel & Geisel,

Bosma, B., & DeVries Guth, N. (1995). *Children's literature in an integrated curriculum: The authentic voice.* New York: International Reading Association & Teachers College Press.

Butzow, C., & Butzow, J. (1989). *Science through children's literature: An integrated approach.* Englewood, CO: Teacher Ideas Press.

Butzow, C., & Butzow, J. (1994). *Intermediate science through children's literature: Over land and sea.* Englewood, CO: Teacher Ideas Press.

Fredericks, A., Meinbach, A., & Rothlein, L. (1993). *Thematic units: An integrated approach to teaching science and social studies.* New York: HarperCollins.

Hefner, C., & Lewis, K. (1995). *Literature-based science: Children's books and activities to enrich the K–5 curriculum.* Phoenix, AZ: Oryx.

LeCroy, B., & Holder, B. (1994). *Bookwebs: A brainstorm of ideas for the primary classroom.* Englewood, CO: Teacher Ideas Press.

Shaw, D. G., & Dybdahl, C. S. (1996). *Integrating science and language arts: A sourcebook for K–6 teachers.* Boston: Allyn & Bacon.

Figure 3–4
Resources for teaching science with children's literature.

1977). Once the story is read, a mixture of cornstarch and water (made beforehand) is handed out for student exploration. The students interact with the mixture and determine its properties. Through this experience, they are working on many scientific skills. They also explore content knowledge as they discuss new words and ideas in a small-group social setting. Finally, the students are developing values and attitudes as they begin to use their natural curiosity to explore scientific phenomena.

Mathematics can be integrated by measuring the amounts of water and cornstarch it takes to make a "good" mixture. Social studies is integrated in a discussion of kingdoms because the story is based on a king. Art can be integrated when students create mosaics with water-based paints and the cornstarch mixture. The sourcebook for arranging this experience is *Oobleck: What Do Scientists Do?* (Sneider, 1985). See Figure 3–5 for a sample lesson plan.

The assessment of this integrated experience should be in keeping with its constructivist nature. Students should be assessed on the product (knowledge), process (skill), and attitude (value) of the experience. Literature/language activities can become an assessment exercise as students write (or orally present) a creative story. Students could also write descriptive adjectives about the goo. These are used to create poetry, such as cinquains or diamantes.

Scientific attitudes can be assessed as students are asked how they feel about the fact that even scientists cannot agree on why the mixture acts the way it does. Students should also be challenged to come up with their own explanation as to why the material behaves the way it does.

Concept maps (see Chap. 5) would be an appropriate way to determine content knowledge in this case. Students can be provided a key word such as *mixture* and asked to develop links based on what they know.

Contextual Framework

Overview of the Lesson

Children can become scientists as they explore the world around them. When they encounter a new situation, they can observe, classify, measure, infer, predict, communicate, and experiment to solve problems and gain new information or ideas. Children's curiosity is stimulated as they complete activities. This activity is designed to acquaint children with a substance that does not behave as other substances do. Specifically, the mixture gets harder as it is manipulated and softer when it is left alone. This is in direct opposition to materials such as Play-Doh or clay.

Science Themes

> *Systems*—Green goo is a physical/chemical system made up of molecules that interact with each other and the environment. To understand the nature of the substance, we must consider its behavior as an integrated system composed of interacting parts and energy.
> *Models*—In considering the way molecules or atoms are arranged in the mixture, students will create pictorial or mental models of the structure of this particular type of matter.
> *Consistency*—Although we can cause temporary changes in the substance by inputting energy in one form or another, students will notice that the system tends to maintain its properties and reorganize itself into the same physical consistency and structure as before the system was disturbed.
> *Patterns of Change*—Green goo seems to be both solid and liquid at the same time. It can be compared to other substances, and the patterns of change that are represented as liquid and solid states are interchanged.
> *Scale*—The behavior of green goo may be caused by scale. The sizes of the molecules allow them to interact in ways that a larger substance cannot.

Benchmarks for Science Literacy

By the end of fifth grade, students should know that

- Heating and cooling causes changes in the properties of materials. Many kinds of changes occur faster under hotter conditions.
- When a new material is made by combining two or more materials, it has properties that are different from the original materials. For that reason, a lot of different materials can be made from a small number of basic kinds of materials. (AAAS, 1993, p. 77)

National Science Education Standards

As a result of the activities in Grades K–4, all students should develop

- Abilities necessary to do scientific inquiry
- Understanding of properties of objects and materials (NRC, 1996, pp. 121 & 123)

Scientific Skills

> *Classification*—Students will compare and contrast this substance and other materials in an attempt to classify it according to its properties.
> *Observation*—Students will use all their senses to observe the substance (provide a caution against tasting the material).
> *Inference/Prediction*—Students will infer from the collected data such nonobservable properties of the mixture as what it is made of or how the atoms might be arranged.
> *Communication*—Students will communicate their findings to the group. They will also communicate with each other when developing theories of why it behaves the way it does.
> *Experimenting*—Students will design and carry out experiments to alter the mixture, to find its properties, and to explain its behavior.

Figure 3–5
Thematic lesson plan for green goo.

(continued)

Curricular Integrations

> For *language arts,* the teacher can record the words used to describe green goo and discuss descriptive adjectives. Descriptive poetry, such as cinquains or diamantes, can be developed.
> *Mathematics* activities can be developed as students compare densities of other substances to that of green goo.
> *Art* can be integrated into this lesson as students experiment with water-based paints and the green goo mixture.
> *Physical education* is promoted as students act out the behavior of green goo molecules.
> *Social studies* is a natural integration as kingdoms are discussed. Also, the interaction between science and society can be stressed.
> *Safety* during the green goo activity is stressed when using heating devices. Also, cautions against eating the substance or getting it on clothing should be noted.

Materials

Supplies

Two or three boxes of cornstarch; green food coloring; water; small objects such as marbles, coins, rubber stoppers; other common substances or materials that can be used to explore. (Note: Prepare the mixture by placing one or two boxes of cornstarch in a mixing bowl and mixing in small amounts of green-colored water. Continue until the consistency is like a thick plaster.)

Equipment

Thermometers, heat source (microwave), balance, graduated cylinders

Procedure

Problem to Solve

> 1. The problem to be solved is to use the materials provided to find out as much about the substance as possible. While students explore, walk around the room, questioning students about what they are doing, why they are doing it, and what else they can do to gain information about green goo.

Closed-Ended Question

> A. What happens to the green goo as you continue to squeeze it in your hands? (It hardens.)

Open-Ended Question

> A. What did you find out about the green goo?

Problem to Solve (continued)

> 2. Continue exploration with the green goo and develop a theory to explain why it behaves the way it does.

Open-Ended Questions

> A. What do you think causes the green goo to behave this way? Have students explain why it behaves as it does and suggest what materials it might be made from.
> B. What possible explanations do you think scientists give for the behavior of green goo? Discuss scientific theory and why scientists cannot completely agree on why it behaves as it does. Discuss the tentative nature of science, theoretical models and their use, and the scientific search for explanations.

Figure 3–5   (continued)

Problem to Solve (continued)

    3. Experiment with other materials, looking for ones that behave the same way as green goo.

Open-Ended Questions

    A. What other substances do you think behave like green goo?
    B. How could the king have eliminated this material from the kingdom?

Problem to Solve (continued)

    4. Record the words used to describe green goo and discuss descriptive adjectives.
    5. Art/PE extensions from Curricular Integrations above.

Closed-Ended Question

    A. What is a kingdom?

Open-Ended Question

    A. Why do you think America is a democracy and not a kingdom?

Assessment

Student Assessment

    1. Assign group reports that explain why the mixture behaves as it does. Require such items as a hypothesis, data collected, a summary of the data, and conclusions.
    2. Write a story about your own day in the kingdom as the messy substance fell. What did you find out?
    3. Take a small amount home and ask a parent or friend to provide his or her thoughts on green goo.
    4. Find out more about Newtonian and non-Newtonian fluids.
    5. Leave the mixture out for 1 week. What effect does this have on the substance? Explain why this happens.
    6. Use descriptive adjectives to develop poetry, such as cinquains or diamantes.

Teacher Assessment

Audiotape the lesson and review the tape with the following questions in mind: How did the students react to the investigation? What percentage of the time was I dominating the discussion and how often were students actively discussing green goo?

Bibliography

Geisel, T. S., & Geisel, A. S. (1977). *Bartholomew and the Oobleck.* New York: Random House. (Original work published in 1949 by Dr. Suess)
Kerr, D. A. (1983). Quick clay. *Scientific American, 209*(5), 132–142.
Sneider, C. I. (1985). *Oobleck: What do scientists do?* Berkeley, CA: Lawrence Hall of Science.
Walker, J. (1978). The amateur scientist. *Scientific American, 239*(5), 186–198.
Walker, J. (1982). The amateur scientist. *Scientific America, 246*(1), 174–180.

Planning Units

Making and teaching a unit is a surer way to become competent than merely reading about it. When you begin a unit, keep the following in mind.

- Is the unit based on a small number of concepts?
- Do the lessons relate to students' experiences, provide feedback about their current knowledge, and move smoothly into the first activity of each sequence?
- Are some open-ended activities included?
- Can a variety of science processes be used in the activities?
- Are the activities appropriate for the students' abilities?
- Are useful activities from other subject areas integrated into learning sequences?
- Do students apply their knowledge in assessments, or simply recall it?
- Does the unit plan allow enough time for students to learn what is proposed?

In deciding how to make your own textbook-based units, here are three main things you need to know:

1. How to determine which generalizations to use

2. How to gather more activities, if needed, to teach each generalization

3. How to introduce, or bridge into, each generalization's sequence of activities

See the Planning and Management, Pacing and Time section of the companion CD for examples related to planning units of study.

Determining Generalizations

The chapters or units of most textbooks are organized around 3 to 10 main *generalizations* or concepts. Make a tentative list of such generalizations. Then, go through the chapter to see whether your list reflects the main parts of the chapter. Change your list of generalizations as needed to match what you find in the chapter if you want to stick closely to the textbook's contents. Alternatively, you may want to supplement the chapter's concepts with other generalizations found in ancillary materials. You may also want to look for science generalizations in thematic resources. In any event, your task is to wind up with as few big ideas as possible without combining unrelated ideas. When making a unit, you need to know the generalizations in order to compile extra activities.

Whether you use text chapters or a main integrated theme as a base for a unit, it is important to think through the basic organization. This sort of analysis boosts your confidence by providing a sense of direction. It leads to the feeling that, if needed, you can make a few changes and add some ideas. It helps you decide what is important and what is not.

Finding Activities

See *http://www.prenhall.com/peters* for other activity source links.

Activities can come from a wide variety of sources, including trade books and the teacher's guide to the students' science text. Many other activity books are available from the National Science Teachers Association (1840 Wilson Blvd., Arlington, VA 22201, *http://www.nsta.org/*). A series of activity books are also available from the Activities Integrating Math and Science (AIMS) Education Foundation (P.O. Box 8120, Fresno, CA 93747-8120, *http://www.aimsedu.org/*) and the Great Explorations in Math and Science (GEMS) group (Lawrence Hall of Science, University of California, Berkeley, CA 94720, *http://www.lhs.berkeley.edu/GEMS/*).

How many open-ended investigations should you plan for? That depends a lot on how diverse your class is. Cultural diversity and disadvantaged populations in the classroom may require more experiences to make connections.

After you have researched the topic and grouped some good learning activities under each generalization, arrange them in some logical teaching order. The sequence of content in the class textbook can provide the overall direction here. Remember to cluster concrete activities ahead of reading and other secondhand activities when possible.

Determining Bridges or Introductions

Now that you have located some activities for each generalization, you will need some way to introduce each of these main parts of the unit to students and move smoothly into each accompanying set of activities. Teachers call this phase "bridging" because it takes the children from where they are now to the beginning of where they need to go next.

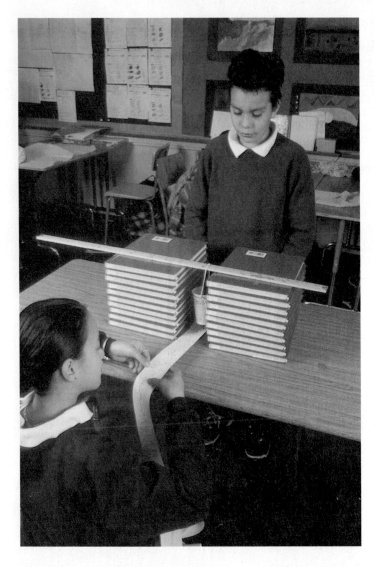

Children use an earthquake activity as a supplement to a textbook unit on the earth's changing surface.

A useful introduction, or bridge, relates to students' experiences and current understandings. It stimulates them to use their current constructions as you interact with them. Students' responses and questions give you some insight into what the students already know about the generalization or topic to be studied, including their misconceptions. The last part of the bridge also leads into the first activity in each sequence.

You may want to introduce your students to the entire unit at one time by asking questions based on all the generalizations. Many teachers believe, however, that it is easier and more meaningful to the children to introduce only one section at a time. Of course, a brief statement about the overall unit topic should be made in any case.

Ideas for bridging into each set of activities usually can be found in the textbook, a text's teacher's edition, or an activity book. Most programs reflect the constructivist view. They are likely to begin a unit or lesson with an opportunity for the teacher to find out what children already know and relate this to what they will learn.

When supplementing a textbook unit, consider these suggestions:

See
http://www.prenhall.com/peters
for links to the *Atlas of Science Literacy* (AAAS). This document is a collection of strand maps that show how students' understanding of the ideas and skills that lead to scientific literacy grow over time.

1.   Thoroughly read the unit to grasp what it is about.

2.   Look for places where you can use local resources.

3.   Look for opportunities to integrate reading, mathematics, language, and other subjects into lessons.

4.   Look for chances to use some concrete activities.

5.   Estimate the total time needed to teach the unit and then fit the text's lessons into the block of available time.

Some teachers feel restricted by the book format. Without the publisher's full array of multimedia resources to draw from, they see mostly closed-ended activities that illustrate ideas in the book rather than broad chances for real inquiry. They see relatively short, tightly controlled lessons when they want students to ask more questions and pursue strong interests over longer periods of time. These teachers are aware of some ways to augment the book unit, but for them these measures don't go far enough. They want the book to be one tool among several, rather than the main event. What they really want is a practical way to design their own multimedia unit and a format that allows them to work flexibly with their students.

A Sample Unit

See the Planning and Management, Finding and Organizing Materials, and Pacing and Time sections of the companion CD for examples related to unit planning.

For a sample unit developed in this way, see Figure 3–6. Notice that the unit is written on index cards. This is a convenient way to keep track of generalizations, activities, and bridges. Suggestions for using the format follow.

Write one broad generalization at the top of each 5-inch-by-8-inch card. This is for your reference only, not for teaching to the children. Sections of the book may be headed by problems, topics, or themes. If one seems useful, you might prefer to first write this heading, then the generalization. Next, write your sequentially arranged activities under each generalization, leaving a space for the bridge. Then write the bridge. Be sure to relate the last part of the bridge to the first activity so that you can move smoothly into it.

Earth's Changing Surface

This is a fourth-grade unit on the forces that tear down and build up the earth's surface. Children also learn how rocks are formed and several ways soil is conserved. Fifteen periods of about 50 minutes each are planned for the unit. (See block plan on back of this card.)

(Front of card)

	April 6–10	April 13–17	April 20–24
Monday	Generalization I, Activity 1 (Ask class for materials for Act. 2.)	Gen. II, Act. 1	III, Act. 3 (Ask for rocks and jars Gen. IV, Act. 2, 4.)
Tuesday	I, Act. 2 (See custodian for materials for Act. 3.)	II, Act. 2	III, Act. 6, assess. (Ask for rocks and jars, IV, Act. 2, 4.)
Wednesday	I, Act. 3 (Ask class for materials for Act. 6.)	II, Act. 3 or 5	Gen. IV, Act. 1, 2
Thursday	I, Act. 4 or 5	II, Act. 4, assess.	IV, Act. 2, 3
Friday	I, Act. 5 or 6, assess. (Ask for materials for Gen. II, Act. 1, and milk cartons from cafeteria.)	Gen. III, Act. 1, 2 (Ask volunteers to bring materials for Act. 3.)	IV, Act 4, 5 assess. (Follow up on crystal growth next week.)

Order library books. Also AV materials by March 6 for I (4), II (3), III (1, 2). Phone II (5), III (4).

(Back of card)

Figure 3–6
Sample unit: Volcanoes.

(continued)

Gen. I. Weathering and erosion constantly wear down the earth's surface. (Class text pages 61–68.)

Bridge

How far down do you think the soil goes? What is beneath the soil? What are some ways rock may get broken up? How might broken up rocks and soil be removed? What does *weathering* mean? What is *erosion?*

Activities

(obs.)	1.	Define weathering and erosion. Tour school grounds for examples. (Open-ended.)
(exp.)	2.	Plants break rocks experiment, text p. 63. (Open-ended.)
(infer.)	3.	Dirt mountain erosion demonstration, Schmidt p. 56.
	4.	Films: Face of Earth (15 min.), Work of Rivers (10 min.).
	5.	Read text pp. 61–68 and library books. SUMMARIZE weathering and erosion forces.
(class.)	6.	Kids find and sort picture examples of forces that bring change. Display. (Open-ended.)
	7.	Haiku poetry on forces that change the earth's surface.

(Front of card)

Materials

Act. 2. Plaster of paris; bean seeds; paper cups.
Act. 3. Shovel; hose. (See custodian.)
Act. 4. MP204; MP206 (AV center).
Act. 6. *Nat'l Geographic, Arizona Highways* back issues; scissors; construction paper; paste.

Assessment

How many examples of weathering and erosion can you find on the school grounds? Find some examples we did not observe on our first tour. Make a record. Also use end-of-section questions, p. 68.

Figure 3–6 (continued)

(Back of card)

Gen. II. Topsoil is composed of mineral, vegetable, and animal matter; topsoil is conserved in several ways. (Pages 69–77.)

Bridge

What are some reasons farmers might be interested in erosion? How might they guard against soil erosion? What makes up soil? Let's see for ourselves.

Activities

(class.) 1. Small-group analysis of soil samples. Sort objects found. (Open-ended.)
(exp.)   2. Plant seeds in poor and good soil samples, text p. 72. (Open-ended.)
         3. Introduce six study points on soil erosion. See "Conserving Our Soil" videotape.
         4. Read text, pages 69–77, and library books. SUMMARIZE ways to conserve soil.
         5. Possible visit by agent, Soil Conservation Service. (Practice interview and listening skills.)

(Front of card)

Materials

Act. 1. Magnifiers; old spoons; sack of good topsoil; newspapers; clean pint milk cartons.
Act. 2. Bean seeds; sack each of good and bad soil; milk cartons.
Act. 3. SP (set of 6) 117; Vid. 440.1 (AV center).
Act. 5. Bill Johnson, Soil Cons. Service, 555-6600.

Assessment

What are some ways you might prevent erosion on our school grounds? Think about the examples you found before. Discuss these ways with two partners. Then give a report.
We don't live on farms. What difference would it make to us if most farm soil erodes? Also use end-of-section questions, p. 77.

(Back of card)

Gen. III. Lava flows and crustal movements continually build up the earth's surface. (Pages 77–84.)

Bridge

Does anyone know what a volcano is? What do you think makes a volcano happen? What is an earthquake? Has anyone been where there was an earthquake? Let's find out some surprising ways the earth's surface changes.

Activities

1. Film: Earthquakes and volcanoes (30 min.).
2. Explore Internet for related information (25 min.).
(meas.) 3. Make clay models of volcanoes, p. 79. Also "seismograph," special project Hone, p. 28. (Art and construction.)
4. Guest speaker with northern California earthquake slides. (Or locate earthquake pictures.)
5. Use maps to locate active volcanoes.
6. Read text, pages 77–84, and library books. SUMMARIZE how mountains are formed.

(Front of card)

Materials

Act. 1. MP 254 (AV center).
Act. 2. Internet-connected computer.
Act. 3. Two colors of clay; newspapers; rulers; scissors. (Seismograph volunteers, check Hone book for materials.)
Act. 4. Orville McCreedy, 286-6147. (Or, past *Nat'l Geographics,* 1989 issues.)

Assessment

Children will construct cutaway models of volcanoes and, using the models, explain how volcanoes may happen. Also use end-of-section questions, p. 84.

Figure 3–6 (continued)

(Back of card)

Gen. IV. Three kinds of rocks are formed as the earth's surface wears down and builds up.

Bridge

Thank you for bringing so many different rocks. What makes them look different? Which of these might have come from volcanoes? How else might some have been made? Before we find out, let's see how many different properties of these rocks you can observe.

Activities

(comm.) 1. Partners do rock description game. (20 questions—lang. develop.)
(exper.) 2. Crystal growing activity, p. 91. (Open-ended.)
        3. Read text, pages 85–93, and library books.
(class.) 4. Sort rocks as to basic type, p. 90. (Open-ended.)
        5. SUMMARIZE Gen. IV and whole unit.

(Front of card)

Materials

Act. 2. Baby food jars; string; paper clips; sugar; hot plate; teakettle; newspaper.
Act. 4. Children's rock samples—stress variety; heavy paper sacks; several hammers.

Assessment

Children will be able to control the size of "rock" crystals by varying the cooling rates of hot sugar solutions.
Children will be able to identify some properties of rocks and explain how these are clues to the rocks' formation.
Also use unit test questions, p. 93.

(Back of card)

The use of cards has advantages. Cards can be shuffled in any desired sequence. It is easy to add and take away generalizations and activities. Special sections can be fitted in: bulletin board ideas, news clippings, notes, whatever else is desired to make the unit complete and easier to teach.

Also, notice the marginal notes for science processes written next to some activities. These can remind you of what to stress in such activities. Several "open-ended" notes serve the same function. Open-ended activities are often the easiest and best way to meet students' individual differences in unit teaching.

Finally, note the specific assessment section for each of the four main parts of this unit. For Generalizations I and II, assessments are stated as questions. For Generalizations III and IV, they are stated as student behaviors to observe. Which method do you prefer? Some teachers use both.

Summary

1. Closed-ended problems and activities lead to a single response. They foster convergent thinking. Open-ended activities and problems lead to a wide variety of responses. They produce divergent thinking.
2. Lessons can be taught in a direct teaching, guided discovery, or problem-centered learning fashion. As you reduce teacher control and increase student autonomy, students are required to take charge of their learning. More meaningful relationships can be formed with problem-centered learning.
3. When planning a unit, the three main things you need to know are these: (a) how to determine which generalizations to use, (b) how to gather more activities to teach each generalization, and (c) how to introduce, or bridge into, each generalization's sequence of activities.

Reflection

1. Take a lesson plan that you have recently completed and rewrite it in the form of a problem-centered lesson to share with the class.
2. Search the Internet for some lesson plan databases. A good starting point is to use the key words *lesson, plan, elementary,* and *science.*
3. Observe the next five science lessons while at your practicum site. Note the use of open-ended and closed-ended activities. How could more open-ended activities be incorporated?
4. Ask several adults one of the misconceptions questions. Do you notice any pattern in their answers? Did your classmates have similar experiences?
5. Read *Multiple Intelligences in the Classroom* (Armstrong, 1994, Alexandria, VA: ASCD), *Teaching With the Brain in Mind* (Jensen, 1998, Alexandria, VA: ASCD), or *Use Both Sides of Your Brain* (Buzan, 1989, New York: Plume) and research ways that curriculum and planning can be modified to better meet students' needs.
6. Integrate multiple intelligences activities into your curriculum by using a resource such as *Celebrating Multiple Intelligences: Teaching for Success* (Faculty of the New City School, 1994, St. Louis, MO: Author), *Succeeding With Multiple Intelligences: Teaching Through the Personal Intelligences* (Faculty of the New City School, 1996, St. Louis, MO: Author), or *If the Shoe Fits . . . How to Develop Multiple Intelligences in the Classroom* (Chapman, 1993, Arlington Heights, IL: IRI/Skylight).

References

Alfving, A., Eitzen, L., Hyman, J., Patron, R., Holve, H., & Nelson, P. (1987). *Fun with foods: A recipe for math & science.* Fresno, CA: AIMS Education Foundation.

Aliki. (1976). *Corn is maize.* New York: HarperCollins.

American Association for the Advancement of Science (AAAS). (1989). *Science for all Americans.* Washington, DC: Author.

American Association for the Advancement of Science (AAAS). (1993). *Benchmarks for science literacy.* New York: Oxford University Press.

American Association for the Advancement of Science (AAAS). (1998). *Blueprints for reform.* New York: Oxford University Press.

Barrett, J. (1978). *Cloudy with a chance of meatballs.* New York: Aladdin Paperbacks.

Barrett, J. (1997). *Pickles to Pittsburgh.* New York: Atheneum Books.

Briscoe, C., Peters, J., & O'Brien, G. (1993). An elementary program emphasizing teacher's pedagogical content knowledge within a constructivist epistemological rubric. In P. Rubba, L. Campbell, & T. Dana (Eds.), *Excellence in educating teachers of science* (pp. 1–20). Columbus, OH: ERIC Clearinghouse.

Brown, M. (1997). *Stone soup.* New York: Aladdin Paperbacks.

Burns, M. (1997). *Spaghetti and meatballs for all! A mathematical story.* New York: Scholastic.

Charbonneau, M., & Reider, B. (1995). *The integrated elementary classroom: A developmental model of education for the 21st century.* Boston: Allyn & Bacon.

Cobb, V. (1979). *More science experiments you can eat.* New York: HarperTrophy.

Cobb, V. (1994). *Science experiments you can eat* (Rev. ed.). New York: HarperTrophy.

Cole, J. (1996). *The magic school bus gets eaten.* New York: Scholastic.

Dooley, N. (1991). *Everybody cooks rice.* Minneapolis, MN: Carolrhoda Books.

Geisel, T. S., & Geisel, A. S. (1977). *Bartholomew and the Oobleck.* New York: Random House.

Giganti, P. (1992). *Each orange had 8 slices: A counting book.* New York: Mulberry Books.

Jenkins, S. (1997). *What do you do when something wants to eat you?* Boston: Houghton Mifflin.

Johmann, C., & Rieth, E. (1996). *Gobble up science.* Santa Barbara, CA: Learning Works.

Jones, R. (1990). *Teaming up!* LaPorte, TX: ITGROUP.

Kahle, J., & Meece, J. (1994). Research on gender issues in the classroom. In D. Gabel (Ed.), *Handbook of research on science teaching and learning* (pp. 542–557). Arlington, VA: National Science Teachers Association.

Keig, P. (1994). Introducing elementary teachers to thematic science instruction. In L. Schafer (Ed.), *Behind the methods class door: Educating elementary and middle school science teachers* (pp. 79–88). Columbus, OH: ERIC Clearinghouse.

Lauber, P. (1995). *Who eats what?* New York: HarperCollins.

Levine, S., & Johnstone, L. (1995). *Silly science: Strange and startling projects to amaze your family and friends.* New York: John Wiley.

Lind, M., Knecht, P., Dodge, B., Williams, A., & Wiebe, A. (1994). *Out of this world.* Fresno, CA: AIMS Education Foundation.

Markle, S. (1996). *Icky, squishy science.* New York: Hyperion.

Mathews, L. (1979). *Gator pie.* Littleton, MA: Sundance.

National Research Council (NRC). (1996). *National science education standards.* Washington, DC: National Academy Press.

National Research Council (NRC). (2000). *Inquiry and the national science education standards: A guide for teaching and learning.* Washington, DC: National Academy Press.

Paulsen, G. (1995). *The tortilla factory.* New York: Voyager Books.

Penner, L. R. (1991). *Eating the plates: A pilgrim book of food and manners.* New York: Aladdin Paperbacks.

Post, T., Ellis, A., Humphreys, A., & Buggey, L. (1997). *Interdisciplinary approaches to curriculum: Themes for teaching.* Upper Saddle River, NJ: Merrill/Prentice-Hall.

Roberts, P., & Kellough, R. (2000). *A guide for developing interdisciplinary thematic units* (2nd ed.). Upper Saddle River, NJ: Merrill/Prentice-Hall.

Sneider, C. I. (1985). *Oobleck: What do scientists do?* Berkeley, CA: Lawrence Hall of Science.

Sterling, M. (2000). *Food and nutrition.* Westminster, CA: Teacher Created Materials.

Sunal, C., Powell, D., McClelland, S., Rule, A., Rovegno, I., Smith, C., & Sunal, D. (2000). *Integrating academic units in the elementary school curriculum.* New York: Harcourt College Publishers.

Tchudi, S., & Lafer, S. (1996). *The interdisciplinary teacher's handbook: Integrating teaching across the curriculum.* Portsmouth, NH: Heinemann.

Tobin, K., Tippins, D., & Gallard, J. (1994). Research on instructional strategies for teaching science. In D. Gabel (Ed.), *Handbook of research on science teaching and learning* (pp. 45–93). New York: Macmillan.

Westcott, N. (1994). *Never take a pig to lunch and other poems about the fun of eating.* New York: Orchard Books.

Willrich, L. (1993). *Food.* Westminster, CA: Teacher Created Materials.

Suggested Readings

Eby, J., & Martin, D. (2001). *Reflective planning, teaching, and evaluation for the elementary school: A relational approach* (3rd ed.). Upper Saddle River, NJ: Merrill/Prentice-Hall. (This book promotes reflective thought in the planning process.)

Freeland, K., & Hammons, K. (1998). *Curriculum for integrated learning: A lesson-based approach.* New York: Delmar. (A guide to K–8 integration based on an integrated lesson plan structure.)

Mason, C., & Markowsky, J. (1998). *Everybody's somebody's lunch: Teacher's guide.* Gardiner, ME: Tilbury House. (A book of activities and information on food chains, predators, and prey.)

National Science Teachers Association (NSTA). (1996). *Pathways to the science standards: Guidelines for moving the vision into practice.* Arlington, VA: Author. (A practical guide to help put the national standards into practice during teaching and assessment.)

Shymansky, J. A. (1996). "Transforming science education in ways that work: Science reform in the elementary school." In J. Rhoton & P. Bowers (Eds.), *Issues in science education* (pp. 185–191). Arlington, VA: National Science Teachers Association. (This chapter discusses curriculum and instruction in the light of science education reform.)

Chapter 4

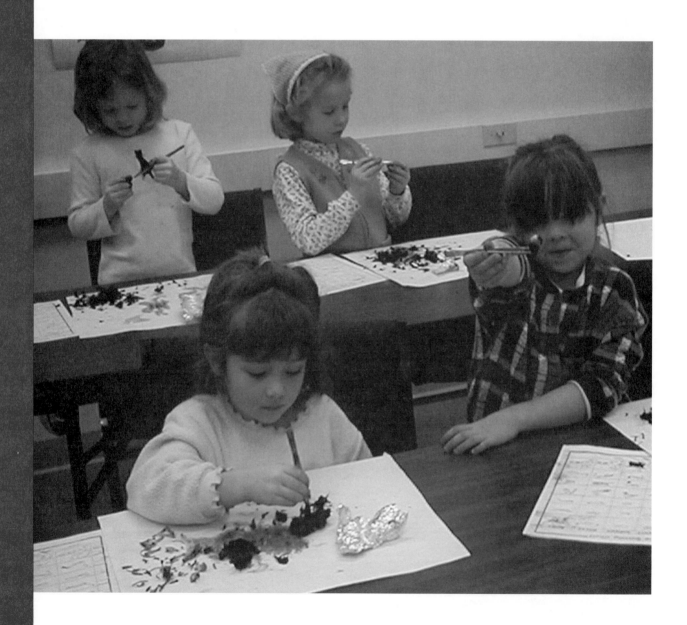

Developing Inquiry Skills

VIGNETTE 4–1

Scientific Skill Development

Dr. George E. O'Brien
Florida International University, Miami

Angela M. Alexander
Pine Villa Montessori School, Dade County (Florida) Public Schools

Students Working with Mystery Objects

Picture a small community school just 30 miles from downtown Miami but in a rural, farm region of south Florida. The students in the school typically do not venture outside the neighborhood, and trips to the local supermarket and department stores are rare. Frequently, when teachers bring hands-on, minds-on activities (Flick, 1993) to class, their students anticipate the fun that is coming next. This particular day, the fourth-grade teacher has arranged her students into cooperative learning groups, and they are excited, curious, and anxious about what is going to happen in the science lesson.

Each group receives plastic gloves, dissecting needles, hand lenses, and an oval-shaped object wrapped in aluminum foil. Can the students predict and/or infer what the objects are? The students are told to unwrap the foil from the objects carefully and to inspect the objects. An initial reaction from many students is, "Wow, I don't know if I really want to touch this." These reactions fade fast. The students are now told to use dissecting needles to separate parts that make up the whole of the oval-shaped objects and then to record observations and make inferences concerning what the objects or their contents might be and why they think so. Quickly, some students discover or infer that they are working with bones. Some say they are working with wishbones, and one student says these are hog bones (because hogs have a lot of bones). Some students think they can make out a bird's head, and one student thinks she can see parts of a hamster. Some students guess that they are working with dinosaur teeth, human teeth, or some kind of fossil.

The students from each group sort the bones. The task of sorting and organizing the bones into recognizable entities is a problem-solving challenge. The challenge of discovering the mystery objects piques the students' curiosity. Although on this day no one infers the objects to be owl pellets, the pieces of bones lead to more discoveries about the animals that are consumed by barn owls.

Up the road from the elementary school, a professor of elementary science methods at the university has set up the activity in the same way as the fourth-grade teacher. He leads his students through the same challenge of identifying the contents of owl pellets. As bones are uncovered and carefully removed and placed to the side on sheets of plain white paper, university students use dichotomous keys (classification) to identify skulls removed from the barn owl pellets. There is much debate and negotiation (communication) in the cooperating groups concerning the identity of the skulls. As skulls of small mammals, including moles and shrews (Order Insectivora), and rats, voles, and mice (Order Rodentia) are identified, the students take pride in their individual and group accomplishments. As a follow-up activity, the students are to diagram food webs with a barn owl at the highest trophic level and grass seeds at the lowest level. The sequence of activities helps the students construct knowledge of diets of barn owls and other birds of prey, food webs showing that energy passes from one organism to another on a higher level through consumption of that lower organism, and other ecological concepts.

In the fourth-grade classroom, the teacher brought books for her students to research owls. Could the students identify the contents of the owl pellets? Yes. In much the same ways that the university students had identified prey, the children were able to identify the skulls of different animals. All the students—at the elementary school and university—solved the mystery of finding out the contents of the pellets. The students, by collecting information from the evidence (in this case, produced by barn owls about 12 hours after consuming a meal by casting, or regurgitating, indigestible hair and bones as a pellet) and using science process skills (in this activity, analyzing, communicating, observing, inferring, classifying, predicting, extrapolating, synthesizing, evaluating, measuring, interpreting information, and making conclusions) enjoyed participation in the active, intellectual process of science. Science surveys and interviews conducted by the instructors after these lessons emphasized hands-on, inquiry-based science, revealed positive attitudes toward science (in both groups) and positive attitudes toward science teaching (in the university group).

Learning Science Is an Active Process
Teachers of science—whether at the elementary school or the university—should believe that learning science must be an active process. Learning science is something students do, not something that is done to them. When an instructor focuses on actively engaging students in doing science, then a natural connection of learning concepts, scientific skills, and attitudes follows. In such classrooms, a focal question in planning science lessons is "What will the students be doing?" Will the students be observing, classifying, measuring, predicting, inferring, collecting data, graphing, experimenting, and/or communicating? The better the teacher understands the level of skill development that the students have, the better she can choose activities to match the needs of her students.

Primary and lower elementary teachers should seek to construct activities that engage students in observing, classifying, measuring, using numbers, making inferences, predicting, indicating time and space relations, graphing, collecting data, and communicating. Teachers of the lower elementary grades should not hesitate to construct many lessons that engage students heavily in making careful observations (using each of the five senses of sight, hearing, smell, touch, and taste), recording observations in numerous ways (e.g., drawings, pictures, poems, rhymes, songs, graphics, essays, field journals), measuring objects with numerous tools in the English and metric systems, and communicating results of activities in many modalities (written, pictorial, graphic, and oral). Upper elementary teachers should plan activities that engage students in the basic process skills as listed above, along with more integrated science process skills including formulating hypotheses, identifying, manipulating and controlling variables, designing experiments, interpreting data from experiments, making operational definitions, and constructing models. Teachers should periodically assess the process skills of the students to better match activities to the students' development. Teachers need to indicate to the students the importance of concurrently developing process skills and scientific attitudes. This advocacy of science education serves the greater goal of promoting scientific literacy for all students.

Making Connections to Other Important Elements of Science Instruction/Learning

Just as it is important for students to be active in their learning, it is equally important for the teacher to be an active inquirer and a visible partner to the students during the instructional process. What follows are some comments from the fourth-grade teacher who taught the lesson on owl pellets.

"I approach teaching science in a way that empowers the students. The students will be given the power to create their own learning environment. The exploration chosen often comes from the students' needs. For example, if my students asked whether fire would go out if it were covered, that would be the area of discovery in a future lesson. These ideas on what to teach come from discussions I have with my students many times a day.

"When the children are working on activities that require an experimental design, I go to each group to discuss how they will set up the experiment. While the students are working on this task, I go from group to group and question the groups on why they chose to set up their experiment this way. The questions are not prepared questions, but are asked so that I have a full understanding of the experimental set-up, including the materials that the students will need. I hope these questions will lead the groups to identify the variables that can be considered, but if they do not consider the variables, it is OK. Some experimental set-ups will be better than others, but all projects will be acceptable. Each group of students will be working from what their group knows. They will be exposed to all the other groups' experiments, which will encourage them to consider other variables in their next exploration. I feel it is also important for the students in the group to self-evaluate their group's experiment. This includes what they think was best about their experiment and what they think they need to improve upon. This helps me to know where the group is in the learning process and what they will be focusing on in the next experiment.

"Before they begin the experiment, the groups need to predict what they think will happen. They may also predict why they think it will happen. When the children start the experiment, I go from group to group, asking each group questions about their experiment so I can understand their thinking and/or explanations. I keep notes on each group and record their responses to questions and any misconceptions that I detect. The group devises a plan and collects data according to the plan. Then the students explain what they think happened in the experiment and share any data collected and recorded by the group with other groups.

"In my class, I feel the students are in charge of their own learning. The teacher sets up situations in which the students are in charge of their learning. The teacher manages situations in which the students can discover and invent on their own to reach understanding. Science process skills are important in my classroom, as is development of critical thinking. The students are encouraged to reach understandings that allow them to be better able to explain their theories. I encourage students to reconsider any misconceptions they might have, and I have students discuss different opinions to see if a consensus can be reached."

The classroom setting described above includes the following characteristics:

- Students are engaged in a motivating classroom environment that provides encouragement and frequent student–teacher interaction.
- Students can integrate science processes and problem-solving skills.
- Students are encouraged to actively construct knowledge and explanations.
- Students can use familiar objects in real-life settings.
- Students are given the opportunity to encounter natural phenomena through firsthand experiences.
- Students are involved in varied classroom settings, including individualized instruction, cooperative learning, whole-class demonstrations, and interest centers.
- Students employ risk taking, divergent thinking, and self-initiated questioning.
- Student activities are developmentally appropriate and capitalize on student interest.
- Students are encouraged to create a learning community where everyone's opinions, questions, and conceptions are valued.

Obviously, an elementary classroom teacher preparing a science lesson has to focus on the question "What will the students be doing?" But just as important, the teacher needs to be cognizant of other important factors. These include selection of instructional materials, physical limitations of the students (e.g., in using manipulatives), choice of management strategy, assessment techniques, cognitive developmental levels of the students, decisions on prerequisites and hierarchy of tasks, and relevant or related science misconceptions. The selection of the overall instructional strategy (e.g., learning cycle or constructivist learning model) is also an important part of inquiry-based hands-on science.

Vignette 4–1 discusses how the use of scientific skills makes science meaningful and active. It is from both a classroom teacher's and a professor's point of view. What did you notice about the use of the skills of observation, classification, measurement, communication, inference, prediction, and experimentation.

In 1929, John Dewey noted that education emphasized the learning *of fixed conclusions* rather than the advancement of intelligence as a *method of action.* He went on to say that schools *separate knowledge from the very activities that would give the knowledge meaning.* By this, he meant that teachers concentrated on teaching facts and conclusions. They were not teaching concepts through experimentation. Students were not developing the skills necessary to investigate facts or to develop new knowledge.

In a more recent discussion of how science should be taught, National Research Council (NRC) members explain the necessity and interaction of activities and content even more specifically. Their views are summarized in the following quote:

> Those developing the national standards were committed to including inquiry as both science content and as a way to learn science. Therefore, rather than simply extolling the virtues of "hands-on" or "laboratory-based" teaching as the way to teach "science content and process," the writers of the *Standards* treated inquiry as both a learning goal and as a teaching method. (NRC, 2000, p. 18)

See
http://www.prenhall.com/peters
for links from the NRC.

In this millennium, educators should take seriously the NRC suggestion and Dewey's advice. Teachers need to continue the practice of inquiry teaching in their own classrooms. As the authors of both *National Science Education Standards* (NRC, 1996) and *Benchmarks for Science Literacy* (American Association for the Advancement of Science [AAAS], 1993) indicate, inquiry teaching is essential to scientific literacy for all students.

The goal of all science programs *should* be problem solving and developing the inquiry skills necessary for competing effectively in the global marketplace. Scientific ventures such as genetic engineering, drug research, telecommunications, nuclear fusion, and environmental monitoring are increasingly done as cooperative ventures between many nations. Today, more than ever, educators must prepare a diverse workforce capable of scientific research, investigation, and informed decision making.

To paraphrase Dewey, intelligent action is the lone definitive resource of humankind (1929). This action of education refers to such entities as the science process skills. These are what scientists, adults, and children use to do science.

Did you notice the skills being taught in the owl pellet activity in Vignette 4–1? Would this activity be one that you would use in your classroom? What instructional strategy or strategies are being used? Is the strategy consistent with the constructivist learning model as presented in Chapter 2? What is the **learning cycle** approach to inquiry mentioned in Vignette 4–1? How could the learning cycle be used in teaching skills to children?

The **learning cycle** is an inductive approach to instruction involving exploration, concept introduction, and concept application phases.

Using the Learning Cycle

The learning cycle is based on an *inquiry* approach to learning consistent with the standards (see the Science Inquiry Standards Link). The learning cycle helps students develop a quest for knowledge, data, or truth. All students are naturally curious, and this approach to learning scientific skills leads to a *conceptual understanding* (Karplus, 1977). An advantage of the learning cycle

The assumption behind the learning cycle is that it is consistent with the ways students learn and can modify false beliefs (see Rosenthal, 1993).

is that it is a methodology that can translate the skills and vocabulary used by scientists into a more meaningful learning experience for students. The learning cycle began several years ago as part of the Science Curriculum Improvement Study, or SCIS (Karplus & Their, 1967) and continues gaining in popularity (Odom & Settlage, 1996). In fact, this instructional strategy is in use in many current programs, such as the Full Option Science System (FOSS) by the Lawrence Hall of Science and some Biological Sciences Curriculum Study (BSCS) projects.

Charles Barman (1989) has modified the original terminology of the learning cycle to make it more understandable for elementary teachers. He suggests three phases as follows:

1. *Exploration Phase. The first phase of the cycle is student centered; the teacher plays the role of a facilitator, observing, questioning, and assisting students as needed. The students interact with materials and each other during this phase.*

In our owl pellet story, this phase occurred when the students were interacting with the owl pellets. For example, they were observing the contents of the owl pellets, classifying the bones with a key, and communicating with each other what they had found. In both the elementary classroom and the university classroom, the students were actively involved in inquiry, with the teacher playing the role of facilitator.

 See the Model Inquiry Unit section of the companion CD for a model based on the learning cycle.

2. *Concept Introduction Phase. This teacher-centered phase is characterized by naming things and events. The teacher's function is to gather information for students that pertains to their explorations in the first phase. The teacher works with students to develop vocabulary and to introduce pertinent information.*

Referring back to the students in Vignette 4–1, we find that the fourth-grade teacher brings in books for the students to begin naming things and events surrounding the formation of the pellet. The university class also engages in learning new names such as *Rodentia* and *Insectivora* as they continue the lesson.

3. *Concept Application Phase. This activity-oriented phase is, again, student centered and allows students to apply freshly learned information to new situations. The teacher presents a new problem to solve, allowing students time to apply what they have learned.*

The university students depict this phase as they diagram food webs to illustrate the barn owls' diet. They are applying what they have found out in the second phase. The fourth-grade students also begin to apply what they have learned as they further research the characteristics of the owl through children's literature and nature books.

As you can see in Figure 4–1, this cycle also has an *evaluation and discussion* aspect. This is an interactive component throughout each phase. The evaluation and discussion help identify current false beliefs and prevent the construction of new misconceptions. In each of the phases, the teacher may rely on various means of assessment (see Chap. 5) to assist in student understanding. Clearly, the cycle is supported by a continuous evaluation. That way, there can be a return to a previous phase, when needed, or an appropriate further application in a new phase.

In the previous examples, both the fourth-grade teacher and the university professor facilitated discussions throughout the owl pellet activity. They were careful to monitor what the students were saying and to ask pertinent questions wherever they thought

See
http://www.prenhall.com/peters
for other learning cycle links.

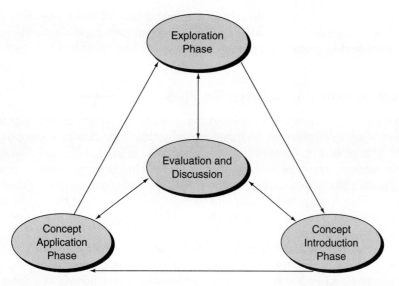

Figure 4–1
The learning cycle.
Source: Adapted from a figure by Charles Barman in "A Procedure for Helping Prospective Elementary Teachers Integrate the Learning Cycle into Science Textbooks," *Journal of Science Teacher Education, 1*(2), p. 22.

misconceptions were present. The ongoing assessment allows for a holistic, or complete, approach to evaluation that includes activity-based evaluation. Consider other possible evaluation strategies as we further explore the three phases.

Exploration Phase ————

As we discussed earlier, the **exploration phase** is a student-oriented phase. Remember the constructivist model presented in Chapter 2? The exploration phase of the learning cycle is similar to the exploration component of the constructivist learning model in which students are *actively engaged*. The teacher's function in either model is to scaffold the learning environment based on the concepts she or he believes are important for the students to learn at that time.

Students can be involved in observing, classifying what they have observed, measuring, making informal inferences based on their observations, conducting experiments, collecting and organizing data, and communicating their findings to their peers as part of the learning cycle exploration phase. It is important for you as the facilitator to build the foundation by making the connections between the activities and the students' everyday lives.

For example, if you want to develop an understanding of floating and sinking, you could first discuss the students' trips to a pool or the beach. What floated on the water? What sank? Next, have the students observe pictures of various objects either floating or sinking. Then, you could ask a series of questions designed to engage the students in a discussion of the phenomena. Here, they would begin to make inferences about why objects floated or sank. It would be important for you to identify the various students' inferences, noting similarities and differences in their perceptions or explanations. The students could

The **exploration phase** of the learning cycle allows children the opportunity to experience events to initiate their thought processes.

See the Model Inquiry Unit, Exploration section of the companion CD for an example of this phase of the learning cycle.

even test several objects during this phase and make a chart of which ones float or sink. Assessment during this phase could be as informal as open-ended questions or as structured as individual student interviews.

Concept Introduction or Invention Phase ——————

The **concept invention phase** of the learning cycle allows children the opportunity to determine relationships among the objects or events that they explored in the exploration phase.

See the Model Inquiry Unit, Concept Invention section of the companion CD for an example of this phase of the learning cycle.

During the **concept invention phase,** the teacher is a facilitator. She or he begins to focus the questioning, to organize the information, and to guide the class into an agreed-upon concept. This process of making connections and sense of things is termed *concept invention.* The teacher assists the students in naming the objects and concepts (vocabulary development) and in experimenting with the newly formed concepts, relating them to the experiences from the exploration phase. In terms of the constructivist model, the students are now in the "proposing explanations and solutions" phase and are looking for ways to construct new explanations.

In the floating and sinking example, the teacher would introduce terminology and concepts such as *weight, surface tension,* and *density.* Specific definitions would accompany these terms and relate to the students' explorations. Questioning why the students think some objects float and some sink would be based on both the new vocabulary and definitions and the explorations. Students would measure various densities in support of concept development. Finally, the students would construct the notion that objects that are denser than water will sink in water and that those that are less dense than water will float in water.

Concept Application Phase ——————

The **concept application phase** of the learning cycle allows children the opportunity to apply the concept or skill that they developed in the concept invention phase.

Now it is time for the students to apply their new knowledge and skills in the **concept application phase.** Students are provided similar situations and challenged to implement their new concepts. In terms of the constructivist model, the students are now taking action on what they have learned. They make decisions about the new explorations and apply newly learned knowledge and skills.

In terms of the floating and sinking example, the teacher may provide new items for students to hypothesize about and test. The teacher may also complete a performance-based evaluation (see Chap. 5) at this point, checking how many objects the students can correctly identify as "floaters" and "sinkers." Different experiments may test the new knowledge or lead back to the exploration phase of the cycle. For example, the teacher may ask the students to float a paper clip in a cup of water. The students know that the paper clip is denser than water, so now they have to experiment with surface tension, bringing them back to the exploration phase.

A Variation of the Learning Cycle

See the Model Inquiry Unit, Concept Application section of the companion CD for an example of this phase of the learning cycle.

One way to make the learning cycle more complete is through the addition of stages to capture the students' attention and assess what the students have learned after instruction (Staver & Shroyer, 1994). A variation of the learning cycle with these additions is the five-stage model developed by BSCS (Bybee et al., 1989). This five-stage model incorporates the engage, explore, explain, elaborate, and evaluate stages. The *engage* stage is matched with the invitation stage of the constructivist learning model. Students observing surroundings and looking for interesting phenomena are characteristics of both models. Here, teachers begin with questions to capture the students' attention.

The *explore, explain,* and *elaborate* stages are equivalent to the original learning cycle. The added *evaluate* stage is included to provide additional opportunity for assessment. It allows the teacher to find out what the students have learned and sets the stage to begin the cycle once again.

See *http://www.prenhall.com/peters* for examples of learning cycle models.

The Learning Cycle and Textbooks

In many elementary schools, a textbook series makes up the science program. Such books contain many activities. Their purpose is to illustrate ideas presented in the books in concrete terms. Teachers sometimes call the worst of these activities "cookbook experiments" because the problems, materials, directions, and even conclusions are furnished. Children are given little chance to construct meaningful knowledge or sharpen scientific skills. All that children are required to do is follow the recipe. Although more authors now use activities that require thinking, there are ways to modify cookbook activities into meaningful experiences. One way is to employ the learning cycle.

Do not start with reading the text. Rather, start with related explorations designed to invite students to want to explore more. Try an experiment out of the book as a discovery activity and not as a set of directions to follow. Then, use the text to develop the related language and reinforce the concepts. Finally, try some associated experiments from the text or supplemental materials.

If you are involved in selecting the textbook for your science program, pay attention to the ways authors lead into the activities and the comments following them. Look for questions that are posed before the experiment, with extending information following the experiment. This enables you to use the author's questions to explore beforehand, then introduce the experiment, and finally use the book's information to extend the children's learning after the experiment is completed.

See the Model Inquiry Unit, Four Days of Science section of the companion CD for an example of how the learning cycle can be used in an elementary science classroom.

The Learning Cycle and Skill Development

In short, we want to use the learning cycle to develop students' scientific understandings and skills. The learning cycle is generalized as a *do-talk-do* cycle (Ramsey, 1993). In the "do" parts of the cycle, skills are being used. What specifically are the scientific skills? Which skills are appropriate for the elementary student? What are some other ways to develop these skills?

In preparing for your own first elementary science unit, like the authors of Vignette 4–1, you may decide to use owls as a theme. You want to focus on observation skills. You will probably begin to ask yourself the following questions about observation:

How will this skill fit into my elementary curriculum?

Do I fully understand this skill, and am I prepared to teach it to children?

What are some examples of activities I can do to promote this specific skill?

Observing

The process of **observation** is the taking in of sense perceptions. It is our job to help our students use all their senses when they observe similarities, differences, and changes in objects or events. Students can learn that each of the senses is a gateway to observing different properties of objects. Seeing allows them to notice properties such as size, shape,

Observation is defined here as carefully exploring the properties of an object or phenomenon, such as texture, color, sound, taste, smell, length, mass, or volume.

An owl rests in its natural habitat as children observe its characteristics.

and color of objects and how the objects may interact. Hearing makes knowable properties of sounds, such as loudness, pitch, and rhythm. Touching teaches the meaning of texture and is another way to discover sizes and shapes of objects. Tasting shows how labels such as bitter, salty, sour, and sweet can be used to describe foods. Smelling calls for associating objects with odors, such as smells "like perfume" or "like cigar smoke."

Properties enable children to compare and describe likenesses and differences among objects. This leads to explorations that require several of the other processes, such as classifying and communicating. You can ask broad and narrow questions to guide learning in such science processes as observation.

In keeping with our owl theme, you may want to begin with a children's literature approach to the study of owls. *Owl Eyes* (Gates, 1994) is a good starting point. This story describes a Mohawk legend in which animals can choose their own colors and body form. It assists the students in observations of the owl and its characteristics. *Owl Moon* (Yolen, 1987) is another story rich in observation that describes a walk in the woods in search of owls. *Good-Night Owl!* (Hutchins, 1972) is a story about animal noises and would be a good introduction to student observations of animal sounds in the schoolyard.

As you begin to explore the owl pellets with children in a primary-level class, invite everyone to observe by saying something such as the following:

See *http://www.prenhall.com/peters* for links related to owl pellet availability and activities.

What do you notice about the object wrapped in foil?

Does it make any noise?

What do you think you will see inside?

Is what you see inside different from what you expected to see?

Later, pose more questions:

How does the object feel?

How many bones did you find?

What do the bones look like?

What does it smell like?

In a middle-level class, begin to make observations more specific:

What animal skeletons in the guide compare to the skeletons that you found?

How many animal remains did you find in the pellet?

In an upper-level class, explore with even more specific observations:

In what specific ways are the bones alike?

How do the skulls that you found compare with the ones shown in the guide?

Classifying

Most primary students can select and group real objects by some common property. **Classification** imposes order on collections of objects or events through characteristics such as color, shape, and size. Dichotomous classifications divide objects or events into two groupings. Elementary students should be proficient at dichotomous classification and multigroup classifications in which they observe and group items on the basis of different properties.

Classification is seen as constructing an order based on similarities and differences between objects or events.

With our owl lessons, we can introduce *The Book of North American Owls* (Sattler, 1995) and *Owls* (Kalman, 1987). The students can classify the owls on the basis of habitat or physical features. Through reading *Town Mouse & Country Mouse* (Brett, 1994), the students can set up a dichotomous key listing comparisons of the two types of habitats that the mice—and accompanying owl and cat—live in as presented in the story.

A Primary-Level Example

In a primary-level class, the students can look over the contents of the pellet and sort the contents by properties. The teacher can prompt the students with the following:

Think of one property, such as hardness. Sort all the objects that have that property into one pile. Leave what's left in another pile.

Later, to expand on the activity, the teacher can say:

What other properties can you use to sort your objects?

In another primary-level class, the students look over the contents of the pellet and sort the contents into animal and plant remains.

Middle- and Upper-Level Examples ───────────

Many middle-level students can classify an object into more than one category at the same time and hold this in mind. In a middle-level class, some students have classified owls into three groups, based on the geographic range of their habitat, with two subgroups each: urban and rural. They completed this independently in response to their teacher's question:

How can you group owls by habitat?

Next, the teacher will explore owl coloration subgroups. Some upper-level students can also reclassify according to other properties that fit their purposes. In an upper-level class, the students have a collection of pictures of animals that owls may prey upon. They start off by dividing them into groups by order but then decide that this will not fit their purpose. They have to reclassify according to the prey's location on the food chain. This example demonstrates a major point about classification: It is done to fit a purpose. What works to fulfill the intent of the classifier is what counts. Objects can be classified in many ways.

Measuring

Measurement is the specific determination of the length, mass, volume, speed, time, or other property of an object or event. See the companion Web site for additional information.

Thinking about properties in a quantitative way naturally leads to measuring them. **Measurement** is used to compare things. At first, at the primary level, children may be unable to compare an object with a standard measuring tool, such as a meterstick or yardstick. Instead, they find out who is taller by standing back-to-back. They find out which of two objects is heavier by holding each object in their hands. Eventually, they begin to use nonstandard measuring devices, such as paper clips or lengths of string, to measure their desks.

There is good reason to start off measuring in this way. Remember that primary students may not conserve several concepts that deal with quantity. Changing the appearance of an object still fools them. Children who think that merely spreading out some material gives them more, for example, have to be taught differently than children who conserve quantity. Most young children find it difficult to work meaningfully with standard units of measurement such as centimeters and inches until about age 7.

Primary students can build readiness for working with standard units by using parts of their bodies or familiar objects as arbitrary units to measure things. A primary child may say, "The classroom is 28 of *my* feet wide."

Concrete Referents and Improvised Tools ───────────

One way to improve the ability of children to measure and estimate accurately is to have numerous concrete objects in your classroom for them to refer to as needed. Metersticks, yardsticks, and trundle wheels are useful for thinking about length. Containers marked with metric and English units are good for measuring liquid volumes.

Similar references are needed for other concepts involving quantity. A kilometer is a round trip from the school to the police station. A mile is the distance from the school to the post office. Meanings associated with time can be developed by many references to water or sand clocks (containers with holes punched in the bottom) and real clocks. Temperature differences become meaningful through using several kinds of thermometers.

Measurement Motivators: From Dinosaurs to Decimals (Palumbo, 1989) and *Measurement: 35 Hands-On Activities* (Garcia, 1997) can be helpful resources when developing meaningful measurement experiences with your students. The concept of measurement as a part of everyday life is also seen in *How Big Is a Foot* (Myller, 1990), in which a foot is used to measure a bed. As students become interested in more detailed information, refer to such sources as *The World of Measurements* (Klein, 1974). This source contains details on units, their history, and their use.

By the time they leave elementary school, most children will have had some experience with a variety of measuring instruments such as the ruler, meterstick, yardstick, balance, clock, thermometer, graduated cylinder, protractor, directional compass, and wind gauge. When possible, children themselves should choose the right measuring tool for the activity under way. Sometimes they can make their own tools when they need them. Inventing and making a measuring instrument can be challenging and interesting.

Measurement and the Metric System

Scientists everywhere have long used the metric system because it is simpler and faster than the English system because its units are defined in multiples of 10. The three basic units most commonly used in the metric system are the meter, liter, and gram.

A meter is used to measure length, a liter is used to measure liquid volume, and a gram is used to measure weight or mass. Strictly speaking, the terms *mass* and *weight* mean different things in science. Mass is the amount of material or matter that makes up an object. Weight is the gravitational force that pulls the mass. On the moon, for example, an astronaut's weight is only about one sixth of what it is on the earth, but the astronaut's mass stays unchanged.

The Celsius (C) thermometer, named after its inventor, Anders Celsius, commonly measures temperature in the metric system. It has a scale marked into 100 evenly spaced subdivisions.

Prefixes are used in the metric system to show larger or smaller quantities. The three most common prefixes and their meanings are these:

- *milli-*: one-thousandth (0.001)
- *centi-*: one-hundredth (0.01)
- *kilo-*: one-thousand (1000)

Take a closer look at Figure 4–2 to see how the prefixes are used in combination with the basic units.

Before your students use different metric standards, have them consider the right standard for the job. Children will usually discover that the metric system is easier to use than the English system. Conversions from or to the English system should be avoided because they are confusing. If your curriculum calls for work with both metric and English measures, give your students a lot of practice with concrete materials for both systems. Try to treat each system separately instead of shifting back and forth. For example, when the students are comparing indoor and outdoor Fahrenheit temperatures as part of a weather activity, do not automatically ask what the temperature would be in degrees Celsius.

Length

1 millimeter (mm)	= The diameter of paper clip wire
1 centimeter (cm)	= The width of a formed paper clip
1 meter (m)	= 1000 millimeters (mm)
1 meter (m)	= 100 centimeters (cm)
1 kilometer (km)	= 1000 meters (m)
1 kilometer (km)	= About the length of nine football fields
1 kilometer (km)	= About six tenths of a mile

Volume

1 milliliter (ml)	= About one fifth of a teaspoon
1 liter (l)	= 1000 milliliters (ml)
1 liter (l)	= 100 centiliters (cl)
1 liter (l)	= Slightly over a quart
1 kiloliter (kl)	= 1000 liters (l)

Weight (Mass)

1 milligram (mg)	= About 1/1000 of the mass of a paper clip
1 gram (g)	= 1000 milligrams (mg)
1 gram (g)	= 100 centigrams (cg)
1 kilogram (kg)	= 1000 grams (g)
1 kilogram (kg)	= About 2.2 pounds

Temperature

0 degrees Celsius	= Freezing point of water
100 degrees Celsius	= Boiling point of water

Figure 4–2
Comparison of length, volume, mass, and temperature.

Instead, at a later time, develop a chart of Celsius temperatures outside over the period of a month and discuss the temperatures and any temperature changes.

The story *A Toad for Tuesday* (Erickson, 1998) can be a starting place for measurement activities related to the owl theme. Potential measurement activities could include the distance of the toad's journey through the woods before meeting the owl, the time the owl waits before changing his mind about his vow to eat the toad, the potential temperatures of the woods, the relative sizes of the toad and owl, and the appropriate weights of the owl and toad.

Communicating

Communication is the sharing of information through written or spoken means such as an oral report, charts, graphs, reports, and publications.

Communication is putting the information or data obtained from our observations into some form that another person can understand or some form that we can understand at a later date. Children learn to communicate in many ways. They learn to draw accurate pictures, diagrams, and maps; make proper charts and graphs; construct accurate models and exhibits; and use clear language when describing objects or events. The last of these activities is usually stressed in elementary science.

It is important to say things or show data in the clearest possible way. We can help our students learn this by giving them many chances to communicate and by helping them evaluate what they have said or done.

The book *The Man Who Could Call Down Owls* (Bunting, 1984) is a good introduction to communication. *Turtle in July* (Singer, 1989) also involves month-by-month communication from animals' points of view, including a poem from an owl.

Think of a primary-level class where some students are seated on a rug. They are viewing a series of pictures of the life cycle of an owl from an LCD projector. The teacher has scanned the pictures into the computer from *See How They Grow: Owl* (Ling, 1992) and is projecting them for all the students to see. She suggests a game in which a child communicates the properties of a life stage, such as "I am fluffy, hunched over, and my eyes are closed." Others try to identify the stage. The child who identifies the growth period first gets to be the new describer. Reminding the children to carefully consider the description discourages guessing. After each identification, the teacher asks questions, such as these:

What did she say that helped you figure out this stage?

What else would be helpful to say?

Did anyone get mixed up?

How do you think that happened?

The teacher summarizes the communications activity by reading *Owl Babies* (Waddell, 1994) and having the children describe the owlets.

In an upper-level class, the students want to find out the locations of owls. They are collaborating with students from throughout the region via the Internet. Students are collecting real-time data on sightings of owls and hearing owls' screeches. Together they will make maps, charts, and graphs on their findings and communicate the results.

In another upper-level class, the students want to find out the warmest time of the day. Temperature readings are made on the hour from 10 a.m. until 3 p.m. for 5 days in a row and then averaged. They decide to record their results on a line graph, but they don't know whether to put the temperature along the side (vertical axis) or along the bottom (horizontal axis) of the graph. Is there a "regular" way? The teacher helps them see how graphs are arranged in their mathematics text. Scientists call the change being tested the *manipulated variable*. In this case, time is usually placed along the horizontal axis. The change that results from the test is called the *responding variable*. In this situation, temperature is the responding variable and is placed along the vertical axis.

See
http://www.prenhall.com/peters
for links related to graphing.

Defining Operationally

Defining operationally is a subprocess of communicating, usually introduced after the primary grades. To define a word operationally is to describe it by an action (operation) rather than just by other words. For example, suppose you invite some students to hold an evaporation contest: Who can dry water-soaked paper towels fastest? They begin to speculate excitedly. But there is just one thing they will have to agree on before the fun begins: How will everyone know when a towel is "dry"? This question stumps the students, so you pose another open question that hints at *actions* they could take: What are some things they could *do to the towel* to tell if it is dry? Now, they start coming up with operations (actions) to try:

Squeeze the towel into a ball and see if water comes out.

Rub it on the chalkboard; see if it makes a wet mark.

Tear it and compare the sound to a dry towel you tear.

Hold it up to the light and compare its color to an unsoaked towel.

See if it can be set on fire as fast as an unsoaked towel.

Put an unsoaked towel on one end of a balance beam; see if the other towel balances it.

The children agree that the last operation is easiest to observe and the least arguable. It is stated as an operational definition: "A towel is dry if it balances an unsoaked towel from the same package." Now the activity can begin.

Had the open question not worked, one or two narrow questions such as "How would squeezing the towel show if it is dry?" could have been posed, followed later with a broad question like "What else could you do to the towel to tell if it is dry besides squeezing it?"

When operational definitions are not used, it is easy to fall into the trap of **circular reasoning:** What is the condition of a *dry* towel? It contains no moisture. What is the condition of a towel that *contains no moisture?* It is dry. Or, to borrow from children's humor, consider this example:

He is the best scientist we've ever had.

Who is?

He is.

Who is "He"?

The best scientist we've ever had.

There are some predictable times when the need for operational definitions will come up. Watch the children's use of relative terms such as *tall, short* (How tall? short?), *light, heavy, fast, slow, good,* and *bad* (What is "*bad*" luck?).

Circular reasoning is like a specious argument where the child's answer is plausible to a child but the argument has a logical flaw.

Recording Activities ——————

Recording is another subprocess of communicating. When activities require time to gather data (e.g., growing plants over many weeks) or when there are many data to consider (e.g., discovering how much Vitamin C many juices contain), it is often sensible to make a record of what is happening. Without a record, it is difficult to remember what has happened and to draw conclusions. In a way, recording can be considered communicating with oneself. Many teachers ask their students to make records in a notebook or *data log.* Records can be in picture or graph form, as well as in writing. But whichever way the data are recorded, they should be clear.

In a primary-level class, some children are recording the growth of their plants with strips of colored paper. Every other day, they hold a new strip of paper next to each plant and tear off a bit to match the plant's height. They date the strips and paste them in order on large paper sheets. A growth record of the plants is clearly visible to all the students.

Table 4–1

Acidity of Mystery Liquids

Group	1	2	3	4	5	
Miranda	A	B	N	B	A	A: Acid
Tasha	A	B	N	B	A	B: Base
Evan	A	A	N	A	A	N: Neutral
Brian	A	B	N	A	A	
Britton	B	B	N	B	B	

Other children in the class have drawn pictures of their plants at different stages, from seed to mature plant. These pictures are made into record booklets at the teacher's suggestion. The children describe each picture for the teacher, who swiftly writes their short statements on paper slips. The children paste these beneath their pictures. The result is a "My Plant Storybook" for each child, who can proudly read it to impressed parents.

In a middle-level class, five groups are at work with narrow strips of litmus paper. (This chemically treated paper changes color when dipped into acidic or basic liquids.) The children want to find out whether five mystery liquids in numbered jars are acidic, basic, or neutral. Each group has a recorder who notes the findings on a data sheet. At the end of the work session, the teacher asks how the results of all the groups should be recorded on the chalkboard. It is decided as outlined in Table 4–1. Notice that by having a code (A: Acid, B: Base, N: Neutral) written to one side, the teacher cuts down on the time needed to record the findings. The data are now compared, differences noted, and possible reasons discussed. Careful retesting is planned to straighten out the differences.

In an upper-level class, some students want to find out whether there is a pattern to the clouds passing over the city in the spring. They have made a chart that has three columns: one each for March, April, and May. In each column is a numbered space for each day of that month. Next to about half of the days, the students have drawn the weather bureau cloud symbols for the cloud cover, if any, on those days. Even though the record chart is only partly completed, a sequential pattern is taking shape. After the chart is completed, the students will compare it with data gathered by the local weather bureau office for the same months in previous years.

Inferring

The usual meaning of **inference** is to interpret or explain what we observe. If Wallie smiles when she greets us (observation), we may infer that she is pleased to see us (explanation). The accuracy of our inferences usually improves with more chances to observe. Several like observations may also lead us to the *prediction* that the next time we see her, she will smile (observation) because she will be pleased to see us (explanation). For convenience, then, view the process of inferring as having two parts: We may make an *inference* from what we observe, and we may predict an *observation* from what we

Inference is an explanation of an observation based on the available information.

infer. Let's now look at children *explaining* observations and then, later, in another section, *predicting* them.

Inferring as Explaining ————————

In at least three common ways, we as educators can help children infer properly from observations. Primary-level students, however, may have a very limited overall understanding of this process.

Look at the Constructivist Pedagogy, Private Speech section of the companion CD. Are the students engaged in observations or inferences?

First, we can get students to distinguish between their observation and an inference. In a middle-level class, two children are looking at a picture of shoeprints in the snow. One set of prints is much smaller than the other (observation). One child says, "One of these sets of shoeprints must have been made by a man and the other by a boy" (an inference). The other child says, "That's true" (another inference). Hearing this, the teacher asks an open question to make them aware of other possibilities:

In what other ways could these prints have been made?

They think for a moment and come up with other inferences: Perhaps two children made the prints—one wore his father's shoes; or maybe it was a girl and her mother; or it could have been a girl and her older brother.

The teacher points out that what they have observed is still the same but that there is more than one way to explain the observation. If the children look at the tracks closely, they may *conclude* that one of their inferences is more likely than the others. A *conclusion* is simply the inference in which one has the most confidence after considering all the evidence.

Second, we can get students to interpret data they have observed or recorded. Remember the students who were using litmus paper to identify mystery liquids? When several groups recorded their data, they noticed that some data were inconsistent. Some liquids were labeled both acidic and basic. The children inferred from this that the litmus test was done incorrectly by one of the groups. After the tests were redone, all the data became consistent. So, the children inferred that their final labeling of the mystery liquids was probably correct.

Recall the cloud data study. The sequential pattern the children saw when they examined their data was an inferred pattern. Later, when they compare their pattern with the weather bureau's report, they will be able to evaluate the quality of their inference.

Third, we can let students observe and interpret only indirect evidence or clues. Scientists must often depend on clues rather than clear evidence in forming possible inferences. For example, no scientist has visited the middle of the earth, yet earth scientists have inferred much about its properties.

Children can learn to make inferences from incomplete or indirect evidence, and they can also learn to become wary of hasty conclusions. In a primary-level class, some students are working with two closed shoeboxes. One box contains a smooth-sided, cylindrical pencil; the other box contains a six-sided, cylindrical pencil. The children's problem is, Which box contains which kind of pencil?

They tip the boxes back and forth and listen intently, inferring correctly the contents of the two boxes. When the teacher asks them what made them decide as they did, one child says, "You could feel which one was the bumpy pencil when it rolled." The other child says, "The bumpy one made more noise."

Later, the teacher puts into the boxes two pencils that are identical except for length. The students now find that correct inferring is more difficult, so they become more cautious. What observations must they rely on now?

In the middle and upper grades, students can do an excellent job of inferring the identity or interactions of hidden objects from indirect observational clues. In science, this way of inferring is called *model building*.

Explore owl inferences with your students. Why is the beak shaped a particular way? Why are the feathers of one owl different than those of another? How do owls differ from eagles or other birds of prey? Read *A First Look at Owls, Eagles, and Other Hunters of the Sky* (Selsam & Hunt, 1986) to follow up on your inferences.

Predicting

A **prediction** is a forecast of a future observation based on inferences from the available data. The more data that are available, the more confidence we have in the prediction; the reverse is also true. We can be very confident that spring will follow winter, but not at all confident that spring fashions this year will be exactly like those of a year ago. Without some data, we can only guess about future observations; to predict is impossible. When students put their data in graph form, they usually have many chances to predict.

Upper-level students measure and record on a graph the time candles burn under inverted glass jars. After they have recorded the times for 100-, 200-, and 300-milliliter jars, the teacher asks, "How long do you think the candle will burn under a 250-milliliter jar?"

Notice that predicting the time for a 250-milliliter jar would require the students to read the graph between the current data—they have the times for a 200- and a 300-milliliter jar. This is called *interpolating*. If the teacher had asked the students to predict the candle-burning time of a 400-milliliter jar, the students would have needed to go beyond the current data. This is called *extrapolating* from data. Using these processes to predict is more accurate than guessing.

Children often need assistance when predicting. Simple diagrams can help them reason through data. If they cannot calculate precise predictions, just asking them to predict the direction of change is useful to them. Primary-level students might be asked, "Will *more* or *less* water evaporate when the wind blows?" Middle-level students might be asked, "Will a *higher, lower,* or the *same* temperature result when these two water samples of different temperatures are mixed?"

> A **prediction** is an estimate of a future observation.

Experimenting

Experimentation is the quintessence of inquiry teaching. In the Inquiry Teaching Standard, the authors of the standards list investigations, inquiry, accessibility of science resources, and the learning environment as important teaching considerations. When we think of inquiry, we often think of experiments. But just what is involved with an "experiment?"

To a child, experimenting means "doing something to see what happens." Although this definition is overly simple, it does capture the difference between experimenting and the other six science processes. In experimenting, we change objects or events to learn how nature changes them. This section is about how children can discover the various conditions of change. Experimentation builds on the concept of open-ended investigations.

Experimenting is often called an *integrated* process skill because it may require us to use some or all of the other process skills: observing, classifying, inferring and

> **Experimentation** is finding a conclusion to a hypothesis through the integration of all the scientific skills.

Inquiry Teaching Standard

Teachers of science design and manage learning environments that provide students with the time, space, and resources needed for learning science. In doing this, teachers:

- **Structure the time available so that students are able to engage in extended investigations.**

- **Create a setting for student work that is flexible and supportive of science inquiry.**

- **Ensure a safe working environment.**

- **Make the available science tools, materials, media, and technological resources accessible to students.**

- **Identify and use resources outside the school.**

- **Engage students in designing the learning environment.**

(Teaching Standard D, National Research Council, 1996, p. 43)

predicting, measuring, and communicating. That is one reason some curriculum writers may reserve experimentation for upper-grade activities. But experimental investigations can vary in difficulty. With guidance, even primary students will benefit from experimentation. This does not mean any hands-on activity may properly be called experimenting. Two generally accepted criteria that separate hands-on activities from experimentation are these:

> *Children should have an idea they want to test (hypothesizing).*
>
> *Children should vary only one condition at a time (controlling variables).*

To many educators, almost any investigation is experimenting, as long as the child changes an object for a purpose and can compare its changed state to the original one. This is the position taken in this book.

Hypothesizing

How do we get students to form ideas they want to test before they manipulate objects? There are several ways of getting children to state operations that they want to try. For elementary students, stating operations as questions such as "Will dropping a magnet make it weaker?" or "Does adding salt to water make objects float higher?" is a clear and easy way for them to state hypotheses. It makes them focus on what they want to do to produce some effect, or on what effect to observe and connect to a cause.

In science, a hypothesis is often stated in an "if–then" manner: *If* I do this, *then* I believe this will happen. *If* a magnet is dropped, *then* it will get weaker. You may want to use the if–then form with upper-level students. But for most children, stating a hypothesis as an operational question is easier and more understandable.

Allowing students to explore the properties of real objects stimulates them to suggest their own ideas for changing the properties. Their curiosity usually prompts them to state operations they want to try or to be receptive to broad or narrow questions that you ask. For example, in a primary-level class, some children have been making and playing with toy parachutes. They tie the four corners of a handkerchief with strings and attach these to a sewing spool. Some release their parachutes while standing on top of the playground slide and watch them fall slowly to the ground. Others simply wad the cloth around the spool and throw their parachutes up into the air.

A few children have made their parachutes from different materials. They are quick to notice that some parachutes stay in the air longer than others. After they go back to the classroom, they discuss their experiences. Then, the teacher says:

> *We have plenty of materials to make more parachutes on the science table. How can you make a parachute that will fall more slowly than the one you have now?*

Students discover the properties of a parachute as part of an extension to a parachute lab.

The children will respond in different ways: "Make it bigger," "Make it smaller," "Use a lighter spool," or "Make it like Martha's." These are the children's hypotheses. Some children may say nothing, but peer intently at the materials. They are hypothesizing, too, only nonverbally. The children's ideas need testing so that they can find out what works. Now the children have purposes for doing further work with parachutes.

Where did the children's hypotheses come from? When the children were first observing their parachutes in action, they did much inferring. ("Jimmy's parachute is bigger than mine. It stays up longer." "Corinne has a big spool. Her chute falls fast.") It is natural for people to be curious about the correctness of their inferences. *Hypotheses are simply inferences that people want to test.*

Exploring the properties of concrete materials provides the background that most children need to construct new concepts. They may not be able to offer broad explanatory hypotheses to test concepts or theories. This calls for additional scaffolding and prior knowledge and experience. For this reason, some *what* questions, such as "What makes a ship float?" are difficult for children to answer. Instead of broad, generalizable hypotheses, elementary students are likely to offer limited hypotheses based on the objects they have observed or manipulated.

Primary students are far more limited in this ability than upper-elementary thinkers. Scaffolding is more effective with real materials to think about during their discussion, instead of relying on discussion alone. Most primary students can only think about one variable at a time. This limits the experimenting they can do, because they are unlikely to control other variables that might affect the outcome. So, primary-level investigations usually lean more heavily on the other six science processes.

Controlling Variables ————

To find out exactly what condition makes a difference in an experiment, we must change or vary that condition alone. Other conditions must not vary; in other words, they must be *controlled* during the experiment.

Suppose you think that varying the size of a parachute will affect its falling rate. A good way to test the variable is to build two parachutes that are identical in every way except size. These could then be released at the same time from the same height. After repeated trials, you can infer whether size makes a difference in the test.

Don't expect primary-level students to reason in this way. They will not think of the many variables or conditions that can influence their experiment. They may unwittingly change several variables at the same time. Their intent is simply to make a parachute that will fall more slowly than another, not to isolate variable conditions. Young children, in contrast, will grasp the need to control some variables. Typically, they will insist on releasing their parachutes from the same height and at the same time. Otherwise, "it won't be fair," they will tell you.

The parachute experiment is more than just a trial-and-error activity. The children have observed parachutes and have done some inferring about their observations. The changes they try will reflect thinking we can call hypothesizing. And although they may not think of controlling *all* the possible variables, they are conscious of *some*. This is the nature of children. How well they do and how fast they progress is influenced by how we as teachers scaffold their experiences. Following are more examples of teachers helping their students construct the idea of experimentation.

In a middle-level class, the children have worked with seeds and plants for about 2 weeks. The teacher says:

> *We've done well in getting our plants started. But suppose we didn't want our seeds to sprout and grow. Sometimes in nature seeds get damaged or conditions are not right for seeds to grow. What could you do to keep seeds from sprouting and growing?*

The children begin suggesting operations to try, as shown in Figure 4–3. These are their hypotheses; at this point, they need not be framed as operational questions. The teacher writes all of these on the chalkboard, regardless of content. The teacher then has the class screen the hypotheses for those that may have possibilities:

> *With which conditions might the seed have some chance to live? Suppose Jimmy squashed his seed just a little. Would the seed sprout? Would the plant look squashed? Would this happen with any kind of a seed? How about some of the rest of these conditions?*

This mixture of broad and narrow questions is posed slowly to give the children time to think. The children discuss a number of possibilities. After a while, the teacher says:

> *How can we test our ideas?*

Squashing it	Cutting it in half
Chewing it	Not watering it
Freezing it	Watering it with salt water
Boiling it	Microwaving it

Figure 4–3
Things that may keep a seed from growing.

It soon becomes obvious that some children are going to do several things at one time to their seeds, so the teacher says:

Suppose Beth squashes her seed and also freezes it. How will she know which one stopped the seed from growing?

The children decide to change just one condition at a time. Pairs of children quickly form operational questions from hypotheses they want to test:

Will squashing a bean seed keep it from sprouting? Will cutting a bean seed in half keep it from sprouting?

Interest is high as experimenting begins.

In an upper-level class, the students are working in pairs. They are testing their reaction time by catching dropped rulers. In each pair, one student holds the ruler just above his partner's hand. When he releases the ruler, the partner catches the ruler between her thumb and forefinger. The ruler number closest to the top of her pinched fingers is recorded. This is her "reaction time." After a few minutes, the teacher asks the students to give their reaction times. He writes these on the board in the form of a histogram, as shown in Table 4–2. Histograms are used to classify data in a way that encourages thinking about the differences in the data.

After a few moments, in a discussion with the students on how the scores are distributed, the teacher says:

Suppose everything and everyone were the same in our experiment. How would the histogram look? Well, are there differences that may have given us these results? What conditions might affect reaction time?

The students start forming hypotheses:

"Not everybody did it the same way," "Some people have faster reaction times," "Some kids have more practice," "I was tired today."

After a discussion to narrow down and clarify different ideas, the teacher says:

How are you going to test your ideas?

The students state their ideas as operational questions: Will people have the same reaction time if they do the experiment in exactly the same way? Does practice give you a faster reaction time? Do people who feel "tired" (defined as having fewer than 8 hours of

---

Table 4–2

Reaction Time Histogram

1	2	3	4	5	6	7	8	9	10	11	12
						X					
						X					
						X					
				X		X					
				X	X	X	X				
		X		X	X	X	X				
		X		X	X	X	X	X	X		
X		X		X	X	X	X	X	X		X

sleep) have slower times than when they don't feel tired? Everybody agrees that they must do the experiment in the same way each time to control the test variables. Then each question is tested separately under the controlled conditions.

When developing your students' scientific skills, consider experiments involving owl pellets. Ask the students to explore the question "What is the relationship between the size of the pellet and the number of skeletons inside?" Have the students brainstorm other ways to experiment related to owls, their environment, or the food chain. There are benefits to involving students in the learning process. One positive outcome is in the area of student attitudes toward science.

Scientific Attitudes

Exploring your students' attitudes and resolving any negative attitudes toward science will assist in positive teaching experiences throughout the school year.

As seen in the Inquiry and Attitudes Standard, an important part of inquiry is acquiring positive scientific attitudes. Experimentation and other skills are not fully developed if they are completed in a negative framework or only finished to "get it over with." Science is different from such activities as learning to spell, in which the task is simple and there is only one correct answer. Science includes developing attitudes and questioning those attitudes. The development of these attitudes is part of the job for elementary teachers. We will consider five categories related to attitudes.

Curiosity

"To be a child is to touch, smell, taste, and hear everything you can between the time you get up and when your parents make you go to bed. I don't have to *teach* curiosity. It's there already." The kindergarten teacher who made that statement about curiosity echoes the feeling of many of her elementary school colleagues. Yet, in some classes, there are children who lack interest in science.

Walk into two adjoining classrooms: one with a hands-on science program and another where students just read and do worksheets during science time. Handing concrete materials to children is like rowing downstream or cycling with the wind at your back. Making children sit still and be quiet for long periods is like rowing upstream or riding into the wind: You can do it, but it's best avoided. Children lose much of their curiosity unless they are allowed to do what comes naturally.

Teachers who maintain or spark students' curiosity apply science to everyday life. These teachers also use several open-ended investigations during a teaching unit. As you can see, we often use children's literature as a way to initiate curiosity about a topic. For example, reading *Poppy* (Avi, 1995) explores the relationship between an owl and a deer mouse. Students will immediately begin to wonder about the relationship between these two animals.

Inventiveness ──────

To be inventive is to solve problems in creative or novel ways. This contrasts with simply taking a known solution and applying it to a problem at hand: It's good to apply what you know about a car jack to change a flat tire, but what do you do when there's no jack? Inventive people may apply their knowledge to solve problems much as other persons do. But they are more likely to show **fluency, flexibility,** and **originality** in their thinking.

Critical Thinking ──────

To think critically is to evaluate or judge whether something is adequate, correct, useful, or desirable. A judge does this when she decides whether the evidence is adequate to find guilt; the judge has a standard in mind against which she makes a judgment. This is key to critical thinking: Know the accepted standard and decide whether or to what degree it is being met.

A problem we face as teachers of elementary children is the numerous standards of behavior in science. Many are highly sophisticated. Let's see if we can reduce them to a manageable few and restate them on a level that makes sense to young minds.

Science has three overall standards for critical thinking that most children can gradually understand and learn to make decisions about: *open-mindedness, objectivity,* and *willingness to suspend judgment* until enough facts are known.

The *open-minded* person listens to others and is willing to change his mind if warranted. An *objective* person tries to be free of bias, considers both sides in arguments, and realizes that strong personal preferences may interfere with the proper collecting and processing of data. Someone who *suspends judgment* understands that additional data may confirm or deny what first appears. Looking for further data improves the chances for drawing proper conclusions.

Try having several groups work on the same activity and then report and compare findings. The degree of open-mindedness soon becomes obvious when people refuse to listen to others, push their own ideas, or jump to conclusions before all groups have their say.

Critical and creative thinking go hand in hand. It's artificial to separate them. When problem solving or experimenting, for example, children should be encouraged to generate several possibilities, rather than just consider the first idea suggested. You also want them to appraise all the ideas critically so that they can tackle what looks most promising. Controlling variables in experimenting gives students another chance to generate suggestions, but they must also think: "Will these controls do the job?" Later, if groups come up with different findings, critical thinking is again needed to answer why. Perhaps one or more variables were not controlled after all. You can see that creative and critical thinking are different sides of the same coin.

When students seek information, a variety of sources are available to them, including each other, printed matter, audiovisual materials, electronic information, and knowledgeable adults. Certainly, students can be cautioned to check copyright dates and agreement with what is known, to consult more than one source, and to note conflicts in fact. This is especially important when exploring the Internet, where information can be

Fluency refers to the number of ideas a child gives when challenged with a problem. We can promote fluency by asking open-ended questions.

Flexibility is the inclination to shift one's focus from the usual.

Originality is shown when children generate ideas that are new to them. We can promote originality by encouraging children to use their imagination and combine others' ideas in new ways, and by withholding evaluative comments until we have all the ideas.

posted from anyone who has access to it. Children often do not critically appraise information. As educators, we can help children learn ways to consult these sources efficiently and to understand what the sources say.

Spend time reading fictional materials with your students. *Owls in the Family* (Mowat, 1981) is a humorous tale of two owls. Critical thinking is promoted as students begin to separate fact from fiction in this story.

Persistence ─────────

Most elementary science activities can be completed within a short time. But some require a sustained and vigorous effort. To do our best work often takes persistence. Children sometimes lack the persistence to stick with a worthwhile goal. Primary-level students often want instant results. Their short attention span and need for physical activity can easily convert into impatience. You can combat this impatience by arousing children's interests with meaningful science activities.

Uncertainty ─────────

Another important attitude to develop is the ability to understand or accept uncertainty. Much of this centers on students understanding the nature of elementary statistics. Some events can be predicted well; some cannot. We do not always know all the variables in a given situation, nor do we always have representative data of a population. For instance, the weather announcer on television only predicts rain tomorrow on the basis of the percentage of times it has rained with similar weather conditions (e.g., air pressure, wind patterns, cold/warm fronts).

Elementary students should be aware that evidence is not always complete and that therefore predictions may not always be precise. Experiments are influenced by the lack of an accurate observation, missing information of compounding factors, or a model to explain the variables effectively. Scientists do not always have all the answers, but must theorize on the observations and experimental results they do have.

Developing Attitudes ─────────

Early learning of attitudes begins with imitation and later comes from experiences with the consequences of having or not having the attitudes. The open-minded, accepting teacher who reflects positive attitudes is more likely to influence students in positive ways than one who lacks these qualities.

See the Nature of Science section of the companion CD for examples related to scientific attitudes.

Open-ended activities bring out positive attitudes. Success in science is bound up with curiosity, inventiveness, critical thinking, persistence, and tolerance for uncertainty. Children learn, in a more limited way, the same habits of mind as scientists and other reflective people. Successfully practicing these attitudes helps build self-esteem.

Summary

1. In observing, students learn to use all their senses, note similarities and differences in objects, and become aware of change.
2. In classifying, students group things by properties or functions. Students may also arrange them in order of value.

3. Measuring teaches students to use nonstandard and standard units to find or estimate quantity. Measurement is often applied in combination with skills introduced in the mathematics program.
4. Communicating teaches students to put observed information into some clear form that another person can understand.
5. By inferring, students interpret or explain what they observe. When students infer from data that something will happen, usually the term *predicting* is used. When people state an inference they want to test, usually the term *hypothesizing* is used. Therefore, predicting and hypothesizing are special forms of inferring.
6. In experimenting, we often guide students to state their hypotheses as operational (testable) questions and help them control variables within their understanding.

Reflection

1. Safety is an important consideration when experimenting or developing other scientific skills in the elementary classroom. Purchase a copy of *Safety in the Elementary Science Classroom* (1997, available from the National Science Teachers Association and at *http://www.nsta.org*) and identify potential safety hazards in your practicum classroom. Also visit the companion Web site (*http://www.prenhall.com/peters*) for more safety information.
2. What other scientific skills can you think of to teach children? What approaches could you take to develop these skills in elementary students?
3. How well do you know the science processes? Experiment with one of the activities from the books listed in the Suggested Readings. Repeat your experiment with students at your practicum site and compare their results with your classmates'.
4. Interview an elementary student and compare her scientific attitudes with those in this chapter. Share these results with the class or your instructor.
5. Try some activities in *Floaters and Sinkers* (Cordel & Hillen, 1995, Fresno, CA: AIMS Education Foundation) as an initial source to learning cycle activities related to mass, volume, and density.
6. A fun way to introduce the metric system is to have a classroom or schoolwide Olympics. The book *Math + Science: A Solution* (Ecklund & Wiebe, 1987, Fresno, CA: AIMS Education Foundation) has metric measurement activities related to the Olympics. *Olympic Math* (Vogt, 1996, Grandview, IL: GoodYear Books) also has measurement and graphing activities. The *Math Counts* series (Pluckrose, 1995, Chicago, Children's Press) has many titles related to introductory measurement, such as *Length, Weight, Time,* and *Capacity,* that can assist students in identifying concepts as part of the Olympics experience.
7. Try using the "Deliver Woodsy's Message" activity in the *Woodsy Owl Activity Guide* (Children's Television Network, 1977, Washington, DC: USDA Forest Service) as a communication activity. Students can make posters, create mobiles, write poetry, or perform a play based on a "lend a hand—care for the land" theme.

References

American Association for the Advancement of Science (AAAS). (1993). *Benchmarks for science literacy.* New York: Oxford University Press.

Avi. (1995). *Poppy.* New York: Orchard Books.

Barman, C. R. (1989). A procedure for helping prospective elementary teachers integrate the learning cycle into science textbooks. *Journal of Science Teacher Education, 1*(2), 21–26.

Brett, J. (1994). *Town mouse & country mouse.* New York: G. P. Putnam.

Bunting, E. (1984). *The man who could call down owls.* New York: Macmillan.

Bybee, R. W., Buchwald, C. E., Crissman, S., Heil, D. R., Kuerbis, P. J., Matsumoto, C., & McInerney, J. D. (1989). *Science and technology education for the elementary years: Frameworks for curriculum and instruction.* Washington, DC: National Center for Improving Science Education.

Dewey, J. (1929). *The quest for certainty: A study of the relation of knowledge and action.* New York: G. P. Putnam.

Erickson, R. E. (1998). *A toad for Tuesday.* New York: Lothrop, Lee & Shepard Books.

Flick, L. B. (1993). The meaning of hands-on science. *Journal of Science Teacher Education, 4*(1), 1–8.

Garcia, A. (1997). *Measurement: 35 hands-on activities.* Cypress, CA: Creative Teaching Press.

Gates, F. (1994). *Owl eyes.* New York: Lothrop, Lee & Shepard Books.

Hutchins, P. (1972). *Good-night owl!* New York: Macmillan.

Kalman, B. (1987). *Owls.* New York: Crabtree.

Karplus, R. (1977). Science teaching and the development of reasoning. *Journal of Research in Science Teaching, 14*(2), 169–175.

Karplus, R., & Their, H. D. (1967). *A new look at elementary school science: Science Curriculum Improvement Study.* Chicago: Rand McNally.

Klein, A. (1974). *The world of measurements.* New York: Simon & Schuster.

Ling, M. (1992). *See how they grow: Owl.* New York: Dorling Kindersley.

Mowat, F. (1981). *Owls in the family.* New York: Bantam.

Myller, R. (1990). *How big is a foot.* New York: Dell.

National Research Council (NRC). (1996). *National science education standards.* Washington, DC: National Academy Press.

National Research Council (NRC). (2000). *Inquiry and the national science education standards: A guide for teaching and learning.* Washington, DC: National Academy Press.

Odom, A. L., & Settlage, J., Jr. (1996). Teachers' understandings of the learning cycle as assessed with a two-tier test. *Journal of Science Teacher Education, 7*(2), 123–142.

Palumbo, T. (1989). *Measurement motivators: From dinosaurs to decimals.* Torrance, CA: Good Apple.

Ramsey, J. (1993). Developing conceptual storylines with the learning cycle. *Journal of Elementary Science Education, 5*(2), 1–20.

Rosenthal, D. (1993). A learning cycle approach to dealing with pseudoscience beliefs of prospective elementary teachers. *Journal of Science Teacher Education, 4*(2), 33–36.

Sattler, H. R. (1995). *The book of North American owls.* New York: Clarion Books.

Selsam, M. E., & Hunt, J. (1986). *A first look at owls, eagles, and other hunters of the sky.* New York: Walker.

Singer, M. (1989). *Turtle in July.* New York: Macmillan.

Staver, J. R., & Shroyer, M. G. (1994). Teaching elementary teachers how to use the learning cycle for guided inquiry instruction in science. In L. Schafer (Ed.), *Behind the methods class door: Educating elementary and middle school science teachers* (pp. 1–11). Columbus, OH: ERIC Clearinghouse.

Waddell, M. (1994). *Owl babies.* Compton, CA: Santillana.

Yolen, J. (1987). *Owl moon.* New York: Philomel Books.

Suggested Readings

Council for Environmental Education. (1992). Owl pellets. In *Project WILD K–12 activity guide* (pp. 144–145). Bethesda, MD: Author. (This is a guide to owl pellet activities.)

Gabel, D. L. (1993). *Introductory science skills* (2nd ed.). Prospect Heights, IL: Waveland Press. (A comprehensive workbook of scientific skill development and assessment.)

Goldsworthy, A., & Feasey, R. (1997). *Making sense of primary science investigations.* Hatfield, Herts., UK: Association for Science Education. (A guide to primary science investigations and the skills involved.)

Ostlund, K. L. (1992). *Science process skills.* Menlo Park, CA: Addison-Wesley. (Ways to assess each of the science processes, with material lists and reproducible worksheets.)

Ostlund, K., & Mercier, S. (1996). *Rising to the challenge of the national science education standards:* *The process of inquiry.* Fresno, CA: S & K Associates. (Thirty-six activities that promote the processes of science inquiry.)

Rezba, R. J., Sprague, C., Fiel, R. L., Funk, H. J., Okey, J. R., & Jaus, H. H. (1995). *Learning and assessing science process skills* (3rd ed.). Dubuque, IA: Kendall/Hunt. (A workbook of scientific skill development and assessment.)

Ruchlis, H. (1991). *How do you know it's true? Discovering the difference between science and superstition.* Buffalo, NY: Prometheus Books. (An easy-to-follow account of how scientific theories are based on facts and observations.)

Smith, B. (1989). *Measurement motivators: From dinosaurs to decimals.* Torrance, CA: Good Apple. (A book of measurement activities.)

Chapter 5

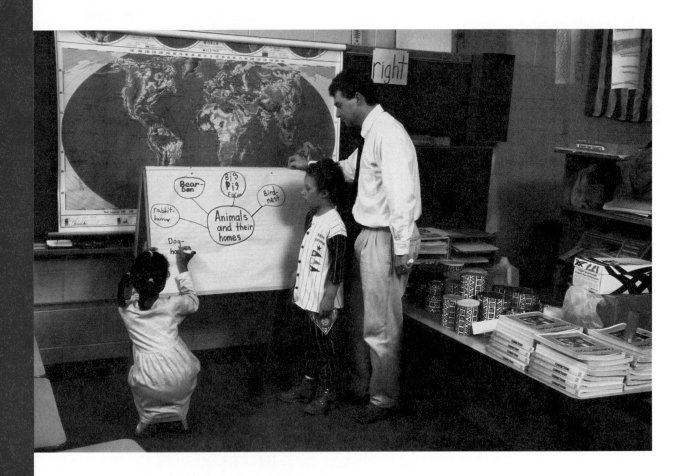

Assessment

Portfolio Assessment

Christine Peters
Harborcreek School District, Pennsylvania

Portfolios

During the last several years, I've been using portfolio assessment more and more. At first, I felt somewhat uncomfortable with the notion. I worried about when I'd find the time in our hectic day to collect, sort, choose, meet, and interview. Now that I've been using this form of individualized assessment, I see that my students are the ones who are responsible for the selection process. This is actually the most important aspect of using portfolios. By involving the children in the decision-making process, they achieve a deeper sense of pride, a feeling of ownership about their work, and a desire for excellence.

In building portfolios, I am concentrating on the *process* of the child's learning, as well as the *product*. My students are better able to focus on a specific goal, rather than on a letter grade. I am also promoting a closer relationship with my students because my assessment focuses on the development of a student's work over time. Not only do my students feel a great sense of pride, but I feel like the world's best teacher when I compare one of their spelling assessments from September with one from May, or when I listen to one of my student's oral reading cassettes from the first week of school—when she knew very few words and didn't have enough skills to sound them out—and compare it with the middle or end of the tape when she is able to read anything she picks up from the library.

The toughest part of using portfolio assessment is deciding when to fit the interviewing and selection process into your day. I have tried many approaches, and what I like the best is what I call "free choice time." Every other Friday afternoon, the boys and girls in my classroom are free to do what they would like to do. Of course, I give them some guidance in what they are choosing from, and if there is any unfinished work for the day or week, that must be completed first. I will often invite one or two other adults into my classroom to help with the interviewing and selection process. Administrators, instructional and learning support teachers, and parents have all been involved in this process in my classroom in the past. It is valuable to use the same volunteers so that little time will be re-spent on "training," even though this is not always possible.

A typical free choice time in my classroom will look like this:

- A small group working in the science center on a food pyramid with pictures they've cut out of magazines; several children playing Pictionary using the sand trays and shaving cream boards in the corner; a group of children making numbers out of clay to take to another classroom; two children taping themselves reading one of the big books our class wrote entitled *Ten Black Dots* (also to take to another classroom); and several children reading books from our classroom library that they will then present to their classmates by using puppets or posters they've made.

- At the same time, I (along with my adult volunteers) will be meeting individually with each of my 22 students. Before the students are individually interviewed, they are told what materials are required for their meeting. They have an idea of which (products) works they will want to place into their portfolios, and they have thought about why they have chosen such pieces. During their interviews, I go over the selected pieces and together (later in the year, the students fill this out independently) we write out a "Portfolio and Goals Survey." This survey states the date, the title of the piece, why the piece was chosen, the favorite part of the piece, what the piece shows, what the child has learned so far, what he wants to learn next, and things that will help him learn better.

- If I have several adult helpers and if time permits, then I also find it very valuable to go over one of my checklists with each child. One week, I may share each child's oral reading checklist with him or her, and the next week I'll share their writing or cooperative learning checklists. These are forms that I keep in their portfolios to record learning skills and behaviors that I observe in their daily work and in how they work with each other.

I love using portfolios in my elementary classroom! The students enjoy having a collection of their work that progresses throughout the year. Even my students with learning difficulties can't help but see the progression of skill in their work. They all feel successful and are always trying to do their best, hoping that what they are currently working on will be added to their portfolio. Parents are even excited about the portfolio assessment going on in my classroom. They can see their child's learning in concrete terms and become partners in the learning process. Parents are invited in often to view their child's works, and a few times a year, the portfolio is sent home along with a letter in which the parents are encouraged to give feedback.

It doesn't take much preparation to begin using portfolios in your classroom. All you need are some file and pocket folders, composition books, cassette and/or videotapes, large manila envelopes, and lots of stick-on notes. To store the portfolios, I use a large plastic crate. A cardboard box would even fit the purpose.

Some of the items that go into my students' portfolios are my observations; their writing samples; journals; reading, writing, math, and cooperative learning inventories; artwork; parent surveys; rubrics; book evaluations; and child-selected samples of day-to-day work.

Portfolio assessment teaches students how to learn and teaches teachers how to slow down, get to know each student and his or her strengths and needs, and develop a curriculum that appeals to each student's multiple talents. It encourages students—and teachers—to strive for excellence in all they do.

The portfolio process discussed in Vignette 5–1 is representative of **assessment** practice changes in our schools. To better understand the need for these changes, let's use an industry metaphor.

Throughout most of the 20th century, school, like industry, was conceived of as a manufacturing process in which raw materials (students) were operated on by the machinery (teachers). Some of the products were worked on for longer periods of time than others, but in the end, we molded a finished product (a literate citizen).

Twentieth-century education had certainly moved beyond the agrarian practices of the 19th century. Students were no longer in one-room schoolhouses where education was planned around harvest and planting seasons. The children of this era learned in unison as they progressed through the assembly line (curriculum). The primary process used to shape the final product was expository teaching. The bosses (school administrators) told the workers how to run the assembly line under rigid work rules (behavioral aims, goals, and objectives) that gave them little or no stake in the process (see Rubba, Miller, Schmalz, Rosenfeld, & Shyamal, 1991).

Assessment practices, the "quality control" of the educational allegory described above, were consistently used to seek out the degree of factual knowledge students were able to absorb. It is well documented that educators of this generation were in the "we teach what we test" mode. Unfortunately, tests of this nature were "fundamentally incompatible" with reform efforts such as those we now associate with constructivism (Resnick & Resnick, 1989).

Assessment involves the collection and interpretation of information about what students know and can do as it relates to the curriculum.

See *http://www.prenhall.com/peters* **for links related to current assessment research and practice.**

Assessment Today

The paper-and-pencil test method that once dominated classroom testing is downplayed in this century's classrooms. Multiple-choice, true-false, and matching tests are minimized as much as possible. Assessment is no longer something we *do to children,* but something we can *do with children.* Assessment methods, including portfolios, performance-based measures, open-ended questioning, **concept maps, vee maps,** and journals, have replaced the testing some of you may have been familiar with in elementary school.

This chapter reflects the view that the primary purpose of assessment is to improve opportunity to learn and the student's construction of knowledge. One way to do this is to match the assessment with the learning paradigm of constructivism. We would hope to make the linkage between what we want students to know and the assessment tool that would be used to find the answer. Look at the Consistency of Assessment Standard in the Standards Link box. This standard is a good beginning example. Do you think that this standard causes teachers to think about assessment in a different way? Why would they

Concept maps are hierarchical graphic organizers of a person's concepts.

Vee maps are similar to concept maps but have two sides: a conceptual side (the "knowing" side that may contain a concept map) and a methodological side (containing results and actions).

use one procedure or another? What question would they hope to answer through the data collected? How will they analyze the data collected? Is the scoring rubric fair and consistent? Will this approach be helpful to the students and lead to good instructional decisions? It seems like a lot to think about, yet these questions were rarely considered in the past. Instead, teachers may have only sent an end-of-the-chapter test out of the teacher's guide to the office to be copied.

As you read this chapter, think about your own assessment practices. Consider how your beliefs and practices may be different from what you find here and why you and your students should be more involved in assessment. A good starting point is to see why we would use assessment, what assessment involves, and how it is changing.

Assessment of Science Learning ────────

The following are some reasons for using assessment in your classroom:

- Monitoring students' progress
- Increasing communications with students
- Improving instruction and the learning environment
    - Determining the best science program and opportunities to learn
    - Enhancing teacher accountability

For many beginning teachers, it is easier to concentrate on two assessment areas—the knowledge and skills of the students.

You will find that assessment techniques can check students' process skill development, factual knowledge, conceptual knowledge, problem-solving ability, and higher level understanding.

Knowledge Objectives

Knowledge objectives can be overwhelming if you concentrate on discrete facts and definitions. Instead, work toward encompassing concepts and generalizations. For example, instead of focusing on learning every item that a magnet will attract, work toward the generalization. It may be helpful to generalize that magnets attract objects made of iron and steel.

Skill Objectives

Skill objectives, or science process objectives, are also easier to work with if they are kept to a manageable level. During the elementary years, focus on observation, classification, measurement, inference, prediction, communication, and experimentation.

Changing Emphasis ────────

In keeping with the standards-based reform efforts, assessment is one of the most important revisions to the learning environment. The authors of *National Science Education*

Standards sought a changing emphasis in the area of assessment (National Research Council [NRC], 1996). They envisioned less emphasis on assessing discrete or scientific knowledge and more emphasis on assessing scientific understanding, reasoning, and well-structured knowledge.

Today, this means we no longer place as much importance on teacher-tested vocabulary and definitions related to a topic under study. Rather, we look for teacher- and student-assessed genuine understanding. We look at how the phenomenon under study fits into the child's current and future thought processes. With changing assessment procedures, we are no longer looking at what students *do not* know. Instead, we want to know what opportunities students have had to learn and what they *do know* or have achieved. We can build off the knowledge that our children already have, and the possibilities are expanded.

Look at the Achievement and Opportunity to Learn Standard in the Standards Link box. The authors make an interesting point that assessment of the **opportunity to learn** is as important as assessing the learning itself. This means that assessment should be an ongoing process. Meaningful connections should take precedence over "covering the curriculum." The American Association for the Advancement of Science *Benchmarks for Science Literacy* (1993) authors call for reducing the amount of material being covered in science classes. Their goal of "teaching less, but teaching it better" does not mean to teach science less often. It means to teach fewer unrelated facts and to spend more time making connections, refining skills, and providing in-depth study of a topic. Part of this goal is to spend time before, during, and after instruction on assessment, including identifying and resolving misconceptions.

The assessment picture that we are describing can be more difficult but provides a better indication of the true learning occurring in your classroom. To see how assessment can be more student centered and related to understanding, follow along with the students as they study the effects of water on the environment.

Mr. Correa's Water Lesson

Mr. Correa reads *A Drop of Water* (Wick, 1997) to his class and sparks an interest in how water travels through the water cycle. The next day, a student follows up the discussions by telling the class about a book she had recently read called *Water Dance* (Locker, 1997). The student tells the class the story of how water travels throughout the environment.

Later in the week, Mr. Correa facilitates the *Project Learning Tree* activity called "Water Wonders" (American Forest Foundation, 1996). Students become drops of water and cycle through clouds, mountains, oceans, streams, plants, animals, and groundwater stations set up in the classroom. At each stop, they pick out a slip of paper that leads them to the next randomly selected station. They keep track of their journey by taping the slips of paper they select at each station onto a scorecard. After they finish, they each tell a story about their adventures. In the follow-up discussion about streams, one student mentions a stream near his house. He informs the class of hearing his father's concern over a new tax to assist the county

See the Model Inquiry Unit, Ongoing Assessment section of the companion CD for an example of assessment at the elementary level.

Opportunity to learn is the concept that assessment should go beyond individual achievement and include the teacher's presentation of the content and skills through quality instructional delivery.

Standards Link

Achievement and Opportunity to Learn Standard

Achievement and opportunity to learn science must be assessed.

- **Achievement data collected focus on the science content that is most important for students to learn.**

- **Opportunity-to-learn data collected focus on the most powerful indicators.**

- **Equal attention must be given to the assessment of opportunity to learn and to the assessment of student achievement.**

(Assessment Standard B, National Research Council, 1996, p. 79)

Children experiment at a labora-tory streambed as part of their river erosion activities.

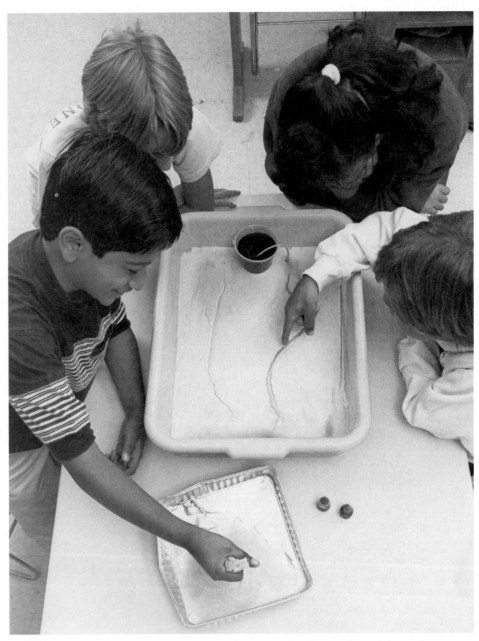

Reprinted from the Great Explorations in Math and Science (GEMS) teacher's guide entitled *River Cutters*, copy-right by The Regents of the University of California, and used with permission. The GEMS series includes more than 70 teacher's guides and handbooks for preschool through eighth grade, available from LHS GEMS, Lawrence Hall of Science, University of California, Berkeley, CA 94720-5200. (510) 642-7771.

with erosion and drainage problems. Taking the discussion a step further, Mr. Correa decides to model the situation with the students.

He engages the students in an activity from *River Cutters* (Lawrence Hall of Science, 1989). The students work together to set up a streambed with diatomaceous earth inside. They place a rubber tube connected to a water source that allows drops of water to flow onto the surface. They carefully observe this model of the effects of water on the earth.

Next, the students draw pictures of what happens with the models. Using tags that Mr. Correa places alongside specific features, the students label the streams, rivers, valleys, and other features that form in the diatomaceous earth. They discuss the features in the streambeds with their small groups and later with their teacher. Mr. Correa asks the students what other experiments they could do with the streambed apparatus.

Mr. Correa now looks on as the students generate ideas for further study. They write a description of what they would like to find out, propose ways to model the situation, and predict outcomes. They want to demonstrate what is occurring near Ninth Street. The students begin to work with the streambeds. They are adjusting the water flow to create the correct model of their neighborhood.

Where has the assessment occurred with the stream activities? What type of assessment was done? Could Mr. Correa have employed **authentic assessment** as part of his water lessons? To answer these questions, let's look further into what is meant by authentic assessment.

River Cutters is one of the Great Explorations in Math and Science (GEMS) series of thematic activity books that are based on a hands-on/cooperative learning format (see *http://www.prenhall.com/peters* for the link to GEMS materials).

Authentic assessment is seen as measuring or testing what the student really knows about a concept or skill, as opposed to testing something inconsistent with what was taught or the goals of the science program.

Authentic Assessment

If you remember learning about the water cycle and erosion in ways similar to how Mr. Correa's class learned, then you were fortunate. More likely, you memorized the water cycle from a definition or illustration in an elementary science textbook and took a test. In fact, testing and assessment were synonymous for most teachers. In paradox to the methods used in the past, the authors of the *National Science Education Standards* (NRC, 1996) and Project 2061 (see AAAS *Blueprints for Reform,* 1998) view assessment as authentic or genuine. They want the data to measure what they are supposed to measure. This view of assessment is indicated in the Quality of the Data and Interpretations Standard.

Assessment should be "similar in form to tasks in which [students] will engage in their lives outside the classroom or are similar to the activities of scientists" (NRC, 1996, p. 83). The term *embedded assessment* refers to how assessment should be "part of the activities that naturally occur in a lesson or a logical extension of the lesson's central activity" (National Science Resources Center, National Academy of Sciences, Smithsonian Institution; 1997, pp. 103, 108). Examples of authentic assessment are included in Figure 5–1.

You can infer from the different types of assessment practices noted in Figure 5–1 that assessment is not just for assigning a grade. In fact, there are two types of assessments according to the Project 2061 authors (AAAS, 1998): *internal purpose assessments* and *external purpose assessments.*

Standards Link

Quality of the Data and Interpretations Standard

The technical quality of the data collected is well matched to the decisions and actions taken on the basis of their interpretation.

- **The feature that is claimed to be measured is actually measured.**
- **Assessment tasks are authentic.**
- **An individual student's performance is similar on two or more tasks that claim to measure the same aspect of student achievement.**
- **Students have adequate opportunity to demonstrate their achievements.**
- **Assessment tasks and methods of presenting them provide data that are sufficiently stable to lead to the same decisions if used at different times.**

(Assessment Standard C, National Research Council, 1996, p. 83)

- Student observations
- Student interviews
- Written reports or journals
- Portfolios
- Performance measurements
- Concept or vee maps

- Multiple-choice tests
- Essay tests
- Short-answer tests
- Attitude surveys
- Creative assessments
- Projects and laboratory experiences

Figure 5–1
Examples of authentic assessment practices.

Internal purpose assessments are classroom-based assessments used by the teacher to measure the progress of students within their class.

External purpose assessments are standardized assessments generally initiated by a school district or state to compare intact classes within a larger system.

See *http://www.prenhall.com/peters* for links related to National Board Certification.

Internal purpose assessments are administered to convey expectations about what is important to learn, to provide information on progress, to help students judge their learning, to guide and improve instruction, and to classify and select students (AAAS, 1998). An example is the everyday assessment completed by teachers as part of the normal classroom experiences.

External purpose assessments include examinations given to provide information for accountability, to guide policy decisions, to gather information for program evaluation, to sort and classify people for admissions, and to certify or hire (AAAS, 1998). This is the assessment resulting from achievement, placement, or certification tests.

Today, both internal purpose and external purpose forms of assessment are receiving much attention. Internal purpose assessment is a key to the reform effort because the assumption "we teach what we test" still holds true in many classrooms. External purpose assessment is likewise becoming increasingly important for teachers at a personal level. Suggested initiatives such as linking assessment results to teacher performance portfolios, or teacher pay raises, are now being proposed or implemented in some states. The ability to provide quality assessment is also a consideration in National Board Certification (National Board for Professional Teaching Standards, 1997). In either internal purpose or external purpose assessment situations, it is important to understand what good assessment is and the many forms of authentic assessment.

Characteristics of Good Assessment

A good rule of thumb for assessment is that it is *reflective* and not *reflexive*. Assessment should not be an automatic, end-of-the-chapter reflexive routine. It should be an everyday experience that is increasingly indistinguishable from the classroom learning activities themselves. It is not a multiple-choice test that comes at the end of the chapter, waiting for our response. Rather, it is a teacher-*and student*-selected means to show that learning has occurred.

Assessment data should support reasonable conclusions of learning that has occurred as seen in the Sound Inferences Standard. The information should help both teacher and students reflect on what they have or have not learned. It should

---

Standards Link

Sound Inferences Standard

The inferences made from assessments about student achievement and opportunity to learn must be sound.

- **When making inferences from assessment data about student achievement and opportunity to learn science, explicit reference needs to be made to the assumptions on which the inferences are based.**

(Assessment Standard E, National Research Council, 1996, p. 86)

- They indicate the student's opportunity to learn.
- They allow for the student to select the best approach to a task.
- They are relevant to the student and are not just a correct answer.
- They accommodate the student's developmental level.
- They account for the student's prior knowledge.
- They are consistent and reliable for the student.
- They take more time to complete than tests.
- They are relevant to the learning goal.
- They promote transfer of learning into new situations.
- They produce measurable evidence of learning.
- They include both individual and group efforts.
- They are a continual process.

Figure 5–2
Characteristics of good classroom assessments.

also help the teacher reflect on what future lessons or activities will assist in student understanding of the concepts being learned. Appraisal of learning should account for the students' individual differences and varied experiences. Figure 5–2 contains some good assessment characteristics.

Types of Authentic Assessment

Essay Items

Essay items provide a bridge between traditional assessment procedures and authentic assessment practices. Essay questions are useful in evaluating whether students are able to express personal ideas clearly. This type of question can be designed to assess higher order thinking, the ability to solve problems, or the capability to reason about the interrelationships between concepts.

As a caution, essay questions can be very subjective because there is not one right or wrong answer. The questions may be too vaguely worded for students to understand exactly what answer the teacher wants. Or, they may be too obvious for students and so the questions are not effective in measuring learning.

Also keep in mind that disabilities, language differences, and cultural diversity will affect students' abilities to answer questions, as pointed out in the Fair Assessment Standard. Students with poor language skills will often do poorly on these items, regardless of content knowledge. Likewise, students with good language skills may be able to bluff through answers that they do not fully understand. Cultural differences are also an important consideration.

As with other tests, careful construction of items will help make the test more meaningful. Compare the following two test items.

What are the phases of the moon?

Explain what we would observe here on Earth as the moon goes through its phases. Explain why it appears this way to us on Earth.

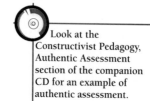 Look at the Constructivist Pedagogy, Authentic Assessment section of the companion CD for an example of authentic assessment.

The first item is open for your students to interpret. They could respond by just listing "new, first quarter, full, last quarter." The second item requires your students to provide an explanation for why the phases occur and what they would look like, as well as the names of the phases. Essay tests that are well constructed match what was learned in class. They also ask well-defined, explicit questions that are understandable to all students. Additionally, good essay questions indicate, either in writing or through discourse, exactly what the teacher is looking for as an acceptable response.

The teacher should set and communicate to the students her expectations for length, detail, and spelling prior to the test. A grading rubric should also be developed that lists the specifics of what is expected. Use of a checklist will eliminate most subjectivity.

Are essay questions and other paper-and-pencil tests the best indication of learning? Could the students actually *do something* as part of the assessment?

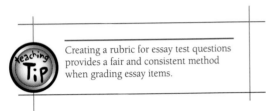

Creating a rubric for essay test questions provides a fair and consistent method when grading essay items.

Performance-Based Assessment

Reflecting back on Mr. Correa, we see that the students are being assessed as they complete the activities. How? The students are challenged to create a model streambed that is consistent with the severe erosion patterns in their neighborhood. Their *performance* on this task is one form of authentic assessment.

A performance-based assessment will generate an answer by the students. This type of assessment will also indicate the process used by the students to arrive at that answer. Performance-based assessment is often associated with the phrase "know and be able to do" (Ochs, 1996). Because students are doing something, we can assess the procedure as well as the product. There are ways to assess the procedure a student uses to arrive at an answer. This procedure is often more important than the answer itself. In fact, many times more than one answer will be correct.

In the streambed example, as in other performance-based measures, there are three basic steps to follow (McMillan, 1997). The first step is to *construct the performance task* for students. In our example, Mr. Correa wanted his students to apply what they learned about erosion, so he asked the students themselves to generate or identify an idea for a task. Brainstorming ideas leads into the second step, which is to *develop a task description*. This is often done as a group effort but can also be completed individually. Third, with Mr. Correa's assistance, the students wrote a task question. Their specific "problem to solve" was to model what was going on in their neighborhood.

Was this the best question to explore? It was meaningful to the students, but other questions are certainly possibilities. Other examples of products that could be developed through this type of assessment include models based on scientific concepts, written material, or a formal decision. Products could also be applications of process skills, such as experiments with definite or undetermined conclusions.

> Assessment of the performance task can be done through teacher observation, student interviews, a written outline for the students to fill in, or daily journal entries.

When used, journals should be written in daily and checked often so that a dialogue can occur between the student and the teacher. This will indicate whether the student has misconceptions or whether the teacher needs to adjust instructional practice in any way or to encourage students to explore further.

Assessing Process Skills

Process skills should also be addressed. Assessing these operations requires students to be placed in contexts that allow them to gather and process data. To help yourself better track your students' achievement of process skills, develop a recording chart similar to the one in Figure 5–3.

In its purest form, a performance measure has a child demonstrate process skills with concrete materials. For instance, the inquiry may ask the child to measure several irregularly shaped rocks to find the one with the greatest volume. Materials for this task include various types of rocks, a widemouthed clear plastic cup, a spoon, a marking pen, and a container of water. To demonstrate this process, the child could partly fill the cup and mark the water level with the pen. Next, she will carefully submerge each of the various rocks into the cup with the spoon, taking care each time to mark the water level and not spill any water. If the process is performed properly, the child identifies the rock with the highest water level as having the most volume.

Another example of a performance measure is to ask a child to infer the identity of three unknown leaves by consulting a chart with descriptions of leaves. A variation of the task is to ask the child to classify a small collection of leaves. Can the child put them into two or more groups and state the observable property or properties used to group them? Will the groupings be consistent with the stated properties?

> See
> *http://www.prenhall.com/peters*
> for links related to assessing student performance in science.

Working with concrete materials may not always be possible. Performance-based measures can also use representations of things. For instance students can classify pictures of leaves or animals. Another idea is to supply a chart that shows data from an investigation and to ask the child to interpret the data and draw a conclusion.

When children are capable writers, some performance measures may be completed entirely with words. For experimenting, this problem might appear as follows:

Suppose you want to find out whether bean plants will grow faster with Fertilizer A or Fertilizer B. How could you set up an experiment to find out?

Name	Classify	Observe	Measure	Infer	Communicate	Experiment
ROSE	(A-C-T)	(A-C-T)	(A-C-T)	(A-C-T)	(A-C-T)	(A-C-T)
DAVE	(A-C-T)	(A-C-T)	(A-C-T)	(A-C-T)	(A-C-T)	(A-C-T)
NINA	(A-C-T)	(A-C-T)	(A-C-T)	(A-C-T)	(A-C-T)	(A-C-T)
JOSH	(A-C-T)	(A-C-T)	(A-C-T)	(A-C-T)	(A-C-T)	(A-C-T)

Note: A = Achieved Skill, C = Continuing to Improve, T = Trouble Applying

Figure 5–3
Process skill checklist.

The problem could also address a specific part of the experiment:

What variables do you need to control in the plant experiment?

In either instance, it is important to place an emphasis on assessing the performance of the students. But if you have a good science program, isn't that enough?

Using Performance-Based Assessment

Some teachers with active, hands-on/minds-on science programs bypass performance measures. They believe that they get all the assessment data they need by observing their students at work and interacting with them during regular activity times and follow-up discussions. This may be possible with a wide array of process-rich activities and systematic observing. But mandated performance explorations are becoming more prevalent at school district, state, and national levels. Avoiding them entirely in the regular science program may cause students to do poorly on such assessments. Reliability of your personal assessments may also be affected if you leave out **performance-based assessment.** This could be due to bias of your observations of certain students because of their personality or prior success. One way to complete this type of assessment and decrease bias is through an instrument such as the example in Figure 5–4.

Note that the particular checklist in Figure 5–4 is for a small-group assignment. You will have to modify the checklist to use individually or with different learning situations. Also, if you are working with early grades, you will find that teacher observation is the primary means of gathering assessment data. In these situations, it is important that you track progress over longer periods of time and record progress as students develop new skills.

Project-Based Science

Whether exploring on an individual basis or as a small group, **project-based science** assists students in investigating authentic questions based on scientific phenomena. The principle behind project-based science is that young learners engage in exploring important and meaningful questions through a process of investigation and collaboration (Krajcik, Czerniak, & Berger, 1999). The result of this approach is that students learn fundamental science concepts and principles that they can apply to their daily lives.

It's a good idea to view science projects as normal and regular extensions of concepts and generalizations studied by the whole class. Projects can be individual self-directed activities, similar to a science fair project. They can also be small-group projects during which students collaborate in learning. One way or the other, they make assessment simpler, less formal, and more frequent. Extended investigations can be useful in pursuing knowledge in greater depth or in focusing on a particular area of interest. But what makes a good project?

Characteristics of a Good Project

An ideal project usually requires self-assessment from start to finish. If guidelines are simple and your comments regarding success are consistent, students will develop judgment in assessing their efforts during projects and when reporting them. The components of a good project are found in Figure 5–5.

Remember that good projects also give students many chances to display the scientific attitudes of critical thinking, such as persistence, inventiveness, curiosity, and questioning techniques. Some sample questions for you to keep in mind during the assessment process are as listed on the next page.

Performance-based assessment is a form of testing that requires students to perform a task rather than select or provide answers from a test. The teacher then judges the quality of the student's work based on an agreed-upon set of criteria. An example would be asking a student to generate scientific hypotheses.

Project-based science organizes science experiences around an authentic question. The students focus on all of the class activities to answer this driving question.

See *http://www.prenhall.com/peters* for links related to project-based science and the PIViT software from the University of Michigan.

Completed by the Student

Student Names
(List the names of the students in your group.)

Problem to Be Solved
(State the problem you are investigating in your own words.)

Method or Strategy
(How will you go about solving the problem?)

Skills
(Identify how you used the following skills while investigating this problem: classifying, observing, measuring, inferring/predicting, communicating, and experimenting)

Results
Written Response
  What did you find from your investigation?
Pictures
  Can you illustrate your findings?

Verification and Communication
Did you compare your answer with other groups? Did you verify it with the teacher?

Teacher Checklist

_____   Students understood the problem.
               (0—no; 1—somewhat; 2—completely)
_____   Students developed a method/strategy to solve the problem.
               (0—no; 1—somewhat; 2—completely)
_____   Students used scientific skills in solving the problem.
               (0—no; 1—somewhat; 2—completely)
_____   Students were able to come to a conclusion.
               (0—no; 1—somewhat; 2—completely)
_____   Students communicated and verified their results.
               (0—no; 1—somewhat; 2—completely)
_____   Total (possible 10)

Figure 5–4
Performance-based assessment checklist (upper elementary).

1. Are the parts of the report or presentation logical and consistent?

2. Does the display or model show evidence of learning?

3. Is there evidence that the child overcame difficulties or was successful at problem solving?

4. Was the child resourceful in substituting materials as needed?

5. Does the child or other children ask further questions based on the project?

When you notice behaviors like these and give positive comments, you will reinforce the students' success at projects. Returning to our situation with Mr. Correa, we find that he is going to continue the learning situation with individual projects.

- **Title:** Name of the investigation that is being considered.
- **Problem:** A brief description of the problem to be solved. The student or teacher can determine the problem.
- **Materials:** A listing of what is needed for the investigation.
- **Hypothesis:** A statement that explains what will happen during or as a result of the investigation.
- **Experiment:** The steps that will be taken to investigate the hypothesis. Includes specifics on variables and how measurements will be taken.

- **Data:** An organized listing of the data collected in charts and graphs.
- **Results:** A data-specific explanation of what happened as a result of the experiment.
- **Conclusion:** An explanation of what happened in your own words.
- **Research Results:** A summary of the background information collected as part of the investigation.
- **Communication of Investigation:** A report, display, presentation, or other means to share the results of the investigation.

Figure 5–5
Components of a good project.

As a springboard for ideas, next week Mr. Correa's students will independently read a variety of children's literature, including *Bringing the Rain to Kapiti Plain* (Aardema, 1992), *Mendel's Ladder* (Karlins, 1995), *Peter Spier's Rain* (Spier, 1997), *A Rainy Day* (Markle, 1993), and *The Rains Are Coming* (Stanley, 1993). These and other books related to rain will help initiate creative ideas for individual projects. Keep in mind that as the students design the projects, they can also design complementary assessment procedures.

Peer or Individual Assessments

Do you want your students involved in the assessment process? Try experimenting by allowing your students to design an authentic assessment procedure. Of course, student assessments may not be as elaborate as some procedures that you may design, but they do have some advantages. Often, students will become more involved in the learning process if they are included in the evaluation and decision making that occur in the classroom. Additionally, students are very creative and can develop some very interesting and useful assessments.

There are some considerations to keep in mind with regard to individually created assessment procedures. First, consider that this is a **low stakes** type of **assessment**. By this, we mean that it is only one piece of the assessment package for that student. In contrast, a **high stakes assessment** affects a student's future to a much higher degree. A student's final grade should be determined through a combination of procedures, including different forms of teacher-based assessments.

A second consideration in peer- or self-constructed assessment procedures is to be clear with the directions that are given related to the assessment. Make sure that everyone knows what is required. Ask questions to ensure that your students understand the requirements. Provide guidance to be sure that the students are not undertaking a procedure they cannot complete. Finally, encourage the students and assist them in reaching their goals. A follow-up interview may assist in clarifying the assessment procedure and results.

A **low stakes assessment** is a tool to assist in finding out what a student knows, in determining future curricula, or in diagnosing a student's skills.

A **high stakes assessment** is used to determine passing or failing, to place a student in a remedial or advanced program, to decide on graduation, or otherwise to compare students, classrooms, schools, districts, states, or even nations.

Interviews ———————

Are you having learning or assessment difficulties with your students? Interviews are an effective way to get information directly. They can be especially useful with early elementary students who cannot express their thoughts in writing. Interviews are also helpful for assessing special needs students. Keep in mind that the specific answers provided by the children are less important than the reasons why they responded as they did. Try to look for trends in thinking patterns and to identify misconceptions.

When using interviews as an assessment tool, keep in mind that you should be accepting of all answers and value each child's thoughts and opinions. Put yourself in the child's perspective and ease the sometimes uncomfortable situation by:

Knowing and using the child's name

Selecting nonconflicting times to interview

Sitting at floor level

Talking in a cheerful tone

Informing the child before the interview what you are doing

Intervene only as necessary to keep the discussion focused on the topic. Ask questions that will promote further discussion. Begin with questions such as these:

Tell me about . . .

What do you think about . . .

How do you feel about . . .

Can you explain why . . .

Describe how you would . . .

How did you discover . . .

Maintain the discussion with questions such as these:

What else can you say about . . .

What if you were to . . .

How is this related to . . .

Is there another way to explain . . .

How could we change . . .

What question should I ask the next student about . . .

General questions should be prepared ahead of time; nevertheless, ask additional clarifying questions as needed. Also make sure to provide enough time for the interview.

Try to make students feel relaxed with the interview process. Allow them to create illustrations or to use models as needed. Some early-elementary students may even want to "speak" through a teddy bear or other object if they are too shy to speak directly to you. Do not mistake a child's being afraid to speak as a sign that he or she is unfamiliar with the concept discussed.

If you are using other students or parent volunteers as interviewers, make sure that you have a checklist of interview questions for them to fill out.

A child composes her daily notes as part of her science journal.

Another use for interviews is to supplement regular testing for culturally and linguistically diverse students. For instance, you can do these things:

Provide additional clues to failed test items.

Change the language of test items in an interview.

Ask probing questions in the student's own dialect.

Focus on how the student is attempting to solve a problem. (Gonzalez, Brusca-Vega, & Yawkey, 1997)

Using interviews to help meet the needs of diverse students will not only allow you to better find their strong and weak areas but also will be a boost to their self-confidence when they can understand the assessment procedure. Complement interview discussions with journal writing as the students are able to express themselves with written discourse.

Journals ───────

Do you remember keeping a science notebook when you were in school? Journals similar to the one you may have kept can assist students in recording observations, outlining procedures, drafting hypotheses, developing inferences, writing the results of experiments, or reflecting on what they have done. You know that recording data in a notebook or log is usually necessary when observations occur over time. Doing so makes it more likely that the students will keep track of changes, observe more carefully, and think about what they are doing. Teachers may also ask their students to respond in writing to questions in activities for similar reasons. These recordings are best kept in a journal.

Notice how often questions appear in properly constructed activities. This practice is typical of elementary school science. Students can appraise their recordings by comparing them with those of other group members. When experimental data conflict, it's only natural for students to pursue reasons. Journals can be a way to develop this dialogue with students who want to learn more about a topic. Remember to be flexible and consider that not every journal should look the same.

Today the concept of *writing to learn* is applied in all subjects. It holds much value for science. Many teachers have their students keep science journals. A journal offers opportunities to improve science learning and to practice important writing skills at the same time. Writing requires thinking, which changes with different purposes.

Descriptive writing can be used, among other possibilities, to identify things:

"Can you describe an animal (plant, habitat, etc.) so well, without naming it, that your partner can tell what it is?"

"Make a chart that shows the properties of these rocks. Can your partner match the rocks to your descriptions?"

Assessing these writings is straightforward. If a problem with a conflicting answer arises, the partners can work together to figure out a solution.

Defining concepts in writing, before and after instruction, enables children to assess for themselves what they have gained from their studies. The questions "What is soil, and what is it made of?" may yield quite different results before and after lessons.

Creative writing should also be linked to concepts being studied. If your students are writing stories about an imaginary visit to an outer planet, you might ask them to use recently learned words correctly, such as *orbit, acceleration,* and *zero gravity.*

Use cooperative learning groups in judging whether concepts are used correctly in journals or creative writing activities. Your students should consult with you as needed.

You can also ask students at different developmental levels to write summaries of what they have learned in a lesson, give opinions and defend them, write persuasive letters, and compose interview questions. Each form can be assessed for clarity, logic, and completeness. Journals are also a valuable tool with students who are too shy to express answers publicly. Journals provide a secure channel of communication with the teacher.

It is important to have your students assess their own writing as much as possible through clear directions and standards. You should evaluate or sample their writing often, but at the same time allow them to do most of the work. The following methods will help you provide guidance for them to self-evaluate their work:

How would you describe your level of participation in the activity?

What contributions did you make to the solution of the problem?

What best describes your role in the group (leader, recorder, materials manager, maintenance crew, liaison, or bystander)?

How effectively do you manage time while completing tasks?

What are you learning in science?

One way we use journals in our own work is to include them as part of a folder or three-ring notebook that is a student's **portfolio.**

A **portfolio** is a sampling of work over time that gives observable evidence of knowledge, processes, and attitudes gained by a student over one or more subject-matter units.

Portfolios ————————

Would you like to cultivate more self-assessment abilities like those described in Vignette 5–1? Would you like to motivate your students to increase their effort in learning? Can you show parents tangible and understandable evidence of what their children are learning? If you would like to improve your assessment procedures, consider a portfolio for each child. A portfolio is a "container of evidence of someone's knowledge, skills, and dispositions" (Collins, 1991, p. 293).

The collection can be a student or personal portfolio where children show accomplishments and learning over a long period of time. An example is a graduation portfolio or a yearlong, grade-level portfolio. Another type is the project portfolio where a student demonstrates the sequence of steps that go into a project or independent study. Other examples are graded portfolios, integrated portfolios, cooperative group portfolios, multiyear portfolios, multiple intelligences portfolios, portfolios of intelligent behavior, class profile portfolios, school profile portfolios, time capsule portfolios, and district portfolios (Williams, 2000).

Mr. Correa, from our streamed example earlier in this chapter, uses project portfolios as part of the evaluation of his students. In his view, project portfolios are good assessment tools during the 4-week study of the water cycle.

Artifacts are typical products or results of a student's learning, such as a student story, lab report, or picture of a scientific phenomenon.

What should go into a portfolio? Both the child and you should select items, or **artifacts,** for the portfolio. When the child selects artifacts to demonstrate learning, she can also jot down why she selected the item. This will make the learning and assessment more relevant. You will also find that to have diverse student portfolios, you must have diverse learning opportunities in the classroom. Otherwise, the portfolio becomes a collection of the standard science tests and vocabulary sheets. Collins (1991) warns:

> There is no guarantee that portfolios always will be a mode of authentic assessment; they can become folders in which teachers plunk the same tired stuff they have been doing because they have been instructed by the administration to use portfolios for assessment. (p. 299)

Here are some examples of artifacts that Mr. Correa's students will include:

- Tests—end of lesson, unit, performance
- Activity log pages
- Project or book reports
- Concept maps, other graphic organizers
- Charts
- Graphs
- Science journal pages
- Creative stories
- Science words learned
- Artwork
- Out-of-class assignments
- Computer resources or data
- Videotaped resources or data
- Cartoons and analysis or explanation

In addition to items that the students will include in their portfolios, Mr. Correa will have his students include an artifact form, such as the one shown in Figure 5–6, for some of the items. It will assist the students in determining what items to place in their portfolios.

What are some other points to keep in mind? Everything should be dated so that items in a category can be put in order by time and progress observed. Guide the children to look for improvements in their work and to discuss with their groups the examples they

Name: _____
Date: _____

Portfolio Artifact

I am including this item because . . .

_____
_____
_____

This is how the item shows what I learned . . .

_____
_____
_____

The next time I do this activity, I will change . . .

_____
_____
_____
_____

Figure 5–6
Portfolio artifact form.

have selected. Encourage them to pair an original effort with an improved version when-ever possible; this can make them more conscious of their progress and help develop a sense of pride in their work.

How should the artifacts be arranged? Materials may be stored in a standard expandable folder or a larger folder cut from poster board. Storage considerations may prompt you to consider electronic portfolios. The advantage of electronic portfolios is that they can be easily stored on disk, reducing the amount of paper in the classroom. The dis-advantage is that students' keyboarding skills may be inadequate or computer access may be limited in the elementary classroom.

Should the science portfolio be separate? Or is it better to reserve a section for sci-ence in a more comprehensive portfolio? Primary-level teachers lean more toward compre-hensive portfolios. Either type gets overstuffed and difficult to store or manage unless some material is sent home periodically or discarded. Some teachers ask their students to write thoughtful responses to these two questions:

What do I feel good about?

What do I want to improve?

Responses to the second question can make it easy to set goals with children. At the next periodic review, they can exam-ine their portfolios for evidence that shows whether the goals were met. Also have parents assist in evaluating portfolios. This assistance helps develop better teacher-parent, teacher-child, and

To help your students set goals for them-selves, periodically have them review and think carefully about the work samples they include in their portfolios. This can be done monthly or at the end of a unit.

parent-child communications. A form such as the one in Figure 5–7 can be used for parent portfolio assessments.

Teacher scoring of the portfolio is also a consideration. Figure 5–8 shows a typical scoring method for elementary science portfolios.

Concept Maps

See *http://www.prenhall.com/peters* for links related to the public domain concept map software from the Institute for Human and Machine Cognition at the University of West Florida.

Nodes are the specific locations where the concepts contained on the map are located.

Links or cross-links are the relationships between concepts in different nodes of the concept map.

Propositions are the connecting words, such as *has, can be,* or *is part of.*

One message from researchers in human learning is especially clear: Organization and meaning go together. The better we are able to relate new information to what we already know, the easier we are able to remember and use it. Science programs now commonly employ several different graphic organizers to help children construct meaningful relationships among the facts and concepts they learn. The concept map is probably the most used organizer. It's also an excellent means to assess conceptual knowledge.

Figure 5–9 shows a concept map that was developed by a student independently studying chameleons. It was generated with a computerized concept map program. As you can see from the map, it contains **nodes** representing the individual concepts and **links** connecting the concepts in a meaningful way. This type of assessment provides a richer view of the student's knowledge than typical objective tests.

A concept map, according to Novak and Gowin (1984), is a "schematic device for representing a set of concept meanings embedded in a framework of propositions" (p. 15). The **propositions** are used to link the concepts, and the map in its entirety is like a snapshot of the person's conceptual understandings. Concept maps can be used before, during, or after a learning activity to assess development of understandings. They encourage reflective thinking and foster development of scientific concepts (Mason, 1992).

Parent or Guardian Name: _____

Date: _____

Portfolio Assessment Questions

The item I think is my child's best work is . . .

_____

_____

The item I think my child could improve on is . . .

_____

_____

Overall, I see evidence of my child learning because . . .

_____

_____

_____

I would like to see my child . . .

_____

_____

Figure 5–7
Parent or guardian portfolio assessment rubric.

Portfolio Assessment Scoring

_____ Student organized materials effectively and is proud of his/her work.
  (3—very evident; 2—somewhat evidenced; 1—little evidence; 0—no evidence)

_____ Student stated learning goals for the time period of the portfolio.
  (3—very evident; 2—somewhat evidenced; 1—little evidence; 0—no evidence)

_____ Student provided a rationale for including individual artifacts.
  (3—very evident; 2—somewhat evidenced; 1—little evidence; 0—no evidence)

_____ Student artifacts demonstrate an understanding of the concepts.
  (3—very evident; 2—somewhat evidenced; 1—little evidence; 0—no evidence)

_____ Student included a variety of written, evaluative, and artistic materials.
  (3—very evident; 2—somewhat evidenced; 1—little evidence; 0—no evidence)

_____ Student included a summary that looked for patterns in the artifacts.
  (3—very evident; 2—somewhat evidenced; 1—little evidence; 0—no evidence)

_____ Student demonstrated a positive attitude toward the content area.
  (3—very evident; 2—somewhat evidenced; 1—little evidence; 0—no evidence)

_____ Student worked cooperatively on joint portfolio projects.
  (3—very evident; 2—somewhat evidenced; 1—little evidence; 0—no evidence)

_____ Total (24 possible)

Figure 5–8
Portfolio assessment scoring rubric.

Concept maps are also an effective small-group project. When done by groups, communication and negotiation among members help in identifying student misunderstanding. Working together, they can resolve their misconceptions.

How can you get your students started with concept mapping? So that students can see how concepts maps are formed, it may be good to start with showing students maps related to the context you are teaching. Next, provide the students maps in which some of the words are already filled in. Have the students complete these maps by filling in other words of their choice. Later, provide just the words for them to use in developing their own concept map. For example, Mr. Correa could have provided these words:

water cycle

clouds

streams

oceans

mountains

plants

animals

groundwater

Beginning students could map just these words. Advanced students could add more words as appropriate to complete the concept map. In time, students will be proficient at reflecting their knowledge with concept maps with little assistance from the teacher.

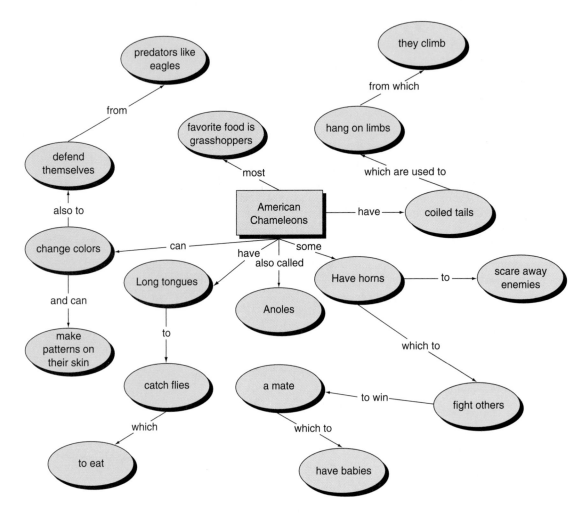

Figure 5–9
Concept map.

Note that students often make different concept maps after receiving the same instruction. This happens even when they understand all the concepts in the way that you intend. They may simply view relationships among the concepts differently. It is important for them to compare their maps on a regular basis with partners and to interact with you to more fully assess what they have learned.

Vee Maps

Vee maps, similar to concept maps, are also useful in developing and conducting investigations. They are a less structured approach to activities. They are likened to a "road map showing the route from prior knowledge to new and future knowledge" (Roth & Verechaka, 1993, p. 25). The following quote summarizes the use of vee maps:

> The left and right sides of the Vee emphasize two interdependent aspects of science learning: knowing and doing, respectively. What students know at any one moment—their existing conceptions, the investigative tools available to them, and their ideas—will determine the quality and quantity of the questions they

ask. Conversely, the answers students obtain to their questions will affect what they know, by changing, adding to, refining, or reconfiguring their knowledge. The Vee should lead students to discover the relationship between doing and knowing science. (Roth & Bowen, 1993, pp. 28–32)

Teacher Observations ─────────

The job of teaching is inexact at best. We view it as a series of consecutively developed hypotheses. That is, each thing we do or say is a kind of hypothesis that we are uncertain will be accepted (learned) by the children. If much teaching takes place before receiving specific feedback that shows learning has occurred, then we could make many unwarranted assumptions about what has been learned by the children.

We can observe, and often help students stay on track, in whole-class settings, but the most productive times are likely to be in individual and small-group situations. There are many chances for informal teacher–child contacts during the activity times in lessons. Notice what your students say and do when they interact with you, a partner, or other members of a small group. What you observe gives you data for fast self-correction or for assisting individual students, if needed.

The quickest way to find out whether students understand the concepts and processes being taught is to ask questions and listen carefully to their responses. Forming follow-up questions to responses may help in detecting misconceptions so that you can quickly address these errors in thinking.

Open-Ended Questions ─────────

An open-ended question has more than one correct response or pathway to a response (Carter & Berenson, 1996). The response may be an answer to a question, a procedure to arrive at a solution to a problem, or an opinion about something. The value of this type of question is that each student can answer it differently.

Open-ended questions are very useful in identifying misconceptions or in promoting divergent thinking.

Assessment of open-ended questions often lies in the completeness of the response. A clear, complete response that includes accurate information and/or the student's opinions is desirable. A rubric for scoring this type of question could simply be a 6-point scale based on information provided by the student, such as the one in Figure 5–10.

Here are some guidelines for writing open-ended questions:

Make sure that the question is understandable to students.

Do not lead students to an answer; let them construct one on their own.

Make the questions interesting whenever possible.

Match each question with the content or process being studied.

Allow sufficient wait time for students to respond.

Allow multiple students time to answer and ask further questions before going on to another question.

Attempt to get at deeper levels of understanding through increasingly complex questions.

Maintain students' interest through meaningful, thought-provoking questions.

Use the following list of five areas to asses a student's response to an open-ended question:

- understands the question
- provides a complete response
- provides accurate information
- justifies the response as needed
- provides additional information as requested

Award 1 point for each objective demonstrated by the student. The scoring ranges from 0 to 5 points for each response, as shown below.

Scoring rubric:

5—all five areas complete
4—one of the above five is missing
3—two of the above five are missing
2—three of the above five are missing
1—four of the above five are missing
0—five of the five are missing or no response

Weather Concepts

Name	Sunshine	Wind	Rain	Snow	Hail	Hurricane	Tornado
Bonnie							
Total:____	____	____	____	____	____	____	____
Doug							
Total:____	____	____	____	____	____	____	____
Shirley							
Total:____	____	____	____	____	____	____	____
Jonathan							
Total:____	____	____	____	____	____	____	____

Figure 5–10
Open-ended question scoring rubric.

Assessing Attitudes

Recall that scientific attitudes of children are often shown by their behaviors in four broad categories: curiosity, inventiveness, critical thinking, and persistence. The sample behaviors listed under these categories are the kinds of actions you look for when you appraise growth in attitudes. Good times to assess attitudes are during hands-on activities and discussions. Remember, though, that broad attitudes cannot be developed quickly. Positive attitudes are a long-range by-product of the quality of learning activities and general atmosphere of your classroom.

Take time to sample attitudes periodically and, if necessary, to develop an informal attitude inventory. It should include items like the following:

Are you curious about nature or scientific phenomena?

Do you enjoy science as much as other subjects?

Do you complete science activities outside class time?

Do you watch science-related shows at home on videotapes or television?

Have you read any science-related books lately?

Do you know a scientist in your neighborhood or community?

Do you like to answer questions during science class?

Have you considered a career in a science field?

In instances where the students cannot read, try using smiling, neutral, and frowning faces on a scoring sheet. The students can respond to items as you read them. What about attitudes toward scientists?

Attitudes and Stereotypes Related to Scientists —————

See
http:www.prenhall.com/peters
for links related to the Draw-a
Scientist Test.

A good way to assess attitudes toward scientists is with the Draw-a-Scientist Test (Mason, Kahle, & Gardner, 1991). In this test, children are provided a blank sheet of paper and asked to "draw a scientist." The test is scored by counting the number of stereotypical indicators, such as lab coats, pencils and pens in a shirt pocket, male gender, facial hair, and glasses. A high score on this test indicates that the student has a very stereotypical or negative image of a scientist. Try this out with your students to see what their image of a scientist is like.

Summary

1. Assessment is no longer something we do to students, but something we can do with students. Assessment should be reflective and not reflexive. With changing assessment procedures, we are no longer looking at what students do not know. Instead, we want to know what opportunities they have had to learn and what they do know or have achieved.

2. Internal purpose assessments are administered to convey expectations about what is important to learn, to provide information on progress, to help students judge their learning, to guide and improve instruction, and to classify and select students. External purpose assessments include examinations that are given to provide information for accountability, to guide policy decisions, to gather information for program evaluation, to sort and classify people for admissions, and to certify or hire.

3. Essay and open-ended questions are useful in evaluating whether students are able to express personal ideas clearly and can be designed to assess higher order thinking, the ability to solve problems, or the capability to reason about the interrelationships between concepts.

4. A performance-based assessment not only will generate an answer by the student but also will indicate the process by which the student arrived at that answer.

5. Project-based assessments assist students in investigating authentic questions based on scientific phenomena and allow young learners to engage in exploring important and meaningful questions through a process of investigation and collaboration.

6. Peer or individual assessments allow students to creatively become involved in the assessment and learning process.

7. Interviews and teacher observations are an effective way to get information directly, to identify misconceptions, and to provide the reasons for student responses.

8. Journals can assist students in recording observations, outlining procedures, drafting hypotheses, developing inferences, writing the results of experiments,

reflecting on what they have done, and developing a dialogue between students and teachers.

9. A portfolio is a sampling of work over time that gives observable evidence of knowledge, processes, and attitudes gained by the students over one or more science units.

10. Concept maps and vee maps assess conceptual knowledge through graphic representations.

Reflection

1. Next time you are at your practicum site, interview a teacher and ask what tools he uses for assessing students. Ask why he selected the particular methods for assessment and whether he thinks the procedures are effective in identifying misconceptions or skill development. Compare his views with your own.

2. Place yourself in the role of the instructor for this course. If you were to assess college students on knowledge of assessment, what form or forms of assessment would you use? Indicate sample test items or authentic procedures. Compare with those of other students in the class.

3. The rapid expansion in the use of computers and the Internet has brought with it the idea of electronic portfolios. Find out what technological resources are available to assist you in developing student portfolios.

4. Using a World Wide Web search protocol, find one or two sites that include assessment information. You may want to refer to the book *Science on the Internet: A Resource for K–12 Teachers* (Ebenezer & Lau, 1999, Upper Saddle River, NJ, Merrill/Prentice Hall). How are they designed? How could you adapt what you found to your classroom? Check *http://www.prenhall.com/peters* for additional links.

References

Aardema, V. (1992). *Bringing the rain to Kapiti Plain*. New York: Dial Press.

American Association for the Advancement of Science (AAAS). (1993). *Benchmarks for science literacy*. New York: Oxford University Press.

American Association for the Advancement of Science (AAAS). (1998). *Blueprints for reform*. New York: Oxford University Press.

American Forest Foundation. (1996). *Project Learning Tree* (4th ed.). Washington, DC: Author.

Carter, G., & Berenson, S. B. (1996). Authentic assessment: Vehicle for reform. In J. Rhoton & P. Bowers (Eds.), *Issues in science education* (pp. 96–106). Arlington, VA: National Science Teachers Association and the National Science Education Leadership Association.

Collins, A. (1991). Portfolios for assessing student learning. In G. Kulm & S. M. Malcom (Eds.), *Science assessment in the service of reform* (pp. 291–300). Washington, DC: American Association for the Advancement of Science.

Gonzalez, V., Brusca-Vega, R., & Yawkey, T. (1997). *Assessment and instruction of culturally and linguistically diverse students with or at-risk of learning problems: From research to practice*. Boston: Allyn & Bacon.

Karlins, M. (1995). *Mendel's ladder*. New York: Simon & Schuster.

Krajcik, J., Czerniak, C., & Berger, C. (1999). *Teaching children science: A project-based approach*. New York: McGraw-Hill.

Lawrence Hall of Science. (1989). *River cutters* (Rev. ed.). Berkeley: University of California.

Locker, T. (1997). *Water dance*. Orlando, FL: Harcourt Brace.

Markle, S. (1993). *A rainy day*. New York: Orchard Books.

Mason, C. L. (1992). Concept mapping: A tool to develop reflective science instruction. *Science Education, 76*(1), 51–63.

Mason, C. L., Kahle, J. B., & Gardner, A. L. (1991). Draw-a-scientist test: Future implications. *School Science and Mathematics, 91*(5), 193–198.

McMillan, J. H. (1997). *Classroom assessment: Principles and practice for effective instruction*. Boston: Allyn & Bacon.

National Board for Professional Teaching Standards. (1997). *What teachers should know and be able to do*. Washington, DC: Author.

National Research Council (NRC). (1996). *National science education standards*. Washington, DC: National Academy Press.

National Science Resources Center, National Academy of Sciences, Smithsonian Institution. (1997). *Science for all children: A guide to improving elementary science education in your school district.* Washington, DC: National Academy Press.

Novak, J. D., & Gowin, D. B. (1984). *Learning how to learn.* New York: Cambridge University Press.

Ochs, V. D. (1996). Assessing habits of mind through performance-based assessment in science. In J. Rhoton & P. Bowers (Eds.), *Issues in science education* (pp. 114–122). Arlington, VA: National Science Teachers Association and the National Science Education Leadership Association.

Resnick, L. B., & Resnick, D. P. (1989). Tests as standards of achievement in schools. In *Proceedings of the 1989 ETS Invitational Conference* (pp. 63–80). Princeton, NJ: Educational Testing Service.

Roth, W. M., & Bowen, M. (1993). The unfolding vee. *Science Scope, 16*(5), 28–32.

Roth, W. M., & Verechaka, G. (1993). Plotting a course with vee maps. *Science and Children, 30*(4), 24–27.

Rubba, P., Miller, E., Schmalz, R., Rosenfeld, L., & Shyamal, K. (1991). Science education in the United States: Editors' reflection. In S. Majumdar, L. Rosenfeld, P. Rubba, E. Miller, & R. Schmalz (Eds.), *Science education in the United States: Issues, crisis, and priorities* (pp. 532–537). Easton, PA: Pennsylvania Academy of Science.

Spier, P. (1997). *Peter Spier's rain.* Garden City, NY: Doubleday.

Stanley, S. (1993). *The rains are coming.* New York: Greenwillow Books.

Wick, W. (1997). *A drop of water: A book of science and wonder.* New York: Scholastic Press.

Williams, J. (2000). Implementing portfolios and student-led conferences. *enc focus, 7*(2), 21–23.

Suggested Readings

Agler, L. (1986). *Liquid explorations.* Berkeley: University of California, Lawrence Hall of Science. (A Great Explorations in Math and Science [GEMS] guide to additional water activities and assessments.)

Anderson, R. D., & Pratt, H. (1995). *Local leadership for science education reform.* Dubuque, IA: Kendall/Hunt. (How changing teaching and assessment practices will assist in the reform process.)

Brandt, R. S. (Ed.). (1992). Using performance assessment. *Educational Leadership, 49*(8). (Special issue on performance assessment.)

Brandt, R. S. (Ed.). (1994). Reporting what students are learning. *Educational Leadership, 52*(2). (Special issue on assessment practices.)

Hein, G., & Price, S. (1994). *Active assessment for active science: A guide for elementary school teachers.* Portsmouth, NH: Heinemann. (A practical guide on the rationale for active assessment. Useful in enabling classroom teachers to develop, interpret, and score their own assessments.)

Herman, J. L., Aschbacher, P. R., & Winters, L. (1992). *A practical guide to alternative assessment.* Alexandria, VA: Association for Supervision and Curriculum Development. (Creation and use of alternative assessment procedures.)

Linn, R. L., & Gronlund, N. E. (2000). *Measurement and assessment in teaching* (8th ed.). Upper Saddle River, NJ: Merrill/Prentice Hall. (A comprehensive text on assessment of learning.)

McShane, J. B. (Ed.). (1994). Assessment issue. *Science and Children, 32*(2), 13–51. (A collection of relevant articles on assessment.)

Raizen, S. A., Baron, J. B., Champagne, A. B., Mullis, I. V. S., & Oakes, J. (1989). *Assessment in elementary school science education.* Washington, DC: National Center for Improving Science Education. (A synthesis of reports and recommendations on assessment.)

Chapter 6

Science Experiences for All Students

VIGNETTE 6-1

Careers for Women in Science

Katherine (Kata) McCarville
South Dakota School of Mines and Technology

My daughter is now 9 years old. She and her friends are about the same age I was when I first read about Marie Curie. Marie Curie, winner of two Nobel Prizes, is one of my personal role models. I would encourage you and your students to discover her inspiring story and those of the many other phenomenal women of science. Look in libraries and on the Web for scientists like geophysicist Inge Lehmann, astronomer Maria Mitchell, physicist Lise Meitner, computer scientist Grace Murray Hopper, and biologist Barbara McClintock.

Knowing several 9-year-olds, however, I suspect that to many elementary school students today—and perhaps even to you—these women may seem quaint and distant, even irrelevant. But on "Crazy Career Day" at her school last year, my daughter chose to dress as her mom. So instead, let me tell you about a contemporary working geoscientist.

She began her professional career in 1978 as a uranium miner in Wyoming. She then became a computer programmer and analyst for an engineering firm. In 1986, she moved to a position in academic computing services at the Colorado School of Mines, a college of engineering. Now, she works as Director of Information Technology Services at the South Dakota School of Mines and Technology, where she is in charge of all the university's computing and networking facilities and an annual budget of $1 million.

While working in highly technical jobs and moving into management, this woman became active in science education through volunteer activities. She developed a personal interest in paleontology over many years through continuing education opportunities. Starting with a bachelor's degree in geology and later earning a master's degree in geology, she is now working toward a doctoral degree in paleontology and is engaged in applying computing techniques, imaging technologies, and scientific visualization to the study of fossils.

Perhaps you have guessed by now—this woman is I. My career path may seem odd or unusual to many people, but my story illustrates many features of today's job markets and career opportunities. To some, it may appear that I have changed jobs too often. In technology-related fields, however, the expectation is a major job change at least every 2 years. In more than 20 years, I have worked for just four primary employers, far below the average.

You may be surprised to know that my current salary places me among the top 5% of salaries for professional women in the United States. Work involving management and business administration is often more highly compensated than technical work. Continuing education in formal programs and informal settings is important for maintaining current knowledge, and volunteer opportunities and activity in professional organizations are ways to develop new skills or explore possible career directions.

The pace of change in today's workplace is accelerating. New jobs are being created that have never existed before. An increasing number of jobs, even those that have been traditionally less rigorous, now require mathematical background, experience with computer technology, and the ability to apply logical reasoning or scientific methods to investigate situations and solve problems. Nearly all positions require communications skills—speaking, reading, and writing. Added to these factors is the growing participation of women and ethnic minorities in the workforce.

What does all that have to do with geosciences and careers for women? And how can you, as a teacher, possibly be expected to prepare every one of your students for future jobs and careers that do not even exist today?

First and most important, your students need to see that you are endlessly curious about the world, always learning something new, and willing to take risks in exploring the unknown. Each student must find and develop one or more areas of interest that provide personal motivation. The earth sciences integrate all the basic sciences and mathematics, with the earth, ocean, and sky as a free laboratory available to everyone for observation, description, and explanation.

My own story illustrates how the geosciences can serve as the foundation for a varied, engaging and successful career. Geology is my "first love"; the ongoing scientific investigation of the geologic past holds a fascination for me like nothing else. During college, that fascination gave me a reason to persevere through difficult courses in mathematics, physics, and chemistry. In the interdisciplinary breadth of geoscience, I could find a real-world example of nearly every equation and principle that was presented in the traditional disciplines. This provided a context within which I could integrate many details into a coherent body of knowledge. Geoscience gives me a unifying theme that lends stability to personal and professional relationships, while leaving ample room for career flexibility and providing a framework for lifelong learning.

Each of your students needs to meet and learn about people who are passionate about their work. It is especially meaningful if these people resemble the student in some way. Clearly, it is important to expose all students to scientists, mathematicians, and engineers, including people representing a wide diversity of backgrounds.

Whenever possible, invite parents and others from the community to participate in classroom or school activities. Try to arrange visits to workplaces in your area. Many professional organizations (see information elsewhere in this chapter, and use libraries and the Web to locate resources) sponsor teaching materials and teacher-education programs. Some groups provide guest speakers, science-fair judges, or sponsor mentoring programs to engage interested students with practicing professionals. Many of these programs now match partners via e-mail; the wide availability of e-mail makes this method extremely cost-effective.

Not very many research-based positions provide opportunities to participate in the advance of science, but encourage all students who show this interest, regardless of gender. These will be the scientists of the future. The results of scientific inquiries are increasingly used in making decisions that directly affect our lives. It is important that people from a wide variety of backgrounds be involved in determining which factors are important and which are not, choosing the questions to be asked, and guiding the direction of investigations.

Geoscience encompasses everything from the purely theoretical contemplation of the origin of the cosmos to the practical application of selecting a safe site for a garbage landfill. Exciting geoscience topics regularly make the headlines, and for good reason: Geoscience affects all of us every day.

Bring geoscience into your classroom as a cornerstone on which to build a comprehensive view of the direct relevance of mathematics and the basic sciences—with the added zing of current topics such as climate change, meteorite impacts, and dinosaurs. From the use of clay minerals in cosmetics to the exploration of the solar system, there is something for everyone in geoscience!

Have you thought about promoting scientific careers for the girls you will teach as suggested in Vignette 6–1?

What are some other ways that you could motivate your students to become interested in science?

You may remember that the science standards and benchmarks have as a primary goal *science for all students*. But, should we limit scientific inquiry to activities that the entire class completes as scheduled? Do you see a need to provide a wider range of science experiences to meet the needs of *all* students? In this chapter, we present four ways to assist you in providing science experiences for all students: science learning centers, science projects, science fairs, and strategies for teaching students with special needs. To begin, let's visit Mrs. Snyder's classroom.

Mandy's Science Fair

Mandy is excited today. Her group will present their science fair project at the school science fair. Mandy's group developed a project in which they compared three types of grasses with respect to ability to reduce soil erosion. They planted a type of turf grass, ryegrass, and crabgrass to see which held sandy soil the best when they ran water on the grass-covered sand hills. Mandy's group developed the idea after participating in activities from the "Agent Erosion" lesson found in the AIMS book *Primarily Earth* (Hoover & Mercier, 1996).

For additional erosion activities, see the GEMS book *River Cutters* (Lawrence Hall of Science, 1989).

Mandy's teacher also arranged for Mrs. Penton to visit her students' science fair projects. Mrs. Penton will talk to the class about a career as a sedimentologist and the

Refer to
http://www.prenhall.com/peters
for addresses for the
Association for Women
Geoscientists, Women in
Mining, Association for
Women in Science, and other
related links.

importance of this type of work to protect the many farms in their area. They will also participate in the AIMS activity "What On Earth Can We Do?" from the book *Down to Earth* (Erickson, Gregg, Helling, King, & Starkweather, 1987). This activity will cause the students to think about the impact of humans' activities on the soil.

Does Mandy's situation remind you of the science activities that you were involved in during your elementary school years? Think about the classroom in which you plan to teach. How will you promote science for all? If you are one to consider science class as "just the facts," then ask yourself the following question: *Will you teach as you were taught in elementary school?* As you contemplate this question, consider how science education was viewed in the past.

Historical Perspective

The authors of the *Thirty-First Yearbook* of the National Society for the Study of Education (NSSE, 1932) recommended a continuous, integrated program for elementary science. Subsequently, the *Forty-Sixth Yearbook* authors advocated a similar program (NSSE, 1947). The *Fifty-Ninth Yearbook,* printed shortly after the launching of the Soviet *Sputnik* satellite (NSSE, 1960), was in response to the contest of the space race. This information again prompted educational professionals to look at the inadequate elementary science program. More recently, reports of research surrounding the National Research Council's (NRC) *National Science Education Standards* (1996) and the American Association for the Advancement of Science's (AAAS) *Benchmarks for Science Literacy* (1993) reflected the common theme of these past reports.

Ask other adults what they remember about science education during the elementary years. Compare this information with your own experiences as you plan your future science program.

The general recommendation of all the above reports is that there should be student-centered, activity-based instruction in science at every grade level and for all students. Surprisingly, most adults cannot remember learning anything but science facts or vocabulary. The problem is that, with current employment trends, every sector of society needs highly skilled individuals who rely heavily on science and technology to perform their jobs.

Teaching and learning also have to respond to societal needs. It is said that a teacher trained 20 years ago could walk into today's classroom and begin teaching without any difficulty. How do you react to this statement? Fortunately, we find that there are teachers who see a need to complement the basic science program. They augment the standard curriculum with supplementary and individualized activities. They find that all children learn differently and adjust their teaching accordingly. One way they accommodate different learning styles is through the use of learning centers.

Science Learning Centers

Refer to
http://www.prenhall.com/peters
for links related to resources
for this lesson.

A classroom learning center is a place where one or several students at a time can do activities independently, working through the materials and directions found there. A learning center is arranged so that children may choose the activities they can do or are interested in and work at a pace that is right for each child. Some teachers also permit children to select the times they go to a center and partners to work with in a cooperative manner.

An example of a science-learning center on weather for an elementary class is shown in Figure 6–1. The center allows children to explore an area of high interest inde-

Figure 6–1
A science learning center.

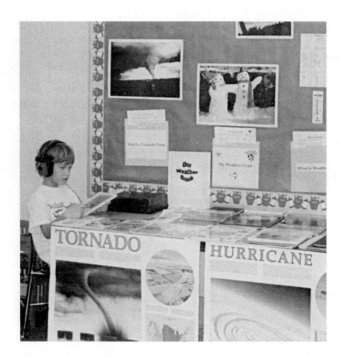

pendently and to develop a background that they may use in a variety of ways. About four children can use this center satisfactorily at one time. Notice the activity sheets on the bulletin board. Children use these to write down data or make drawings. Completed sheets are placed in a basket on the teacher's desk for later examination.

Observe some other features of this center. Children's literature is available for reading either individually or in a peer-tutoring situation. A weather radio is available for listening to the weather service and noting data such as temperatures and rainfall. Individual students can listen to a tape of pertinent weather information. Notice the materials for the students to interact with at the center: alcohol-filled thermometers for measuring temperatures, a wind gauge, and a tornado simulation bottle. Also, a "weather book" contains blank pages on which students can draw and color the weather each day.

To construct this center, the teacher considered these matters:

- Purpose and objectives
- Activity cards and worksheets
- Materials and their resupply
- Record keeping and evaluation
- The physical setup

Will you use learning centers? How will you begin your own learning center?

Refer to
http://www.prenhall.com/peters
**for links related to children's
literature.**

Deciding the Purpose of a Learning Center _____

The first task in making a science-learning center is to decide its purpose. Do you want it for general enrichment? Although this is the most common purpose, centers may also be

If materials are in short supply, then try sharing a learning center with other teachers.

used to complement an instructional unit or to present an entire unit when you only have a few materials.

One example of a learning center activity originated when Mandy's teacher, Ms. Snyder, wanted to have students play the Inside the Earth game from the *Thematic Unit: Geology* book (Gosnell, 1994). Because she only made a few games, she used a center to facilitate this learning activity.

As a rule, avoid activities whose outcomes take more time to happen than the time you assign students to be at the center. Children generally want things to happen *now*. There are, though, occasional exceptions to the rule, such as the example below.

As an extension to the erosion activities, Ms. Snyder started a "Things That Change" learning center (see Figure 6–2). Ms. Snyder got the idea for the center from studying changes that occur with the earth's soil after reading *How to Dig a Hole to the Other Side of the World* (McNulty, 1979) and completing activities related to the story from the book *Thematic Unit: Rocks and Soil* (Hale, 1992). Mandy's classmates Paul and Billy began a "changes" jar. In the jar, they put materials that they thought would deteriorate. Over the course of a month or longer, they will view these slow changes.

Developing Activity Cards and Record Sheets _____

Draw pictures beside key words if the cards are intended for less able readers.

For future use, cover the activity cards with transparent Con-Tact paper or laminate them with your school's laminating machine.

How can you communicate activities in the most understandable and appealing ways? The directions on activity cards must be simple so that independent work is possible. Use short sentences and easy words (see Figure 6–2).

Despite your best efforts, some children may not be able to read your directions. Keeping in mind the scaffolding approach, you may want to pair poor readers with good readers who will help. In some schools, the policy is to have multiage grouping for classes. In other schools, parents, a teacher aid, or a cross-age tutoring program assists students. Teachers at the primary level usually find that they must briefly introduce each new activity to the entire class before most children can do the activity by themselves.

A few teachers find that recording directions on a tape recorder works satisfactorily for nonreaders.

Try to make the design of your activity cards appealing and different for each topic. To do this, you might design the cards to go with the topic. For example, with the topic "volcanoes," make each card look like a cinder cone, shield, or composite volcano. For the rocks and minerals theme, make cards in various crystal shapes. Above all, make the cards as childproof as possible. Cut them from heavy paper or tagboard. Avoid having thin, easily bendable parts. Include as many open-ended activities as you can that have possibilities for process-skill development; these make it possible for children to suggest additional activities, which they enjoy doing.

Record sheets are a convenient way to know what the child has done, if you cannot directly observe the child at work. A record sheet may be simply a plain sheet of paper on which the child has made a drawing or recorded some data after an activity card suggestion.

Some teachers like to have a record sheet for every activity. Other teachers reserve record sheets only for activities in which data recording is necessary for the activity to make sense—graphing temperature or other changes, keeping track of results from testing different materials, or drawing a conclusion from a series of facts. Sometimes record sheets

Figure 6–2
A "changes" jar begun at a center allows children to continually observe slow changes away from the center.

are also called "skill sheets," "laboratory sheets," or "data sheets." See Figure 6–3 for an example of an activity card and its accompanying record sheet.

Materials _____

Kitchen science activities that can be done with common materials are perfect for science centers. The children themselves may be able to bring in most of what is needed. This is a good way to dispel the idea that science is a strange enterprise conducted with expensive and mysterious objects. You can also place in your center printed and audiovisual materials or items lent by local colleges or museums.

Many ordinary learning center materials can be obtained as donations from local retail businesses.

Record Keeping and Evaluation _____

Observing children in action is the best way to learn what they need help with and what they can do. Yet, if many activities are going on, it's difficult to keep track of everything each child has tried.

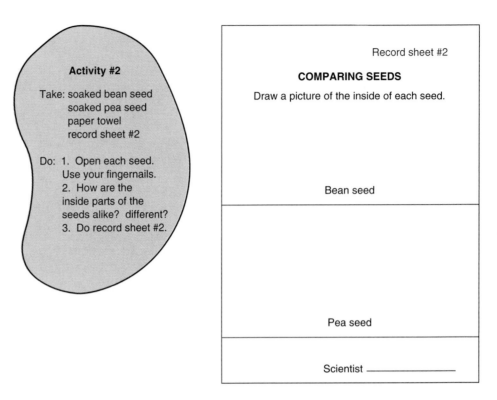

Figure 6–3
An activity card and its accompanying record sheet.

One way to record progress is to have a master list of all the center's activities or objectives with the children's names written to one side. If each activity has a record sheet, the child can file these. Use a folder at the center to collect sheets. Check the record sheet against your master list. The record sheet will show what activity was performed. Develop your own code system for recording the quality of the work, indicating what is incomplete, and denoting what should be done over.

Sometimes it may be better to have a record system in which the child refers only to her own work. To do this, some teachers give each child who uses a center a record sheet containing only activity numbers (see Figure 6–4). A space is left at the top for any center title to be written in by the child. A line is drawn under the last number that equals the center's total activities. On completing an activity, the child circles the activity number on her sheet. This record sheet is kept handy for the teacher to review during informal or scheduled conferences. To save time, only the more important objectives may be sampled. The record sheet is filed in the child's science folder, along with worksheets and other work products.

Monitor student progress to be sure that center activities are meeting your objectives and maintaining the students' interest. What is there about the activities that appeals to the students and gets the job done? Why are the students avoiding or doing poorly with other activities? Ask the students to give their views as well. Together you can continually improve the quality of your center's learning opportunities.

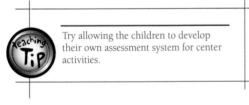

Try allowing the children to develop their own assessment system for center activities.

Record Sheet
Science Learning Center

on _Magnets_

Circle activity finished:

①	8	<u>15</u>
2	9	16
3	⑩ *LM*	17
④ *LM*	11	18
⑤	⑫	19
6	13	20
7	14	21

Scientist _Melinda_

Figure 6–4
A record system in which each child refers only to her or his own work prevents children from making critical comparisons of each other.

Schedule individual conferences periodically to learn more about each child's accomplishments. Can the child profit from further study in the form of an independent project? Such a project can be particularly valuable with the able and older child. This may be the time to set up a "contract" between you and the child. Or, the child may make a preliminary study before deciding with you on the exact topic, time, and goals for the contract.

Arranging the Physical Setup _____

Where is the best place to put a science learning center? How should it look? What are some ways to cut down the work in setting up new centers? These are some questions worth thinking about.

Can children work inside the classroom without interfering with others? Do activity outcomes happen at the center during the allotted times? Locate the center where it will not interfere with other activities and where it is visible to you at all times. Will wall space be needed? Take this into account as you locate the center in your classroom.

You can draw enlarged background pictures by making transparencies of pictures and then projecting the transparencies with an overhead projector. With these, you can enliven your center's background with familiar characters for child appeal. It's also interesting to use mystery, surprise, oddities, contrast, and drama in captions or pictures.

You can purchase a preconstructed backboard for your center or make one yourself with donated wood or heavy cardboard.

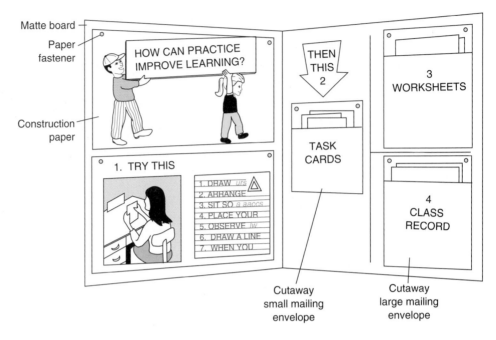

Figure 6–5
Many science investigations can be readily made into learning centers.

Managing the Science Learning Center _____

Use a prearranged signal if things get too noisy at the center.

How can you schedule, introduce the center to children, and keep things running smoothly? It's difficult to say precisely what will be useful in every situation, because schools and individual classrooms vary so much.

If you have never worked with learning centers, start out with a familiar topic. Investigations can be made into learning centers (see Figure 6–5). Always use clear directions and check to see that the students understand the procedure. Demonstrate an activity to get their interest and model appropriate behavior with materials. Finally, keep in mind that the noise level in the classroom may increase slightly. Allow yourself plenty of time at first to ensure a successful learning experience.

Chances are your experience with science learning centers will be rewarding. If so, consider increasing the use of centers through a more flexible arrangement involving several subjects. Some teachers reserve mornings for the three R's and unit teaching. Afternoons are for individualized enrichment and skill-building activities at different learning centers, such as the following:

- Science
- Social studies/multicultural center
- Fine arts center
- Hobby center
- Literature center
- Writing center
- Speaking and listening center
- Math center

Work at the centers may be either assigned or optional. This choice allows you freedom to vary time and other considerations and to assist and confer with individuals. You and each child can cooperatively decide on ways to pursue interests, knowledge, and skills. The best learning usually happens when children themselves take an active part in planning their learning.

Live Animal Centers _____

The use of living creatures such as mealworms, hermit crabs, lizards, fish, mice, hamsters, and rabbits is an excellent way to develop your students' observational skills and responsibility. When using animals, first refer to the school or district policy to determine which animals are acceptable for classrooms. The best policy is to have a veterinarian become your "partner in education" and ensure that the animals in your classroom are safe for student interaction.

Care for the animals should be primarily the students' responsibility; however, you should monitor the cleaning, feeding, and exercise. Help out only when the students cannot provide effective care.

Ideas for animal centers include having the students observe life cycles, compare growth rates, or observe eating patterns. It is a good idea to provide a daily observation log for the students to complete if they are observing animals.

Refer to
Appendix D and
http://www.prenhall.com/peters
for animal care tips.

Science Projects

As professional educators, we have seen withdrawn or listless girls and boys who did not come to life until they began to create science projects. Mandy and her group partners really became involved in science when given the opportunity to complete their project for the science fair. Because they were so interested in geology, Mandy's classmates Shauna and Danielle also completed an informal project on collecting rocks and minerals. The project began at the learning center where her group read *Everybody Needs a Rock* (Baylor, 1985), *Exploring Earth's Treasures* (Olson, 1996), and *The Magic School Bus Inside the Earth* (Cole, 1987). Later, they used *Rocks and Minerals: Mind-Boggling Experiments You Can Turn Into Science Fair Projects* (VanCleave, 1995) in deciding on a particular project. The group spent many hours collecting and identifying rocks and minerals.

What specifically is a project, and how does it differ from other science activities? A *project* is an organized search, construction, or task directed toward a specific purpose. One person or a small team of two or three persons ordinarily completes a project with minimal guidance from the teacher. A project is generally less formal than a "science fair project" and may clarify, extend, or apply a concept. Working on projects causes children to use science processes and develop thinking strategies. Most projects require much independent effort, so they are less appropriate for early-elementary children, who usually lack the skills and perseverance needed to operate independently.

The need for projects most often arises during a regular instructional unit. But projects may also begin with interests expressed by the students. The teacher's job is to provide some realistic project choices, give deadlines for completing the projects, tell how they will be presented, indicate the credit that will be received for projects, and check at times for progress.

Using Investigations and Activities for Projects

Project questions can originate from an informal query such as "What caused the Grand Canyon?"

Investigations that you might use with the whole class or in learning centers often present one or two extra open-ended opportunities to go beyond the basic investigation. Exploration of these questions can be an enriching activity when completed as a project.

Project activities can be short-range, straightforward demonstrations of concepts or procedures. Projects like these allow children to extend their interest by applying interviewing and reference skills to answer real needs.

Curriculum Projects

Project WILD (by the Western Regional Environmental Education Council) is a national program that promotes interdisciplinary, supplementary environmental and conservation activities for all grade levels. Teachers who attend Project WILD workshops are trained to facilitate numerous projects and activities that can be found in the guide provided to participants. The activities are grouped to take elementary students from the awareness of environmental concerns to the action of conservation and remediation.

Project Aquatic WILD (also by the Western Regional Environmental Education Council) is the companion series to Project WILD and is based on water environments. It contains many aquatic-based activities and extensions to terrestrial WILD activities.

Refer to *http://www.prenhall.com/peters* for more information on Project WILD, Aquatic WILD, or Project Learning Tree.

Project Learning Tree (by the American Forest Foundation), similar to WILD, is an environmental education project that has trees as its theme. Teachers who attend these certification workshops are shown how to facilitate integrated projects and activities based on diversity, interrelationships, systems, scale, and patterns of change.

Science Fairs

Refer to *http://www.prenhall.com/peters* for sample volcano projects and links.

Mandy's classmates Lucinda and Raquel are displaying the books *Volcanoes* (Branley, 1985), *The Magic School Bus Blows Its Top* (Cole, 1996), *How Mountains Are Made* (Zoehfeld, 1995), *Volcanoes: Fire From Below* (Wood, 1991), and *Discovering Earthquakes and Volcanoes* (Damon, 1990) at their science fair table. They are also exhibiting charts, graphs, and pictures related to volcanoes. Together, they prepared a science fair project that explains volcanoes. They searched the Internet for ideas and found the Volcano World site where they gathered information and developed their project.

You may want to consider having a science fair to encourage inquiry and display successful projects. The "investigatory aspect of science fairs" supports reform efforts such as the national science education standards and the benchmarks for science literacy (Balas, 1998, p. 1). Science fairs are also exciting for students, as you found out with Mandy's project cited earlier in the chapter. Science fairs are also good public relations tools to promote your science program at school. A well-planned science fair will involve *all students* because they have more options available than with regular instructional periods.

General Guidelines for Science Fairs _____

When beginning to consider a science fair, start small. A single classroom display at an open house is a good way to begin. Then, as you develop confidence, you may want to work with a fellow teacher for a combined event or even organize a schoolwide fair. Either way, allow plenty of time for the students to complete their projects. We suggest at least 6 weeks as follows:

- First Week—Hand out an information sheet and announce the science fair. Allow plenty of time for students to generate ideas and form groups if they are going to work on group projects.
- Second Week—Students turn in preliminary proposals for their projects by the end of the week. Remind students that you will review the proposals with them for quality of the inquiry, completeness of the proposal, and their ability to complete the project.
- Third Week—Hold individual meetings with students and their teacher to discuss proposals and refine projects.
- Fourth Week—Students or groups begin setting up inquiry activities, gathering data, and beginning reports.
- Fifth Week—Students continue projects and begin work on presentations and displays.
- Sixth Week—Students refine displays and presentations, complete reports, and present projects by the end of the week. Displaying projects on Friday afternoon and Saturday morning may increase parent participation.

A "Certificate of Completion" or multiple prizes can formally recognize everyone's efforts, but downplay individual comparisons, which elementary school students find hard to handle.

Invention Conventions _____

As part of the trend to teach science that children can apply to their lives, some science programs today recommend "invention conventions," as well as typical science fairs. Because technology is science applied to solve practical problems, the idea is to give girls and boys chances to develop solutions to their everyday problems and interests:

> *How can I tell how fast the wind is blowing? (A homemade wind gauge, fashioned from cardboard and wood, could fill the bill.)*

> *I'd like to make a weird toy that rolls uphill by itself. (Try a hidden rubber band inside a coffee can.)*

> *I've heard you can make a stool from newspaper that's so strong you can sit on it safely. (Rolled-up newspaper makes surprisingly sturdy columns.)*

For a variety of fun-filled ideas and ways to stimulate inventiveness in your students, see the following resources:

- Caney, S. (1985). *Steven Caney's invention book.* New York: Workman.
- Eichelberger, B., & Larson, C. (1993). *Constructions for children: Projects in design technology.* Menlo Park, CA: Dale Seymour.
- McCormack, A. J. (1981). *Inventor's workshop.* Belmont, CA: David S. Lake.

    If you are interested in a competitive awards program for projects, check the National Science Teachers Association's Web site. There you will find listed current national and regional science competitions.

Refer to *http://www.prenhall.com/peters* for links to NSTA and other award programs.

Science experiences provide special needs students with opportunities that are not found in other content areas.

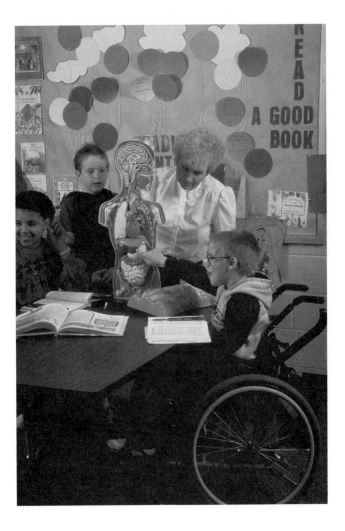

Teaching Students with Special Needs

See the Planning and Management, Special Needs Adaptations section of the companion CD for an example of special needs adaptations.

After listening to *Caves and Caverns* (Gibbons, 1993) being read to the class, Tamika became very excited about speleology. She wanted to know more about stalactites, stalagmites, helictites, speleothems, flowstone, and dripstone. She thought that a career as a speleologist would be perfect because her physical disability would not interfere with spelunking. Fortunately, she is in an inclusive classroom where the teacher recognizes her interest as an opportunity and will support her curiosity. This situation is in keeping with McCann's (1998) statement, "Science classes provide special needs students with opportunities they may not get anywhere else" (p. 1).

Inclusion is education in the least restrictive environment and means that students would, to the extent possible, be educated with their nondisabled peers.

Inclusive Classrooms ——————

Inclusion is a concept that is becoming the standard in most K–12 classrooms. An inclusive classroom has a mix of physical and mental developmental levels of students, accommodating those identified as disabled in some way. According to the U.S. Department of

Education (USDOE), nearly 12% of students were identified as disabled during the period 1991–1994 (USDOE, 1994). The Office of Special Education Programs reports that the number of students with disabilities served under the Individuals with Disabilities Education Act (IDEA) continues to increase at a rate higher than both the general population and school enrollment (USDOE, 1999). IDEA guarantees a free, appropriate education in the least restrictive environment for students with disabilities. Obviously, science instruction is a part of this "appropriate education."

Science instruction for students with disabilities does involve some problems, however. A study by Stefanich and Norman (1996) includes the following information:

- Students with mild disabilities received only 1 minute of science instruction for every 200 minutes of reading instruction.
- Elementary science teachers have little training or experience in teaching students with disabilities.
- Most teachers agree that students with disabilities benefit from hands-on instruction, yet the reality is that they are generally taught from the textbook.

Elementary teachers need to understand that the special education teacher may not take primary responsibility for science instruction, because the students will probably be in regular classrooms for science class. If you are an elementary teacher, you will have to seek out opportunities during college and through in-service to gain a better understanding of disadvantaged children. Likewise, if you are a special education teacher, you will need college and in-service opportunities related to elementary science. The following sections are designed as a first step in assisting you with this.

Assisting Students with Disabilities _____

Mainstreaming presents both opportunities and challenges to people in schools. Mainstreamed children learn to live and work in settings that are more likely to develop their potentials to the fullest. The other children profit from a heightened sensitivity and a greater capacity to live and work with individual differences.

Refer to
http://www.prenhall.com/peters
for links related to IDEA.

The challenges largely come from the diversity of handicaps found in special populations. As an elementary teacher, everyone who comes to your classroom has been identified as a teachable child. To help ensure this, you should share in the placement decision. The disabled students who require the most change in the science curriculum are those who are totally blind or deaf. For most students with disabilities, a solid hands-on program gives the multisensory experiences they need to learn science well.

Also, realize that an individualized education plan (IEP) is developed for each child by a team of persons. Included on the team is at least one person qualified in special education. By working with a team, you are able to draw on more skills, information, and ideas than by working alone. The team shares responsibility for the child's progress. In many states, the IEP is also accompanied by whatever special instructional media and materials the team believes are essential to meet objectives.

The IDEA Amendments of 1997 specify inclusion of at least one regular education teacher on each IEP team.

What are some characteristics of students with disabilities you are likely to teach? How can you generally help them? What resources can you draw on that apply specifically to science? The following sections review students who are visually impaired, hearing impaired, and orthopedically impaired, and those who are mentally disabled.

Visually Impaired

The problems of students who are visually impaired may range from poor eyesight to total blindness. Most mainstreamed students will have at least some functional vision. However, these students frequently lack firsthand experience with many objects. This is reflected in their language. Vocabulary and descriptive capacity, therefore, need considerable strengthening. Keep in mind the following points with students who are visually impaired:

- Use concrete, multisensory experiences to build a greater store of needed percepts.
- Give plenty of time to explore and encourage the use of descriptive language during explorations.
- Encourage communication with the students throughout activity periods.
- Use tactile cues with materials, such as a knotted string for measuring.
- Walk the students through spaces to demonstrate barriers and tactile clues.
- Encourage the use of any remaining vision.
- Encourage other students to be sensitive about their use of phrases such as "over there," "like that one," or any other descriptions that require vision.
- Be tolerant of, and prepared for, spilled or scattered material.
- Use oral language or a recorder for instructions and information.
- Pair each student with a tactful sighted partner who can assist in the scaffolding process.

The American Printing House for the Blind produces several current elementary science series in large print and Braille. Illustrations and graphs are often in the form of touchable raised-line drawings.

Hearing Impaired

The hearing of children who are hearing impaired may range from mildly impaired to totally deaf. Most wear hearing aids and have partial hearing. Communication is easier when the child can read lips and certain facial movements and when sign language is used. Delayed language development is common. When teaching science to students who are hearing impaired, remember the following:

- Use concrete objects—pictures, sketches, signs, and the like—to get across ideas.
- Seat the students close to you or to the sound source.
- Give clear directions and face the students as you speak.
- Speak with usual volume and speed.
- Model, rather than correct, pronunciations for the students who are partially deaf.
- Allow longer periods of wait time.
- Make sure you have the students' attention; use direct eye contact.
- Use gestures and body language, but don't exaggerate these.
- Avoid speaking for the students or having classmates speak for the students.
- Talk with the students frequently about what they are doing.
- Maintain good lighting in the classroom.

Orthopedically Impaired

Students who are orthopedically impaired typically have gross- or fine-motor malfunctions that cause problems in locomotion, coordination, balance, and dexterity. One of the most common impairments is cerebral palsy. Students who are orthopedically disabled may use walkers, wheelchairs, crutches, braces, or other aids. Keep in mind the following when teaching students who are orthopedically impaired:

- Encourage participation in all possible activities.
- Modify activities as much as possible to avoid frustrations.
- Encourage the use of limbs to the fullest ability.
- Find alternative ways to manipulate objects.
- Allow alternative methods for the students to respond.
- Keep traffic lanes clear in the classroom.
- Acknowledge and deal openly with feelings of frustration.
- Have other students assist these students in moving to the next activity if needed.
- Promote the students' confidence and independence whenever possible.
- Use activities that foster problem solving and growth in thinking skills.
- Present materials and activities at a comfortable height for individuals in wheelchairs.

Mentally Disabled

Students who are mentally disabled show significantly subaverage abilities in cognitive tasks and often in motor development. They are likely to have problems in learning, remembering, problem solving, and life skills. Other frequent characteristics are short attention span, poor selective attention, and limited ability to make choices. Often, the child with a mental disability will require shorter work periods, more concrete tasks, more direct and structured instruction, and more frequent reinforcement, because of a short attention span. Keep in mind the following points when teaching science to students who are mentally disabled:

- Use a variety of hands-on teaching methods and materials.
- Be sure you have the students' attention before you give directions, and frequently have them repeat directions back to you.
- Demonstrate and model as you give simple, clear directions.
- Review new concepts and vocabulary.
- Break tasks down to simple, step-by-step parts if necessary.
- Use the least complex language possible when giving instructions.
- Outline expectations clearly for the students before work begins.
- Review and summarize ideas and procedures frequently. Have the students recapitulate experiences.
- Give positive reinforcement immediately after each small success.
- Give responsibility within the students' limits, and let the students observe and assist in a role before giving them responsibility.
- Apply previously constructed concepts to everyday experiences.
- Begin instruction with what the students know and build on that.

Remember that children who are victims of alcoholic or drug-abusing parents may exhibit conditions similar to those of children who are mentally disabled.

Disabled

Children who are disabled are much more likely to have a poor self-concept than other children. Many adults realize this, but they overprotect the disabled in order to compensate. Unfortunately, this overprotection inhibits development and confidence. Children with disabilities, in turn, often learn and accept overdependence, so a cycle develops that feeds on itself. Keep the following in mind when teaching students who are disabled:

- Consider whether help is necessary, rather than convenient.
- Except for obvious needs, get consent from the students before giving help.
- Don't persist if the students decline help; let the students discover whether help is needed.
- Provide prompts instead of answers.
- Allow peers to help or offer help matter-of-factly.

See *http://www.prenhall.com/peters* for a link to the ERIC Clearinghouse on Disabilities and Gifted Education.

The Disabled as Individuals

Many other kinds of disabilities are found in mainstreaming, including the learning disabled, the speech/language impaired, the health impaired, and those with multiple handicaps. Be aware that entire books are devoted to each one of these and the previously described handicaps. Fortunately, you do not have to become an expert in special education to help a specific mainstreamed child. Although it is nice to have some general knowledge about a handicap, it is far more important to know how that handicap affects a particular child and what the child's individual instructional needs are. You learn this by working with the child.

Resources for Science Teaching ─────────

Several sources offer programs and information to better teach the students with disabilities in the regular classroom. An excellent and well-tested program is FOSS, the *Full Option Science System*. Designed for students with and without handicaps in Grades K–6, it was developed at the Lawrence Hall of Science. FOSS is an outgrowth of earlier projects to improve science education for students who are visually impaired and physically disabled. Several modules at each grade level include lesson plans in the earth, life, and physical sciences. Extension activities include work in language, computer, and mathematics applications. The developers worked hard to match activities with students' ability to think at different ages. Further work was done to make the program easy to instruct and manage. The commercial distributor of FOSS is

- Encyclopaedia Britannica Educational Corporation, 310 South Michigan Avenue, Chicago, IL 60604

Further sources that can help you plan lessons for children with different disabilities are listed below:

- Alexander Graham Bell Association for the Deaf, 3417 Volta Place, N.W., Washington, DC 20007
- American Printing House for the Blind, P.O. Box 6085, Louisville, KY 40206
- Center for Multisensory Learning, Lawrence Hall of Science, University of California, Berkeley, CA 94720
- ERIC Clearinghouse on Handicapped and Gifted Children, 1920 Association Drive, Reston, VA 22091
- National Center on Educational Media and Materials for the Handicapped, Ohio State University, 154 West 12th Avenue, Columbus, OH 43210

Refer to *http://www.prenhall.com/peters* for links to FOSS and other resources.

Working with Limited English Proficiency Students ─────────

Not long ago, only a few cities in the United States contained significant numbers of schoolchildren whose native language was not English. Today, they are present in nearly every school. In some schools, foreign-born students who do not speak English may be placed in bilingual classrooms and taught by someone who is proficient in both English and the foreign language. As the students acquire some English proficiency, they are mainstreamed for larger parts of the school day. In other schools, they are taught in all-English classrooms. As a regular classroom teacher, expect to have at least some students of limited English proficiency (LEP) from time to time.

Many LEP students experience some culture shock because what they observe now may differ radically from their earlier environment. They may be reluctant to speak because they are afraid to make mistakes. Your warm acceptance and frequent praise will boost their confidence. Whatever you can do to reduce anxiety, increase meaning of content studied, model good English, and increase chances to interact informally with English speakers will benefit them. Students who are becoming proficient in English require some extra time and attention, but they can also enrich the curriculum by bringing multicultural knowledge and perspectives to what is studied. Here are some things that will work for you:

- Use a listening–speaking–reading–writing sequence in teaching whenever possible. Listening lays the foundation for the other language skills. It's easier to speak what we have first heard, read what we have spoken, and write what we have read.
- Use multisensory, hands-on teaching methods whenever you can. Concrete materials, investigations, demonstrations, audiovisual media, graphs, and diagrams are more likely to foster meaningful learning. One great advantage of hands-on science over most other subjects is that the actual doing demands little verbal ability.
- Pair LEP students with bilingual partners or in cooperative learning groups to increase the scaffolding effect.
- Speak slowly, use short sentences, and rephrase what you say if a student seems unsure, rather than just repeat what you have said. Use body language, props, pictures, and sketches to clarify your words.
- Check more specifically whether a student understands by asking yes-or-no questions or by having the student do something you can observe, such as point to an object.
- Avoid idiomatic expressions; they can be confusing when taken literally: "It's as easy as pie."
- Make whatever you refer to as concrete as possible—what you know the students have done or observed in the past. Give observable examples in the present as well: "The handle of this pencil sharpener is also a lever."
- To help the students build schemata, write key concepts and vocabulary used during a lesson on the chalkboard. Often make a concept map to outline what is to come in a lesson or to summarize the content of a lesson.
- Emphasize and repeat key words of the lesson as you teach. This cues the students about what to remember and how the words sound.
- For the easiest and most meaningful reading, make language experience charts.

Try interactive reading with LEP students.

Sixteen regional resource centers for bilingual education in the United States offer training and technical support services to schools. For the center nearest you, call or write the following:

- National Clearinghouse for Bilingual Education, 1118 22nd Street, N.W., Washington, DC 20037 ([800] 321-6223)

The following references from the National Clearinghouse for Bilingual Education can also further your work with LEP students:

- Hamayan, E., & Perlman, R. (1990). *Helping language minority students after they exit from bilingual/ESL programs: A handbook for teachers.* Washington, DC: National Clearinghouse for Bilingual Education.
- Short, D. J. (1991). *Integrating language and content instruction: Strategies and techniques.* Washington, DC: National Clearinghouse for Bilingual Education.

Working with Gifted Students

What can you expect from mainstreamed students classified as gifted by your district? Children who are gifted display many of the same developmental qualities as most other children. The difference is in the greater degree to which, and the speed with which, these qualities develop. In kindergarten, for example, students who are gifted may perform like second graders. By their senior year in high school, they typically outperform average college seniors on academic tests.

What are some of their attributes? Compared with other students, the gifted child is much more likely to:

- Tolerate ambiguity and complexity
- Have a longer attention span
- Be a highly curious and sharp-eyed observer
- Be a top-notch reader who retains what is read
- Have a well-developed speaking and listening vocabulary
- Have learned the basic skills well

In-depth investigations of rocks and minerals can become an extension activity for gifted students.

- Understand complex directions the first time around
- Be imaginative and receptive to new ideas
- Be interested in broad concepts and issues
- Have one or more hobbies that require thinking

Gifted students who show all or most of these attributes are often placed in a full-time special class or a pull-out program for part of the school day. But many are totally mainstreamed. How can we challenge these children?

A common problem with having gifted children in regular classrooms is that the curriculum is restrictive and unchallenging for them. They soon become bored and often will seek attention in disruptive ways. One way to keep this problem from blossoming is to use many open-ended investigations and activities. Such a program stimulates the kind of creative, divergent thinking gifted students need to grow toward their potential. Fortunately for us as teachers, these and other experiences described next also work well for most nongifted students.

A second important way to help mainstreamed gifted students is to encourage them to build a large knowledge base. This is usually easy because of their broad curiosity, strong ability to locate and understand information, and ability to remember what they find out. A wide variety of open-ended science investigations stimulates them to try multiple observations and experiments and to read for background. Gifted children readily sense how a broad array of knowledge feeds their creative and problem-solving abilities; this motivates them to learn even more.

A third way to help gifted students is to let them manage their own learning through individual and small-group projects, including those done for school science fairs. Independent study also is fostered when we show students how to locate and use references, trade books, and other instructional materials in the school library.

Inquiry activities can be valuable in motivating gifted students.

A fourth way to help gifted students is to expose them to persons in science and other professions who can serve as information sources and future role models. This is particularly important for students who come from economically disadvantaged backgrounds. Gifted children have the interest and quickly develop the capacity to correspond with knowledgeable adults, interview them by telephone or in person, and understand much of what they see and hear.

We can also help gifted students by attending to their social skills as they interact with other children. Some of these students may be advanced academically but be average in social and personal skills. These skills are needed not only for success in many professions but for personal happiness as well. A central objective for mainstreaming the gifted is to help them communicate and get along with persons of all ability levels.

Remember that gifted students may not necessarily be gifted in mathematics and science. Monitor your expectations to make sure you are not expecting too much from a child who may be gifted only in language, art, music, or another area.

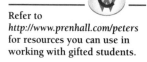
Refer to
http://www.prenhall.com/peters
for resources you can use in
working with gifted students.

Summary

1. A classroom learning center is a place where one or several students at a time can conduct activities independently using materials and directions found at the center. The center may be organized so that the students can choose at least some of the activities and work at their own pace and learning level. Open-ended experiences usually serve best for these purposes.

2. A science project is an organized search, construction, or task directed toward a specific purpose and ordinarily carried out by one to three students. The need for projects often arises in instructional units through interests expressed by students.
3. Science fairs and invention conventions will help you encourage inquiry. They are exciting for students and can be good public relations tools to promote your science program at school.
4. The Individuals with Disabilities Education Act, or IDEA, guarantees a free, appropriate education in the least restrictive environment for students with disabilities. Science instruction is a part of this appropriate education.

Reflection

1. The policy in some schools is to not allow any type of live animal. In this case, you can search the Internet for sites that have permanently mounted cameras for your students to make "live" observations. What other types of environments can you find on the Internet? What other ways can you replace the use of classroom pets? Be ready to share your ideas with classmates.
2. If you were to arrange a science competition in your classroom, what local community resources or industries could help out? Try contacting one or two and see what types of resources are available to you as a classroom teacher.
3. Attend an individualized education program (IEP) meeting for a student. What is expected of the parents, the regular teacher, the special education teacher, and the child?

References

American Association for the Advancement of Science (AAAS). (1993). *Benchmarks for science literacy.* New York: Oxford University Press.

Balas, A. (1998). *Science fairs in the elementary school.* Columbus, OH: ERIC Digest.

Baylor, B. (1985). *Everybody needs a rock.* New York: Atheneum.

Branley, F. (1985). *Volcanoes.* New York: HarperCollins.

Cole, J. (1987). *The magic school bus inside the earth.* New York: Scholastic.

Cole, J. (1996). *The magic school bus blows its top.* New York: Scholastic.

Damon, L. (1990). *Discovering earthquakes and volcanoes.* New York: Troll Associates.

Erickson, S., Gregg, D., Helling, F., King, M., & Starkweather, J. (1987). *Down to earth.* Fresno, CA: AIMS Education Foundation.

Gibbons, G. (1993). *Caves and caverns.* New York: Voyager Books.

Gosnell, K. (1994). *Thematic unit: Geology.* Huntington Beach, CA: Teacher Created Materials.

Hale, J. (1992). *Thematic unit: Rocks and soil.* Huntington Beach, CA: Teacher Created Materials.

Hoover, E., & Mercier, S. (1996). *Primarily earth: AIMS activities grades K–3.* Fresno, CA: AIMS Education Foundation.

Lawrence Hall of Science. (1989). *River cutters* (Rev. ed.). Berkeley: University of California.

McCann, W. (1998). *Science classrooms for students with special needs.* Columbus, OH: ERIC Digest. Available: *http://www.ericse.org/digests/dse98-5.html*

McNulty, F. (1979). *How to dig a hole to the other side of the world.* New York: Harper & Row.

National Research Council (NRC). (1996). *National science education standards.* Washington, DC: National Academy Press.

National Society for the Study of Education (NSSE). (1932). *A program for teaching science.* Chicago: University of Chicago Press.

National Society for the Study of Education (NSSE). (1947). *Science education in American schools.* Chicago: University of Chicago Press.

National Society for the Study of Education (NSSE). (1960). *Rethinking science education.* Chicago: University of Chicago Press.

Olson, D. (1996). *Exploring earth's treasures.* Chicago: Kidsbooks.

Stefanich, G., & Norman, K. (1996). *Teaching science to students with disabilities: Experiences and perceptions of classroom teachers and science educators.* A special publication of the Association for the Education of Teachers in Science. (Available from AETS, Dr. Jon Pedersen, University of Oklahoma, 820 Van Vleet Oval, ECH 114, Norman, OK 73019)

U.S. Department of Education (USDOE). (1994). *Mini-digest of educational statistics: 1994.* Washington, DC: Author.

U.S. Department of Education (USDOE). (1999). *Twenty-first annual report to Congress on the imple-mentation of Individuals with Disabilities Education Act.* Washington, DC: Author. Available: *http://www.ed.gov/offices/OSERS/OSEP/ OSEP99AnlRpt/*

VanCleave, J. (1995). *Rocks and minerals: Mind-boggling experiments you can turn into science fair projects.* New York: John Wiley.

Wood, J. (1991). *Volcanoes: Fire from below.* Milwaukee, WI: Gareth Stevens.

Zoehfeld, K. (1995). *How mountains are made.* New York: HarperCollins.

Suggested Readings

Blume, S. (1991). *Science fair handbook.* New York: Macmillan/McGraw-Hill. (A resource for teachers, principals, and science fair coordinators.)

Bochinski, J. (1991). *The complete handbook of science fair projects.* New York: John Wiley. (How to complete a project plus 50 award-winning examples.)

Carratello, J., & Carratello, P. (1989). *All about science fairs.* Huntington Beach, CA: Teacher Created Materials. (A practical guide to help students and teachers with science fairs.)

DeBruin, J. (1991). *Science fairs with style.* Carthage, IL: Good Apple. (A comprehensive guide for upper-grade projects.)

Fredericks, A., & Asimov, I. (1990). *The complete science fair handbook.* Glenview, IL: Good Year Books. (A good guide to conducting science fairs.)

Hampton, C. H., Hampton, C. D., & Kramer, D. C. (1994). *Classroom creature culture: Algae to anoles* (Rev. ed.). Arlington, VA: National Science Teachers Association. (Guidelines for setting up live animal centers in the classroom. Also available as an ERIC microfiche, ERIC Document Reproduction Service No. ED 370 797.)

National Science Teachers Association (NSTA). (1988). *Science fairs and projects: Grades K–8.* Washington, DC: Author. (A resource book from the NSTA.)

National Science Teachers Association (NSTA). (1990). *Science and math events.* Arlington, VA: Author. (A resource book on science and math events from NSTA.)

Poppe, C. A., & VanMatre, N. A. (1985). *Science learning centers for the primary grades.* West Nyack, NY: Center for Applied Research in Education. (A comprehensive book for those interested in setting up centers.)

Shubkagel, J. F. (1993). *Show me how to write an experimental science fair paper: A fill-in-the-blank handbook.* Independence, MO: Show Me How. (A step-by-step guide for teachers, parents, and students in upper-elementary grades.)

Stone, G. K. (1981). *More science projects you can do.* Upper Saddle River, NJ: Prentice Hall. (A paperback book of many interesting projects for upper-elementary students.)

Tocci, S. (1986). *How to do a science fair project.* New York: Watts. (A useful guide to science fair projects.)

VanCleave, J. (1997). *Guide to the best science fair projects.* New York: John Wiley. (Complete rules, display tips, and experiments on 50 topics.)

Chapter 7

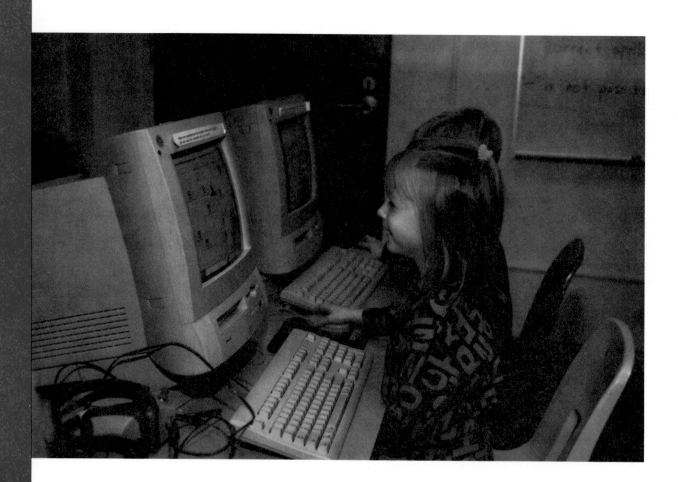

Constructing Technological Understandings

Where the Wildflowers Are

Charlotte Boling
Dr. Pam Northrup,
University of West Florida

To plan the upcoming unit on native wildflowers, the teacher uses STEPS (Support for Teachers Enhancing Performance in Schools), an online tool designed to assist in planning using a standards-driven model. STEPS contains a Lesson Architect that helps the teacher organize his lesson online. He will be able to store the lesson in his personal online folder and even e-mail it to his principal. Resources such as links to Web sites, best practices, and other model units help him in planning the lesson on wildflowers. Tutorial links are especially useful because the teacher is trying out some new technologies in his lesson. The tutorials within STEPS will guide the teacher in how to use technology in the classroom. Using this online tool, he designed a unit that will last for several weeks.

On the first day of the unit, the teacher greets his students at the door and hands each a card with the words "Where the Wildflowers Are." Once everyone is seated, the teacher explains that the class will be embarking on a new unit about wildflowers. He then discusses the strategies the students will be following by using a PowerPoint presentation loaded with pictures and graphics taken from the Internet. The students will be researching wildflowers, learning about where they grow, and actually growing some in their classroom. At the end of the unit, the students will sell their wildflowers. The teacher then poses this question: "As a scientist, how would you go about gathering information, making initial hypotheses, testing the hypotheses, and reporting?" Using Inspiration (a concept mapping software) projected on a big television in the front of the room with a TV-to-computer conversion device, the teacher notes the students' brainstorming answers to the question. The teacher organizes students into cooperative learning groups, and they begin.

A group of students immediately embarks on a virtual field trip to the desert, to the Pitcher Plant Prairie, and to the local garden store's Web site. (All pertinent Web sites had been bookmarked earlier by the teacher to save time.) The students take notes, copy interesting pictures to their group folder on the computer, and begin comparing and contrasting types of wildflowers. One student finally suggests

167

that they begin looking at wildflowers that will grow locally. After a bit of problem solving, the students notice a link to the Global Temperature Cam and to Weather Underground. They are on their way!

Another group begins their investigation by using the CD-ROM Explorapedia. They look up wildflowers, gardening, and seeds to begin their search. This group of students also jots down notes on their palm computers, saves pictures to their computer folders, and even prints some information for later use.

A third group's approach is to go online to the site Ask A Scientist and to study the Biomes projects. They think that the information they gain in other ways will help them better understand wildflowers. They e-mail a scientist who guarantees a 24-hour response. They also go to Global Schoolhouse to see whether other classes are studying the same topic and, they hope, to collaborate with students in other parts of the country.

After the information gathering is complete, the students create HyperStudio stacks to share with each other, with other students, and with new online partners. The stacks include projections of which types of flowers should be grown in their classroom, the soil that should be used, and the type of pot that would work best.

One of the groups establishes a relationship with a classroom in another part of the country. The two classrooms decide that they will plant wildflowers at the same time while predicting, observing, and recording plant data. To make the relationship as visual as possible, the teacher creates a simple Web site containing both classes' selection of wildflowers to grow, the type of soil selected, the HyperStudio lessons that were created, and a simple database for student groups to update weekly and monitor growth. To keep the Web site current, the students take digital pictures each week and load them on the Web site. Both classrooms download NetMeeting and begin daily conversations through their inexpensive Quick Cam camera. The students also create and share pictures of their plants with their new pen pals across the country.

While the plants mature, marketing techniques are established. The students brainstorm the best approach to marketing their wildflowers. Some engage in traditional marketing by creating posters to hang in the school. Others decide to create a bookmark by using a simple desktop publishing program and hand out to everyone that they see: *"Bookmark it! Wildflowers for Sale . . ."* along with the URL of the class Web site. Another group believes that a video is a good approach. Using the resources that have been gathered during the past several weeks, the students go to the ITV room and create a short commercial to be played on the school's ITV network.

The plants are finally ready for sale! The students must keep track of the expenses they incurred while growing the plants (soil, pots, advertising, fertilizer) and make sure they sell the plants at a price that will allow them to make their money back and still have some left over for a class celebration. The students use a spreadsheet to keep up with the expenses and the profits.

"Step right up! This is where the wildflowers are" could be heard and seen on the school ITV system on the day of the sale!

With the possibility of exploring online resources as the students did in Vignette 7–1, children and their teachers have a new world of exciting possibilities open to them. The students in the vignette constructed new knowledge about technology and science. They were excited about using their technologically enhanced learning environment and discovering new things about wildflowers as they developed inquiry skills.

What do you think of when you hear the words *technology* and *education?* If you are like most people, your response would include the use of computers in education. In fact, the response for most preservice teachers is the use of computers in the curriculum. This is just one small part of technology, however. Technology education also includes the **designed world** (Rutherford & Ahlgren, 1990).

The **designed world** refers to the applications of science in the form of technology.

By including the designed world, we mean that technology education includes such areas as agricultural technology, materials technology, manufacturing technology, energy technology, communication technology, health technology, construction technology, and transportation technology. In the first part of this chapter, we look at educational technology, or using computers, laser discs, CDs, DVDs, and similar tools in the classroom. We then explore the science technology society (STS) movement. In the last part of the chapter, we explore the growing field of technology education in the elementary classroom.

Educational Technology and Elementary Science

Most historians agree that a revolution occurred in education soon after the printing press was invented. The printed book became the tool of its time and has since been noted by many groups as the greatest invention of the past millennium. Today, computer technology is the educational tool of the times. Historians tell us of the resistance to books in the 15th century. As people relied more on the printed word for educational opportunity, however, this technological advancement became commonplace. Similarly, resistance to using computers in the classroom is rapidly changing today.

Not that long ago, a single microcomputer for a school was rare. This is no longer the case. Computers of all sizes are located in media centers, labs, and individual classrooms. Computing capacity is now at the point where the average home video game has the computing ability of the most powerful computers manufactured just a few years ago. The automobile you buy today has a greater ability to process data than any computer you may have used in school. What does this mean for you as a teacher? You will be challenged to use this *technology as a learning tool* instead of just *learning about the this tool of technology.*

In some classrooms, although significant advances have been made in instructional technology, actual practice in the classroom is status quo (Kozma & Shank, 1998; Means, 1994). The uses of advanced technologies have not kept pace with the advances. If this is still the case for you, how can you change this? Will your classroom look like the one in the vignette?

The Science Program Resource Standard is included here so that you can refer to it and see the need for educational technology. As noted, inquiry requires the right equipment. Computers can provide access to data and scientists beyond the classroom. The authors of the national science education standards (National Research Council [NRC], 1996) suggest that your students can access scientific information as well as collect, store, analyze, and display data. Think about how the students in Vignette 7–1 used technology

See *http://www.prenhall.com/peters* for links to other programs emphasizing the use of computers in the classroom.

See the Constructivist
Pedagogy and Planning
and Management sections
of the companion CD for
examples of the classroom
teacher's and students' use
of computers.

Standards Link

Science Program Resource Standard

The K–12 science program must give students access to appropriate and sufficient resources, including quality teachers, time, materials and equipment, adequate and safe space, and the community.

- **The most important resource is professional teachers.**

- **Time is a major resource in a science program.**

- **Conducting scientific inquiry requires that students have easy, equitable, and frequent opportunities to use a wide range of equipment, materials, supplies, and other resources for experimentation and direct investigation of phenomena.**

- **Collaborative inquiry requires adequate and safe space.**

- **Good science programs require access to the world beyond the classroom.**

(Program Standard D, National Research Council, 1996, p. 218)

as a learning tool. Does it seem natural for them to use computers? Do the students in the photograph that opens this chapter illustrate how commonplace computers have become in the elementary classroom?

The Uses of Computers

School microcomputers initially served for drill and practice in mathematics and language. Now, they are also being used to teach broader applications through simulations, microcomputer-based laboratories, project-based science, multimedia, spreadsheets, databases, and learning activities related to the Internet. With more machines available, there are improved chances for us to apply them in science activities and in whole-class teaching. You will find that some schools pool their computer resources into laboratories, some distribute their computer resources into classrooms, and some use a combination of these methods. In most cases, you will have at least one machine to allow you to create a center in your classroom.

Setting up a microcomputer center for science raises some of the same practical questions as learning centers for other disciplines:

- What do you want to accomplish with the center?
- Are other means of instruction better?
- What kinds of compatible hardware and software are available?
- Who will use the center and when?
- What will the users need to know?
- How can I best scaffold the learning environment for my students?

Often, the software available to you will dictate your use of the computer. What types of software are available? Consider the kinds of software programs you are now likely to see in your school.

Types of Software

Software is generally purchased on compact discs (CDs) or downloaded directly from the Internet. It may also be on a networked machine in your school. Software is available to assist in learning science processes and concepts in categories such as the following:

- Tutorials and skill-building games
- Multimedia
- Simulations
- Internet access tools
- Spreadsheets
- Databases

- Word processing
- Research tools

Tutorials and Skill-Building Games

Tutorials and skill-building games are used to teach vocabulary, facts, topical information, or skills. Questions follow each chunk of presented information, and student responses trigger what appears next. The computer may also record responses for evaluation. Science topics include simple machines and their applications, the oceans, the human heart, classification of animals, common constellations, and properties of rocks, to name just a few. These programs can be useful in developing the language of science or in remediation of misconceptions.

Multimedia

Programs in which students look up information or further explore science topics in interactive multiple media forms, such as pictures and sounds, are called *multimedia*. They are arranged so that a student can jump from one topic to another and access text, narratives, digital movie clips, laser disc/CD/DVD sequences, or Internet resources such as Web pages. Students have greater control of the learning situation because they can usually move about topics and go to different levels of understanding as necessary.

If you are considering the purchase of a computer for your classroom, you may want to include a DVD drive to be able to play the growing number of titles becoming available for classroom use.

Examples of this category of software are the Explorapedia (Microsoft) and Eyewitness Encyclopedia of Science (Dorling Kindersley), which are children's interactive encyclopedias about the world of science and nature. Grolier's Multimedia Encyclopedia (Grolier) and Encarta (Microsoft) contain information on a wide range of topics and include color pictures and sound clips. Animals in Our World (Sunburst/Edunetics) has both text and video information on characteristics of many animals.

Multimedia software is useful when students are investigating a specific science topic or preparing a class report. Additionally, programs now take advantage of the computer's video and sound capabilities. These programs often play movie sequences and are especially useful for students who cannot read well on their own.

Do you want your students to try to create their own media? HyperStudio (Roger Wagner Publishing) is an example of software that allows students to make their own multimedia presentations. With multimedia, each screen image is considered a card, and a collection of these cards is called a stack. When making stacks, students can type in text, import clip art from other disks, scan their own pictures in, record sounds, control a laser disc/CD player, or link their cards to other programs and Internet resources. The advantages to using hypermedia are listed below:

- The students can research topics and make their own information stacks to share with others at their school or through the Internet.
- Classroom or school collections of hypermedia stacks provide information on a variety of topics from multiple perspectives.
- The students feel good about themselves when they are able to create a simple stack and share it with others.

You may want to try out HyperStudio or a similar program. Often, they are available free on a trial basis. How can you use such a program in your classroom? Here's an example: Have your students develop a classification of some common objects in the schoolyard, such as the rocks they can find. Use *HyperStudio* (Roger Wagner Publishing) to create a stack of cards based on the students' classification system.

Simulations

Simulation software is available in PC or Macintosh format and on CD-ROM or floppy disk. In *simulations*, students play roles in situations where they can explore scientific phenomena or approximate real events. For example, the Magic School Bus series (Scholastic/Microsoft) allows students to explore things like the human body, the solar system, and the ocean. Dangerous Creatures (Microsoft) allows students to explore the world of wildlife. Other programs develop early science skills through the help of an online friend such as Sammy's Science House (Edmark). Space Station Simulator (Maris) allows students to construct and view a space station. Other simulations such as PERIL (University of Guelph) allow players to decide what to do when given certain data. You can use PERIL with your upper-elementary students. They are presented information on health and safety, make appropriate choices, and identify misconceptions related to health risks.

Simulations are an excellent way to present science phenomena that are otherwise too remote, dangerous, complex, costly, or time-consuming. The computer instantly feeds back information as the simulations assist students in constructing knowledge and making real-life decisions without facing real-life consequences.

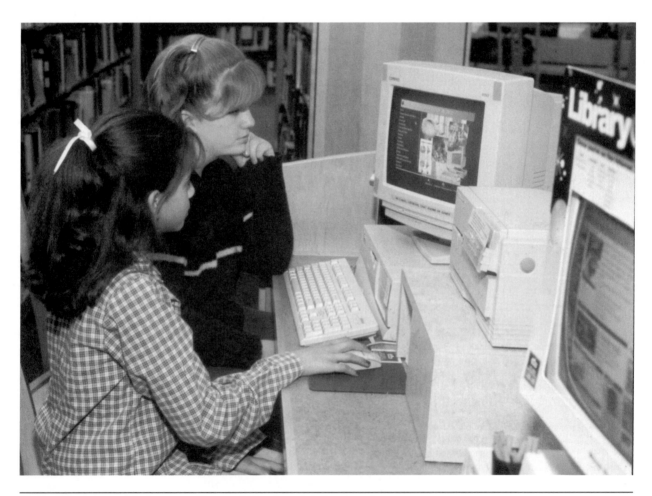

The use of simulations and the Internet provides powerful learning tools in the science classroom.

Internet Access Tools

Connecting to the Internet requires a network link. This is generally an Ethernet cable wired between your school's computer system and your classroom computer. Alternatively, you could use a dial-in Internet connection from your computer. These require a modem, a telephone line, and an Internet provider. Once connected, your students can access thousands of other computers, as well as do all the following:

- Send electronic mail (e-mail) throughout the world
- Participate in newsgroups
- Download files and software through a system called FTP (file transfer protocol)
- Access online databases
- View World Wide Web (WWW) sites
- Communicate through online discussions (chat rooms)
- Use two-way audio/video with NetMeeting (Microsoft) or CUSeeMe (Cornell University)

See *http://www.prenhall.com/peters* **for links to a variety of Web search tools.**

A common program for doing these tasks is a *Web browser* such as Internet Explorer (Microsoft) or Netscape (Netscape). Web browsers are available for all types of computers and generally come preinstalled. They can navigate the various protocols, or data transmission procedures, such as those listed above. **Search engines** are Web resources that work with browsers to allow you to supply key words and find related Internet sites.

Search engines seek out and database the files on Web servers and make this keyword information available to you when requested.

Before you explore the Internet with your students, a word of caution: Promote safe "surfing." Inform your students not to give out their names or personal information or assume that people they meet on the Internet are who they say they are. Monitor student browsing, check the browser's history file frequently, and complete a child/parent agreement form (Haag, 1996). Your school or district may have specific software or regulations concerning the Internet, so do not forget to check.

What is out there in cyberspace? A steadily growing number of people use an electronic mail address with the Internet. These are in the user@location format. Schools, Internet providers, or free services provide the mail addresses. Your students can send e-mail to people, asking for specific information related to the science topics your class is investigating.

Check the companion Web site for links to free Internet providers if your school does not provide this service.

There are also millions of Web sites on the Internet to connect to, including zoos, science centers, museums, schools, research centers, and government agencies.

See *http://www.prenhall.com/peters* **for links to a variety of Internet resources related to zoos, science centers, and museums. You can also find the current addresses to science celebrities at the** *http://www.prenhall.com/peters* **site.**

As you may have already noticed, Web site addresses on the Internet begin with *http://*. This stands for *HyperText Transfer Protocol,* the Internet's multimedia system. Your students can find information or explore many science-related sites for free, once a local Internet connection to your classroom is established. Science celebrities such as Mr. Wizard, Bill Nye the Science Guy, and Beakman's World have Internet addresses.

Perhaps your school already has a *home page.* A home page is a globally accessible file of information on the Internet. Chances are that the college or university you are attending or your practicum site is on the Web. Check with a computer support person to find out the address and how you can access these sites if you do not already know.

Can elementary students build Web pages? Not only can your students access the Web, but they can also become a part of the information superhighway. Students enjoy creating Web pages based on science topics. Teachers also find it to be a fun activity and are delighted by the creativity of the students. The easiest way to develop a file for the Web is

HTML is the worldwide standard necessary for other machines to decode your finished work. It imposes standardized codes to indicate paragraphs, different fonts, picture placement, and other word-processing features.

Check
http://www.prenhall.com/peters
for links to creating and sharing Web pages.

Classroom Connect (*http://www.classroom.net/*) is another resource for well-written Internet-based activities. It produces the *lessonplan.net* series with thematic topics such as Catastrophe (Classroom Connect, 1998) which includes activities on earthquakes, hurricanes, El Niño, floods, and other disasters.

to use a Web page software tool such as FrontPage (Microsoft). This program works like a word-processing program but saves files in a format called **HTML,** or *HyperText Markup Language.* Using HTML, any computer with browser software on the Internet can be used to access a file accurately.

HTML files can be placed on a *Web server* (a machine that is always on and connected to the Internet). Files are shared between classes, within your building, or across the world. Building Web pages helps students develop the scientific skill of communication. They must select relevant information, summarize it, and creatively share it with others.

Intranet is the name given to groups of computers that are not connected to the Internet, but are connected to each other within a school or company. The computers in an Intranet use the same software and hardware as Internet-capable machines, but others cannot access them. Likewise, students could not access the Internet from these machines and can only look at locally stored Web pages. An Intranet is generally used in a safe computing environment where little teacher supervision is needed.

Science activities are abundant on the Internet. We will begin by referring you to *Science on the Internet: A Resource for K–12 Teachers* (Ebenezer & Lau, 1999). Another good reference is *Internet Activities Using Scientific Data* (Froseth & Poppe, 1995). It is available from NOAA (*http://www.noaa.gov/*) and has Internet activities involving real-time data. This guide, developed for teachers, takes you on a journey through the Internet. Your students can learn the basics of the Internet and explore some of the possibilities for science learning.

The chapter "Science and Social Studies" in *Integrating Telecommunications Into Education* (Roberts, Blakeslee, Brown, & Lenk, 1990) includes some exemplary programs, such as the National Geographic Kids Network. This is a project that allows students to share their information with others through the Internet. Students in various schools gather data, transmit the data to a central computer, and share findings with other schools. In one unit, students in schools from around the nation measure the acidity of rain in their local area. They send the data to a scientist collaborating with the program. The data are then pooled through a central computer, organized on charts and maps, and sent back to the students. Electronic collaboration can also be a powerful way for you to improve your own classroom practice in the future (Koufman-Frederick, Lillie, Pattison-Gordon, Watt, & Carter, 1999).

Spreadsheets

The use of *spreadsheets* will allow you to arrange and automatically compute data. A *cell* is an individual data point; it is the juncture of a row and a column. Cells can contain text, numbers, or formulas that are able to compute values based on input or numbers in other cells and display the result. A change in one cell can cause changes in other cells. The use of a spreadsheet for a gradebook is a typical example. As new grades are entered, students' final grades based on the input are automatically calculated. Excel (Microsoft) and ClarisWorks (Claris) are common tools for developing spreadsheets.

The book *ClarisWorks 2.0 in the Classroom* (Claris, 1993) provides examples on how to use spreadsheets to determine the best factors for racing cars, to compare body measurements, or to find the best formulas for bubble mixtures. Spreadsheets can also be used to predict data. If information on plant growth is collected for a period of time, a spreadsheet can determine future trends. A spreadsheet can also be used to determine how long it would take a student to travel to another planet, given the speed of the spacecraft and the distance of the planets.

Databases

A *database* is a way to create, categorize, sort, and view specific records. For example, a collection of records on *Animals A–Z* (Claris, 1993) may contain information like the type of animal, size, number of legs, skin type, and habitats. A database can be used to sort the information and display only records that match certain criteria. For instance, by selecting number of legs as a criterion, the database program will automatically sort the records and list those animals that have two legs.

You can use databases to categorize information on rocks and minerals, weather, and volcano records.

Word Processing

Probably the most-used types of programs are the *word-processing* programs that students use to format text and check for spelling errors. This software is an excellent tool for creating science journals, writing science poetry, or creating science pal files to share over the Internet.

Research Tools

How do scientists use microcomputers? Are children able to use microcomputers in similar ways? Science educators and computer specialists are exploring both questions. The software and other materials coming from their efforts get children into the heart of science: gathering, organizing, and sharing real data.

 Several software programs for students have accompanying hardware called *probes*. These are sensing devices connected through a cable to the computer. When used with the proper software, probes can measure temperature, light, sound, heart rate, acidity, motion, force, pressure, and other properties of matter.

 Several probe-type lab programs, called *microcomputer-based labs,* have had much use in schools from about Grade 3 through college. Bank Street Laboratory (Sunburst) gives students chances to record and analyze graphs of temperature, light, and sound data. Science Toolkit (Broderbund) has rugged, easy-to-use probes for measuring light, temperature, time, and distance. Data are organized into tables, charts, and graphs. Probe labs make it easy to gather a lot of data over short or long periods and then instantly convert the data into analyzable forms.

Software Evaluation

Finding good software for use with elementary students may be a difficult task, given the explosion of software writers and distributors. Because budgets are generally limited for software purchases, it is a good idea to complete a thorough review of the program before purchase.

 A software checklist may be a helpful tool to assist you in selecting software appropriate for your students. It is important to prioritize your software purchases on the basis of the philosophy and needs of your program (Beaty, 1990). Some considerations are provided in the checklist in Figure 7–1.

See *http://www.prenhall.com/peters* for other resources related to software examination and use.

Y/N	Program: Distributor(s) and Price(s): Checklist:
	Is this program developmentally appropriate for children?
	Is the reading level of the program appropriate?
	Does this program meet your specific curricular needs?
	Can the child navigate through the program without adult assistance?
	Will the program hold the child's interest?
	Does the program contain positive reinforcement for children?
	Can you pilot this program to see whether it is compatible with your children?
	Does this software avoid culturally-biased language or examples?
	Does this software avoid gender-biased language or examples?
	Will this program be compatible with your existing hardware?
	Will the RAM be sufficient to run the program?
	Will you have enough hard drive space for the program?
	Are any special input or input devices needed with this program?
	Will your monitor support the graphics in this program?
	Is the level of quality of this program sufficient for classroom use?
	Was this program rated by any external reviewers?
	Are there any technical problems that will make using this program difficult?
	Will other teachers be using this program, and can they help you if needed?
	Is the price of the program compatible with your budget?
	Is an educational discount available for this program?
	Are lab packs available if this program will be used on multiple machines?
	Can you make backup copies of the program for your protection?
	Is any special licensing required for this program?

Figure 7–1
Software checklist.

Computer Accessories _____

If you want your students to use your classroom computer center for word-processing science reports and the like, consider attaching a scanner to the computer. Like a photocopier, a scanner allows the user to incorporate photographs or drawings directly into a written report, multimedia presentation, or Internet Web page.

A digital camera works like a regular camera but saves the image on computer memory instead of film. The pictures can be transferred to a computer and used in other programs, like scanned pictures. The disadvantage of these cameras is that the less expensive models can only store a limited number of pictures at one time before the pictures need to be downloaded to a computer.

Computer video projectors are now affordable for elementary schools. These connect to classroom computers and project the image on a screen. The advantage of a videoprojector over an LCD panel is that the pictures are generally of a much better quality because they have higher resolutions and are not subjected to the heat of an overhead projector. Newer models will even work in normal lighting, so students can take notes while viewing.

Microcomputer Advantages, Disadvantages, and Resources _____

You've already seen some ways computer-assisted instruction can benefit you and your students in both learning centers and larger settings. Let's look at several more advantages and then address a few concerns.

It takes only a brief experience with computers to see how much children delight in this medium. The immediate feedback to their responses prompts them to learn more quickly and confidently. Slow or fast learners may progress at their own developmentally appropriate rates. When they respond incorrectly, a good program branches them into a remedial sequence that reteaches the material in simpler steps. When they respond correctly, a good program moves them quickly into more advanced material. Computers make individualized instruction more accessible.

One of the best uses of the computer in science education is with simulations. The computer-controlled videodisc, CD–ROM, and other resources offer all kinds of opportunities for making decisions and solving problems in realistic settings. Any airline pilot can tell you that what's seen through the cockpit windshield of a flight simulator just after a right or wrong move comes uncannily close to the real thing. Now the chances for children to encounter simulated experiences are increasing.

One problem with computers is that software can be a major part of a school budget. Fortunately, a growing supply of software is available on the Internet, and much of it is available to teachers for free or for a minimal registration fee. One type of software is the Web-based application software called JAVA. Accessing this type of Web page sends *applets,* or small programs, to your computer. Once loaded, applet programs provide specific applications.

Another drawback of some elementary science software is a lack of accompanying hands-on experiences. This is more likely with older and stand-alone materials. The software integrated into today's comprehensive multimedia science programs usually provides for concrete activity.

Nearly everyone needs some extra guidance and practice to apply this remarkable tool creatively. If you are new to computing, it's easy to feel overwhelmed by the sheer quantity of unfamiliar technology and methods employed. But the good news is that plenty of help is available through user groups and schoolwide or districtwide technology coordinators. Both in-service workshops and informal, person-to-person arrangements are common. Don't be surprised to meet students with considerable expertise at microcomputing. By the sixth grade, some children have had several thousand hours of experience with computers at home and at school. They can be invaluable aides to other students and to you. Employ them in cooperative situations as much as possible.

If you are new to a school, ask colleagues and the media specialist what devices and help are available at the school and district levels.

Software Sources and Reviews _____

How can you learn what is currently available and worthwhile? The supply of usable science software continues to grow. Software publishers are producing more materials that reflect the best thinking in constructivist psychology and science education. Science textbook publishers are integrating software titles into text units and chapters. In fact, now these publishers are more accurately called multimedia science program publishers. Some also develop their own software for that purpose.

If you are unsure about a software program, keep in mind that the National Science Teachers Association (NSTA, 1992) presents the following guidelines on the use of computers in science education.

- Computers should enhance, not replace, hands-on activities.
  - Tutorial software should engage students in meaningful interactive dialogue.
  - Simulation software should provide opportunities to explore concepts and models not readily available.
  - Microcomputer-based labs should permit students to collect and analyze data like scientists.
  - Networking should permit students to emulate the way scientists work and reduce classroom isolation.

Check the NSTA site at *http://www.nsta.org/* for other suggestions on the use of technology in the classroom.

Other Technological Devices

The *videodisc* or *laser disc* is a thin aluminum plate, usually about the size of an old vinyl record, sandwiched between two layers of plastic. Each side may contain anything from thousands of recorded still pictures to a full-length movie. A videodisc player can access the recorded material in any order within a few seconds and display it on a television or through a video projector. You control the sequence of events with either a hand-held remote control or a bar-code reader. A teacher's guide may come with either a laser disc or CD. Each photo frame or sequence is given a number and bar code for identification; with the remote control, you punch in the numbers of your selection. Using the bar code reader is even easier: Lightly rub one end of the reader across the code, point the other end at the player, and push a button.

Most nationally published science programs today use videodiscs to some degree. Teacher guides may include whole-class lessons or suggestions for an individual or small-group setting. With your microcomputer center, for example, you might select frames and animated sequences to follow up a lesson on earthquakes and then arrange bar code stickers or numbers in a sequence to guide the students. Some science programs provide student worksheets with bar codes printed on them. In either case, the students can interact with the media. The students might also search out materials themselves to integrate into small-group or individual reports to present to the class. Examples of laser discs we use in elementary science include Voyage of the Mimi (Sunburst), The Planets (National Geographic Society), and Dinosaurs, Gems and Minerals, and National Zoo (Smithsonian Institution).

The CD–ROM (compact disc, read-only memory) is another way to bring a vast amount of computer-controlled audiovisual material into your classroom. About half the size of a videodisc, the CD-ROM is inserted into a CD–ROM drive connected to a computer. The material is accessed through the keyboard and viewed on the computer screen. The CD–ROM is simply a variation of the familiar audio compact disc. Today, almost every computer is sold with a CD–ROM drive. A CD can currently hold about 5 billion bits of information (about 100 books), and technological advances will increase the amount to more than 50 billion bits.

DVD (digital videodisc or digital versatile disc) is a newer form of optical disk storage technology. DVD technology allows video, audio, and computer data to be encoded onto a compact disc. DVD can store greater amounts of data than a common CD. A DVD player is needed to read digital videodiscs. This player is sold as a self-contained, stand-alone device or as an accessory to a computer. Digital videodisc technology may soon replace laser disc, CD-ROM, and audio CDs.

Compact discs and DVD discs contain extensive science information and activities for children.

Science Technology Society

The growing awareness of how *science, technology,* and *society* (STS) interrelate is evident in the STS movement in science education. The NSTA adopted the *Science–Technology–Society: Science Education for the 1980s* position statement in 1982. Ten years later, the International Council of Associations for Science Education (ICASE) developed an STS yearbook (Yager, 1992). The following year, the NSTA developed another STS document for teachers (Yager, 1993), indicating the continued importance of STS in schools. Their shared view is that persons educated in the ideas and processes of science and technology can solve several of the problems we face today.

A Science and Technology Standard (see Standards Link) is included in the national science education standards to show the relationship between the two entities. Scientific and technological literacy is essential for living, working, and decision making in the 1980s and beyond (NSTA, 1982). STS is seen as the teaching and learning of science in the context of human experiences. The NSTA advocates that science should be real to students. An indication of this is providing scientific problems for students to solve that are based on issues of genuine interest to them.

STS in the Classroom _____

STS supplies a context whereby the students can begin to consider such issues as the need for burning coal to produce

---

Standards Link

Science and Technology Standard

As a result of the activities in Grades K–4, all students should develop

- **Abilities of technological design.**

- **Understanding about science and technology.**

- **Abilities to distinguish between natural objects and objects made by humans.**

(Content Standard E, National Research Council, 1996, pp. 135 & 161) electricity against the resulting acid rain, thermal pollution, and greenhouse effect. Elementary students try to answer these questions, follow up by testing their answers to the questions, and then take action based on their findings. The *STS issue investigation and action instruction model* (Rubba, Wiesenmayer, Rye, & Ditty, 1996) is a good example of this teaching strategy because of its four critical factors:

- Foundations
- Awareness
- Investigations
- Action phases (p. 25)

The model begins when the teacher assists students in understanding the nature of science and technology and their interactions during the *foundations* phase. If we continue our electricity production example above, the teacher would facilitate guiding students to find out that electricity production is a result of scientific research. Generating electricity has trade-offs, such as gaseous emissions, that are balanced against society's need for electricity.

The teacher would then discuss and guide students in understanding the concepts and issues related to the topic during the *awareness* phase. The issue would be studied from every aspect, including the scientific and social science points of view. What are the gases emitted? Are other pollutants produced? What are the alternatives to coal-fired plants? What laws and other regulations relate to the topic? What processes are used in generating electricity?

Students then experiment and investigate the STS issue during the *investigations* phase. They visit a plant to see the generation process. Students experiment with making electricity on their own or investigate the effects of production.

Finally, students develop ways to *take action* on the issue during the final phase. Can "green" energy be purchased in their community? If not, how can that be changed? Can energy be conserved to help reduce any negative effects on the environment?

In keeping with current reform efforts, science educators who advocate STS agree that the overall goal for science education is to develop scientifically literate graduates who can apply science to everyday life. These citizens will be able to understand the issues, take responsibility for the issues, and make informed decisions on these issues. These goals are further reflected in the science education benchmarks and standards.

Check
http://www.prenhall.com/peters for other resources related to STS.

Benchmarks, Standards, and Technology _____

According to the authors of the *Benchmarks for Science Literacy* (American Association for the Advancement of Science [AAAS], 1993) and *Blueprints for Reform* (AAAS, 1998), educational research on what students know about technology is insufficient. We need to know more about how technology relates to science, or the structures and functions of the designed world. Because of the lack of research, the author groups suggest that technology is generally ignored in schools.

Check
http://www.prenhall.com/peters for technology education standards and information.

Technology can, nevertheless, be useful in developing scientific inquiry skills and in fostering the understanding of fundamental differences between science and technology. The authors of the standards have analogous concerns about the lack of understanding related to technology. They include science and technology in the content standards for students at every grade level (see the Science and Technology Standard).

Students and Technology _____

You may have witnessed a child taking apart an old appliance, nailing together some old boards, building a bridge for toy cars in a sandbox, or otherwise interacting with technology. You may have even worked during a practicum on AIMS projects from the *Machine Shop* activity book (Battcher et al., 1993). You may also have used the *Under Construction* (Gossett, 1997) or *Inventa Book of Mechanisms* (Catlin, n.d.) resources. You will find that children are, without a doubt, curious about technology and the designed world.

As elementary students begin explorations of technology, they understand what is humanmade and what is natural. Their designs are less elaborate or functional, and they cannot easily distinguish between science and technology. By the end of the elementary years, however, students will use scientific inquiry skills to assist them in a design that will solve a problem. They will also begin to see the important relationship between science and technology. *Science is the quest for answers to questions about the universe.* Science relies on technology to assist us in discovering the universe. *Technology is the application of science.* Technology supports science, helps us satisfy our wants and needs, and extends our capabilities to do those things.

Technology Education and Elementary Science

Are the children *playing* in Vignette 7–2, or does this activity have an objective? Would you consider this lesson carefully structured to promote technological literacy? Should elementary students even be involved in *design* activities?

VIGNETTE 7–2

Experiencing Technology Education for the First Time: The Early Elementary Years

A group of six- and seven-year-olds had completed some grouping and sorting of materials (fabrics, plastics, glass, wood, paper products, and so on) and an exploration of "connectors" (glues, brass fasteners, string, clips, nails, and so forth). They had learned how to use saws, drills, and hammers. They were given a twelve- by eighteen-inch sheet of paper and asked to design something they would like and be able to build that moved in some way. They were told they could use materials from their classroom recycling center such as cartons, containers of all sorts, fabric, dowels, cardboard, wheels, and centimeter wood strips. They could also use materials brought from home. The connectors they had explored were available.

Drawing was not new to these children. They had drawn from nature in their science studies, they had illustrated stories, and drawing materials were always an option for art or classroom choice times. They had built three-dimensional constructions in the block corner and in the classroom recycling center. However, they had never been asked to draw something to be constructed in the future and then to build from their drawings. The process of moving from two to three dimensions and of committing themselves to a plan (as opposed to planning and creating as they went along) were new experiences for these children.

Ben, a six-year-old, drew a rather conventional house with a chimney on the roof and smoke coming out of the chimney. Looking over the materials, he passed by the rectangular boxes and selected a one-liter soda bottle as the basic structure for his house. He cut out freehand a door and some windows from construction paper and taped them to the bottle. Then he chose a dowel, taped a curvy piece of black construction paper to the end and showed his teacher where he wanted the two holes for the dowel to pass through the bottle. He inserted the dowel and proceeded to push and pull it up and down, making the "smoke" extend and retreat from the chimney. He was not bothered at all by the fact that the house looked nothing at all like his drawing. What counted was that the smoke moved in and out of the chimney. With construction successfully completed, his teacher asked him to evaluate his product. Did it come out the way he had planned it? Was there something that moved? A huge smile of satisfaction spread over his face. Yes, this was exactly what he had in mind, he said; the smoke moved out of the chimney (and back in), and he wondered if he could take it home and show his parents what he had made.

Across the room, two eight-year-olds were constructing boats they wanted to move by rubber-band-powered paddle wheels. They had completed their planning and construction and were now ready to test the boats. A small plastic wading pool was filled with water, the paddle wheels were wound up, and the boats were launched. As the boats moved forward, their structures began to come apart; the children realized to their dismay that the glue must be dissolving in the water.

"We should have used a glue gun."

Their teacher watched as they reassembled the boats, connecting the wooden frames with a glue gun, a time-consuming process; they tried them again in the water, and once again watched as they fell apart. The teacher debated whether or not to suggest that they test connecting materials in the water on just a few pieces of wood rather than take the time to reassemble the entire boat. She decided to let them do it their way, and hoped they would come to this realization themselves. If not, she would bring the subject up.

"We'll have to nail them together. Can we have some small nails?"

On the third try, the boat held together and paddled across the classroom pond. Delighted and relieved that their hard work and tenacity had paid off, the boat builders were not at all ready to think about short cuts to finding the right materials to connect wood for use in water. For these students, this lesson would have to wait for another time. For their teacher, there still remained the issue of how much to tell students ahead of time and how much to let them discover, or not discover, for themselves.

The boys' classmate Kylie eyed the recycling center, spotted a shoe box, and decided to build a car that would carry her stuffed bear. She remembered her brother once built a rubber-band-powered car. Her drawing was a rectangle with small wheels. She selected four plastic wheels and found two dowels that fit through their centers. Using a ruler, she carefully planned where to punch holes in the shoe box so the axles would be parallel to the ends of the box. She attached the wheels to the outside of the box, front and back. She then began to puzzle out how to wind up a rubber band. Once she had an idea of how it might work, she asked her teacher if there was another box she could use to try out her ideas because she "didn't want to mess up my car." Unlike the boat builders, Kylie had discovered on her own the concept of building a prototype or model. Once she worked out a rubber band system, making her mistakes somewhere other than on her car, she was ready to complete her project.

Although the entire project was ultimately successful, asking the children to draw their desired object on paper as part of the design for the project may have been too ambitious. Children this age frequently find it difficult to conceptualize three-dimensional construction through two-dimensional drawing, and they become confused by the task. They may worry about their inability to transform their drawing into the object they imagined, and shy away from the task. For example, it is unclear how Ben's drawing helped him in the design of his project, which bore no relation to the picture he drew.

From Technology Education in the Classroom (pp. 68–69), by S. A. Raizen, P. Sellwood, R. D. Todd, & M. Vickers, 1995, San Francisco: Jossey-Bass. Copyright © 1995 by Jossey-Bass. Reprinted by permission of John Wiley & Sons, Inc.

Children's need to explore is a concrete reminder of our need throughout history to explore, understand, and survive in our environment (Dunn & Larson, 1990). Technology has been with us since the Stone Age when humans first began to modify their environment with the tools available to them. Throughout history, technology has played a significant role in the overall societal progress

The study of technological advances is a good topic for social studies and science integration.

of humans, their struggle for freedom, and their advances in scientific knowledge. With technology being so prominent to everyday life, why is it so neglected in our schools?

The term *technopeasants* refers to the common people who are left feeling that they are the victims of technology as a result of their lack of technical literacy (Pucel, 1995). Similarly, educators are viewed as *techno-ostriches* if they hide their heads in the sand when it comes to implementing technologies to create changes in schools (Papert, 1996). Either terminology insinuates that *technology education must play a larger role in the curriculum*. As suggested by some educators, society will not have future technicians if we do not integrate the curriculum and include technology education in today's classrooms (Hall & Bannatyne, 1999).

Resnick, Bruckman, and Martin (1999) question the appropriateness of children learning to play the piano versus learning to play the stereo. They cite that they would rather children become "creators" and not just "consumers" (p. 150) because this allows for a deeper understanding of music. Likewise, we want our students to design rather than just use technology.

We see technology in the schools evolving from two viewpoints. In the science curriculum, technology is used to demonstrate theories of science and to help develop inquiry skills. Technology is also a core element of the less familiar *technology education*. What specifically is technology education? It is a K–12 academic discipline designed to integrate academic and career skills with an emphasis on problem solving and decision making. In short, technology education focuses on working collaboratively through the *application* of technology. Whereas science seeks understanding, technology seeks solutions to problems.

To illustrate, during the elementary years, students should study such areas as "materials and their properties and how they can be used; energy in a variety of forms; control, in the form of switches, catches, valves, and mechanisms; and information used for communication" (Raizen, Sellwood, Todd, & Vickers, 1995, p. 67). Technology education should be a part of your everyday curriculum.

How can you integrate more technology into the curriculum? What are some technological areas that can be explored? The general categories to explore with your students include energy, materials, manufacturing, communication, bio-related, construction, and transportation technology.

Energy Technology ⎯⎯⎯⎯⎯

See *http://www.prenhall.com/peters* for more information on energy teaching ideas and resources.

Energy comes in many forms: chemical, electrical, mechanical, radiant, thermal, nuclear. Energy is one of the most important science and technology issues. Energy conservation awareness allows most people to realize now that we must continue to move away from exploiting the environment and toward conserving or using it wisely. Not only are energy resources of the planet limited, but almost every year we see a greater demand on these resources from all nations. The history of progress in nations closely parallels a rise in energy use. As fuels disappear, more attention will be turned to tapping into relatively inexhaustible sources such as solar, wind, tidal, and geothermal energy. Material progress and swelling populations have also increased air, water, and land pollution, along with the growing problem of managing solid waste.

Working on energy-related activities will help students construct understandings of the importance of energy. The candle-powered steam engine (McCormack, 1981) and the candle-powered steamboat are two design activities that upper-elementary students could

A student engaged in a "mining for energy" activity.

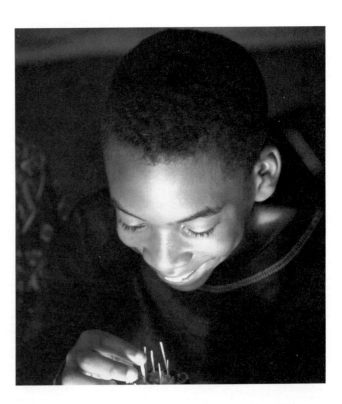

explore. The candle-powered steamboat requires an old-fashioned oilcan, a candle, and a milk carton. The steam engine uses an oilcan, a candle, wire, and an aluminum turbine blade.

We know that the sun is our ultimate source of energy. To demonstrate to our students the power of the sun, try cooking marshmallows (Miller, 1998); the students can design a solar cooker to capture the sun's rays in the cooker.

Remember that safety is a consideration with this solar activity. Be sure to warn the students not to look directly at the sun or to stay out in the sunlight for prolonged periods.

Materials Technology _____

Materials are important to technology because there would be no technical objects without materials. Materials can be the fossil fuel hydrocarbons that are mined or drilled such as coal, oil, and natural gas. Materials can be genetic materials harvested from farming, forestry, or husbandry such as wheat, wood, or wool. They can be minerals that are mined such as metal ores, nonmetallic minerals, precious gems, or ceramics and clays. The study of materials helps students develop their observational skills as they interact with various materials. Students explore physical properties and determine whether materials are artificial or natural. They begin to see the need for specific materials in some designs. They also find that some materials can be used in a variety of ways.

Discussions of materials can originate with the story of the *Three Little Pigs* (Feasey, 1999). Students investigate properties of the items that the pigs used for their houses, as well as several other materials. Ask your students which materials would be best if they were designing a house or a roof. Now have your students make up newspaper headlines about the materials the pigs used or should have used.

The *anoraks* activity (Stringer, 1996) is a primary activity during which students explore the materials of an Eskimo parka or heavy jacket. They are challenged to design an anorak for a season. This activity is a good integration with social studies if you want to develop a thematic unit.

A rough-and-smooth-surface activity is a good way for students to investigate materials (Stringer, 1998). They can even design wooden ramps of various textures and experiment on the effects of friction. Distance traveled, speed of an object down a ramp, height of the ramp, and the relation to surface friction are some beginning variables to explore. Students can also examine the use and integrity of structures and compare such variables as strength, weight, and reinforcement (Tickle, Lancaster, Devereux, & Marshall, 1990).

Upper-elementary students can design an experiment to explore bike helmet materials in relation to safety (Stringer, 1996). They can look at various helmet types and which materials are better at protection of the cranium. This activity is a good lead into the skeletal system and the protection of bones. *Designs in Science: Materials* (Morgan & Morgan, 1994) provides background information on materials and activities to extend materials investigations.

Manufacturing Technology _____

Manufacturing involves using materials to make parts, putting parts together for a finished product that has value, and supplying the products to meet a demand. Primary manufacturing processes involve converting raw materials into industrial materials; this may include changing natural gas into plastic sheets or pellets, wood into paper stock, bauxite into rolled aluminum, or wheat into flour. Secondary manufacturing processes include forming, casting, molding, separating, conditioning, assembling, or finishing the manufactured items. Production can also be **custom** or **continuous**.

Custom production is the making of products one at a time. Intermittent production is the making of a limited quantity of a product at one time.

Continuous production is a steady, assembly-line, mass production of items.

Making paper is one design activity in which elementary students enjoy learning about manufacturing. Making writing paper from toilet paper (Stringer, 1996) is generally less disappointing than making paper from recycled scrap paper.

Activities that model the manufacturing process are good problem-solving tasks for students. Cooperative groups of students can be assigned to design a conveyor belt made from common materials. The conveyer belt should be able to move products effectively from one location to another. Students could also design a robot that is able to pick up and move materials (Miller, 1998). These design challenges involve all the process skills of science. Robotics kits from Lego Dacta™ are one way to integrate the use of the computer in the design (*http://www.pitsco-legodacta.com/*).

Communication Technology

Communications includes the transfer of information from one place to another. This information could be raw data from spacecraft exploring the solar system, organized data called information, or information that is used for a purpose called knowledge. There are many ways to transmit information, or communicate:

- *Printed communications,* or images printed on a material such as paper
- *Telecommunications,* or telephone, computer networks, radio, and television
- *Photographic communications,* or digital and film pictures
- *Technical communications,* or blueprints, technical illustrations, and engineering drawings

Have your students consider communication with people from other countries who do not speak English, along with communication with alien beings. The students can brainstorm what to communicate, how to communicate, and what materials may be needed to design a communications system.

In summary, communication technology is people, their information exchange skills, and the equipment or other tools that help send and receive messages.

What if we were to communicate with space aliens? An interesting design activity for students to consider is how we would communicate with beings from other worlds (Association for Science Education [ASE], 1995).

Students may discuss or make presentations on environmental issues as a way to develop their communication skills (Miller, 1998). Technology has both positive and negative effects on our planet. For this activity, group students on both sides of such issues as the ozone layer, the greenhouse effect, vehicle emissions, and the use of landfills. Have students prepare a debate of the issues to be argued in front of an audience.

Communications is a rapidly changing area of technology. Discuss with your students any changes that they may be aware of or changes that their parents or guardians at home may have talked about. You may want to use this activity to discuss a general timeline for telecommunications (Oxlade, 1997).

Bio-Related Technology

Discuss how science and technology have changed current farming methods.

Bio-related technology includes the disciplines of agricultural technologies, health care technologies, and technologies related to living things, such as genetics. From the food you eat, the water you drink, the clothes you wear, and the health care you receive, biotechnology touches all aspects of our lives.

Technology is present in preserving and preparing foods. If the color or texture is not right, the food will not be pleasing to eat. Experimentation can be done to see the science behind food and what is appealing. Try arranging various foods for birds or other animals to eat and see which is most popular (Stringer, 1996). Does color make a difference? Try using M&Ms to design an experiment involving classmates. What are the variables? The results? Discuss genetic farming (Jefferis, 1999) and the history of past farming methods (Roden, 1996).

Designing an experiment that shows the technology used in producing hand soaps demonstrates biotechnology in action. Students can experiment with eliminating microbes by washing hands (International Council of Associations for Science Education [ICASE], 1988). Try using regular soaps versus antibacterial soaps, liquid soaps versus solid soaps, or short washing periods versus longer washing periods as variables. Agar is a nutrient medium available from scientific suppliers. It is put on sterilized plates for this activity. Students touch the agar on the plates after various hand washes; the microorganism their hands left behind will then grow on the agar.

Students may also want to discuss how biotechnology is used in courtrooms. Rainis and Nassis (1998) discuss the use of DNA testing as a replacement for fingerprints. This is a good area to integrate STS issues.

Have students discuss whether or not cloned humans would have the same fingerprints on their fingers or the same DNA "fingerprint" in their cells.

Construction Technology _____

Construction is the process of producing structures for shelter or transportation such as houses, skyscrapers, or other buildings, stadiums, roads, tunnels, bridges, airports, or monuments. The four generally accepted types of construction are residential, commercial, public, and industrial. Technology plays a key role in helping the structures meet the personal and environmental needs of the construction project. Science is also involved in significant ways. The materials, such as plastics or alloys, used in many structures are the result of scientific research applied technologically. Geologic research on the foundations of structures is important for buildings such as skyscrapers.

Elementary students can further develop observation and inference skills when they investigate natural structures. Looking at bird homes may result in inferences about why the birds construct the nests as they do or build them in the places they do. Adaptation to the environment is evidenced by how animals build their homes. Habitat study is a good scientific exploration for students.

A technological extension to animal and habitat study is to have students create a PowerPoint (Microsoft) or other slide show on the habitats of animals (Donato, 1998).

Lasers are used in many construction projects. An electronic distance meter or laser transit saves time over less technical tools. Many students with access to laser pointers and mirrors can design experiments that will provide results similar to those obtained by the construction equipment.

Bridge activities are a popular technology activity. Designing a bridge that supports the most weight in relation to its own weight is a good upper-elementary activity. Bridges can be built with construction paper (Eichelberger & Larson, 1993) or toothpicks (Pollard, 1985).

Transportation Technology _____

Transportation technology includes air, rail, water, pipeline, space, and automobile or truck transportation. The connections between transportation and science are numerous.

An activity that you can try with elementary students is to send e-mail to other countries and ask students there about their transportation systems. This activity provides a good contrast and comparison to different transportation systems and helps develop communication skills.

For instance, fuel types, the design of the vehicle to reduce friction, and alternative energy sources are examples for scientific discussion and research.

Observation and classification skills are sharpened if primary students cut transportation-related pictures from magazines and classify them in various ways. They can look at air versus water or land vehicles. Sizes of vehicles, the numbers of passengers, or energy use by the vehicle produce other classification schemes. Try to have the students develop their own classification system.

One design challenge that works with upper-elementary students is building mousetrap cars (Balmer, 1997). With the assistance of their parents, students build and race cars that are powered by mousetraps. The car that goes the farthest is the winner.

Rubber band transportation can be explored with rubber-band-powered airplanes or vehicles (Eichelberger & Larson, 1993). Students use simple materials to design and build airplanes or other vehicles that work with the use of rubber bands. Experimentation skills are involved as students explore the effects of winding the rubber band too tight or not enough, reducing friction of the vehicle, placing weight, finding ways to make the vehicles track a straight line, or designing propellers. Balloon-powered cars (Miller, 1998) offer similar experimentation skill development for upper-elementary students.

Building model hovercraft is an interesting design activity related to transportation (ICASE, 1987). Balloons and wooden disks are all that are needed to make simple hovercraft.

Paper airplane design is another great transportation technology activity. Male pilots and astronauts are better known than female pilots and astronauts. Therefore, one way to initiate this design contest is to read about pilots in *Females First in Their Fields: Air and Space* (Buchanan, 1999). Have a challenge to see which team of girls can make the most paper airplanes fly over a 5-meter (20-foot) mark in 1 minute. Supply each team with a stack of copier paper and a marked off area to fly the planes. Group brainstorming and trial sessions beforehand will enhance flight distances.

As with other activities, adjust variables such as times and distances according to your students' developmental needs. It may be helpful to include the 5-stage framework for technological design provided by the standards (NRC, 1996, pp. 137–138, 165–166):

1. Identify a simple problem.

2. Propose a solution.

3. Implement proposed solutions.

4. Evaluate a product or design.

5. Communicate a problem, design, and solution.

The process begins with the students renaming the problem in their own words. Next, the students form possible solutions, given time, costs, and materials. The students then work together to try solutions and see how their design solves the problem. Finally, the students communicate how they solved the problem, including their design and evaluation.

Technology and Career Awareness

Technology is concerned with controlling or managing objects and events in improved ways. With the prevalence of technology in today's society, it is vital to prepare the future workforce for these occupations. Many career opportunities are related to technology (Schwartz & Wolfgang, 1996).

Research scientists, professional engineers, skilled technicians, and computer operators are required to have the scientific knowledge to plan and design useful inventions and creative solutions. Demand will continue to grow for workers qualified in the areas of environmental engineering, biological engineering and biotechnology, energy systems, telecommunications research and maintenance, and advanced transportation systems. Inventions and inventors are good topics to explore for promoting technology awareness and showing careers related to technology.

See *http://www.prenhall.com/peters* **for references to books on invention topics.**

Gender Issues and Technology _____

Technology topics lend themselves to opening up a new world for girls of all age levels because technology is a subject for everyone (Cross, 1998). We need to involve females in technological topics and activities whenever possible, not because the future workforce will rely on highly skilled, technologically literate women, but because we owe it to *all* our students to allow them the opportunity to be able to make good career choices later in life. These career choices will be possible because we have provided a solid scientific and technological background for males and females during the elementary years.

Look at your own practices in the classroom either now or in the future. Ask yourself these questions:

- Do my female students feel comfortable engaging in science and technology activities?
- Do my female students ask the same number of questions or provide a similar number of responses as my male students?
- Do I give equal amount of attention to both male and female students?
- Are female students embarrassed to take part in activities?

It may help to videotape yourself, or have another person observe you, and then complete a checklist to see whether you are being biased. Whether you are a male or female teacher, you may be biased toward boys when it comes to science and technology. Another tactic is to discuss careers and what future courses students should take or activities they should accomplish to be able to achieve their career goals. Also, make sure that you occasionally set up all-female learning groups, forcing girls to participate and not sit back and allow the boys to take control. Use books that focus on successful females in the sciences and technological areas. Make everyone in your class comfortable while learning or asking questions. Finally, begin now to collect resources that will assist you in your classroom.

One good starting point is *Girls and Technology Idea Book* and *Girls and Technology Resource Guide*. These publications are available from the National Coalition of Girls' Schools, 228 Main Street, Concord, MA 01742 or *http://www.ncgs.org*.

Technology and the Curriculum _____

The following notions about teaching science still exist today.

Even a new science textbook is dated by the time it's distributed.

I can't teach science. Who has time to keep up with it?

See
http://www.prenhall.com/peters
for links to current science
news.

Contrary to these views, the basic ideas and processes taught in the science curriculum last a long time. Scientific information and vocabulary do change, but this is expected when you consider the nature of science. This changeability is all the more reason to teach about the nature of science and STS. Discussing the application of science in new technologies helps show students how science theories can be modified. Consider the shift from copper telephone wires to fiber optics, the change in the precise measurement of the speed of light from 186,198 miles per second to 186,282 miles per second, or the discovery of new subatomic particles.

Basic concepts and generalizations in effective science programs are often linked to technological applications, aeronautics, telecommunications, electric circuitry, soil conservation, and food processing. Learning about these applications can change the way children view many of the useful inventions at home and in school. Understanding how systems operate develops a realistic perspective toward the mechanisms of everyday life. A well-constructed elementary curriculum will be rooted in the basic ideas and processes of science. Technological investigations, however, will enhance science understanding by providing concrete examples of science in action.

Summary

1. A microcomputer center can be set up and run much like a regular learning center. Microcomputer software can include such programs as tutorials and games, multimedia, simulations, Internet access tools, spreadsheets, databases, word processing, and research tools.
2. Science technology society (STS) is the teaching and learning of science in the context of human experiences. Advocates of STS think that science should be real to students and that scientific problems provided for students to solve should be based on issues that are of genuine interest to students. The STS issue investigation and action instruction model has four crucial phases: foundations, awareness, investigations, and action phases.
3. Technology use in the science classroom evolves from two viewpoints. One is from using technology to demonstrate theories of science and to help develop inquiry skills. The other is from the applied technology-based curriculum called technology education. Technology education is an academic discipline designed to integrate academic and career skills with an emphasis on problem solving and decision making.
4. Areas of technology include energy, materials, manufacturing, communication, bio-related, construction, and transportation.

Reflection

1. You can learn *from* computers, *with* computers, and *about* computers. You can also learn to think with computers or use computers to manage learning. List examples of how computers and software can be used for each of these categories.
2. Check with your practicum site and college or university to see whether it celebrates National Science and Technology Week (*http://www.nsf.gov/od/lpa/nstw/geninfo/ brochure.htm*). How can you become involved with your future students?
3. Look at the National Science Teachers Association (NSTA) Web site (*http://www.nsta. org/programs/*) for technology-related competitions that would involve your future elementary students. Which competitions are especially helpful in developing technological literacy?

4. Read *The Trouble With Dad* (Cole, 1987, New York: G. P. Putnam) and *It Could Still Be a Robot* (Fowler, 1997, New York, Children's Press). Talk with your class about the use of robots in everyday life. Also discuss society's images of scientists and inventors.

5. Look at *Standards for Technological Literacy: Content for the Study of Technology* from the International Technology Education Association (*http://www.iteawww.org/*) and *National Educational Technology Standards* from the International Society for Technology in Education (*http://cnets.iste.org/*). Compare and contrast these standards and the *National Science Education Standards* from the NRC (*http://stills.nap.edu/html/nses/*).

References

American Association for the Advancement of Science (AAAS). (1993). *Benchmarks for science literacy.* New York: Oxford University Press.

American Association for the Advancement of Science (AAAS). (1998). *Blueprints for reform.* New York: Oxford University Press.

Association for Science Education (ASE). (1995). *Science in space.* Hatfield, Herts., UK: Author.

Balmer, A. (1997). *Mouse-trap cars: A teacher's guide.* Austin, TX: Doc Fizzix Comix.

Battcher, D., Martini, K., Shennan, W. B., Erickson, S., Rogers, C., & Wiebe, A. (1993). *Machine shop.* Fresno, CA: AIMS Education Foundation.

Beaty, J. J. (1990). *Computer as a paintbrush: Creative use for the PC in the preschool classroom.* Upper Saddle River, NJ: Merrill/Prentice-Hall.

Buchanan, D. (1999). *Female firsts in their fields: Air and space.* Philadelphia, PA: Chelsea House.

Catlin, D. (n.d.). *Inventa book of mechanisms.* London: Valiant Technology.

Claris. (1993). *ClarisWorks 2.0 in the classroom.* Santa Clara, CA: Author.

Classroom Connect. (1998). Catastrophe! *lessonplan.net, 2*(5), 1–48.

Cross, A. (1998). *Coordinating design and technology across the primary school.* New York: Falmer Press.

Donato, D. (1998). *Integrating technology into the science curriculum.* Westminster, CA: Teacher Created Materials.

Dunn, S., & Larson, R. (1990). *Design technology: Children's engineering.* New York: Falmer Press.

Ebenezer, J. V., & Lau, E. (1999). *Science on the Internet: A resource for K–12 teachers.* Upper Saddle River, NJ: Merrill/Prentice-Hall.

Eichelberger, B., & Larson, C. (1993). *Constructions for children: Projects in design technology.* Palo Alto, CA: Dale Seymour.

Feasey, R. (1999). *Primary science & literacy links.* Hatfield, Herts., UK: Association for Science Education.

Froseth, S., & Poppe, B. (1995). *Internet activities using scientific data* (National Oceanic and Atmospheric Administration). Washington, DC: Government Printing Office.

Gossett, C. (1997). *Under construction.* Fresno, CA: AIMS Education Foundation.

Haag, T. (1996). *Internet for kids.* Huntington Beach, CA: Teacher Created Materials.

Hall, R., & Bannatyne, M. (1999). Technology education and the 21st century. *Connect, 24*(4), 1–3. Available: *http://www.unesco.org/education/educprog/ste/index.html*

International Council of Associations for Science Education (ICASE). (1987). *Experiments and activities on the three laws of dynamics: A teacher resource book commemorating the 300th anniversary of Newton's Principia 1687–1987.* Hong Kong: Author.

International Council of Associations for Science Education (ICASE). (1988). *Pasteur and microbes: A teacher resource guide commemorating the 100th year of the Pasteur institute 1888–1988.* Hong Kong: Author.

Jefferis, D. (1999). *Cloning: Frontiers of genetic engineering.* New York: Crabtree.

Koufman-Frederick, A., Lillie, M., Pattison-Gordon, L., Watt, D. L., & Carter, R. (1999). *Electronic collaboration: A practical guide for educators.* Providence, RI: LAB at Brown University.

Kozma, R., & Shank, P. (1998). Connecting with the 21st century: Technology in support of educational reform. In C. Dede (Ed.), *1998 ASCD yearbook: Learning with technology* (pp. 3–27). Alexandria, VA: ASCD.

McCormack, A. J. (1981). *Inventors workshop.* Torrance, CA: Fearon Teacher Aids.

Means, B. (1994). Introduction: Using technology to advance educational goals. In B. Means (Ed.), *Technology and education reform* (pp. 1–21). San Francisco: Jossey-Bass.

Miller, L. (1998). *KidTech: Hands-on problem solving with design technology for grades 5–8.* Menlo Park, CA: Dale Seymour.

Morgan, S., & Morgan, A. (1994). *Designs in science: Materials.* New York: Facts on File.

National Research Council (NRC). (1996). *National science education standards.* Washington, DC: National Academy Press.

National Science Teachers Association (NSTA). (1982). *Science–technology–society: Science education for the 1980s. A position statement.* Washington, DC: Author.

National Science Teachers Association (NSTA). (1992). The use of computers in science education. An NSTA position statement [On-line]. Available: *http://www.nsta.org/handbook/ position.asp*

Oxlade, C. (1997). *20th century inventions: Telecommunications.* Austin, TX: Raintree Steck-Vaughn.

Papert. S. (1996). *The connected family: Bridging the digital generation gap.* Marietta, GA: Longstreet Press.

Pollard, J. (1985). *Building toothpick bridges.* Palo Alto, CA: Dale Seymour.

Pucel, D. J. (1995). Developing technological literacy. *The Technology Teacher, 55*(3), 35–43.

Rainis, K. G., & Nassis, G. (1998). *Biotechnology projects for young scientists.* New York: Watts.

Raizen, S. A., Sellwood, P., Todd, R. D., & Vickers, M. (1995). *Technology education in the classroom.* San Francisco: Jossey-Bass.

Resnick, M., Bruckman, A., & Martin, F. (1999). Construction design: Creating new construction kits for kids. In A. Druin (Ed.), *The design of children's technology* (pp. 149–168). San Francisco: Morgan Kaufman.

Roberts, N., Blakeslee, G., Brown, M., & Lenk, C. (1990). *Integrating telecommunications into education.* Upper Saddle River, NJ: Prentice-Hall.

Roden, K. (1996). *Then & now: Farming.* Brookfield, CT: Copper Beech Books.

Rubba, P. A., Wiesenmayer, R. L., Rye, J. A., & Ditty, T. (1996). The leadership institute in STS education: A collaborative teacher enhancement, curriculum development, and research project of Penn State and West Virginia University with rural middle/junior high school science teachers. *Journal of Science Teacher Education, 7*(1), 23–40.

Rutherford, F. J., & Ahlgren, A. (1990). *Science for all Americans.* New York: Oxford University Press.

Schwartz, L., & Wolfgang, T. (1996). *Children's occupational outlook handbook.* Auburn, CA: CFKR Career Materials.

Stringer, J. (Ed.). (1996). *Science & technology ideas for the under 85.* Hatfield, Herts., UK: Association for Science Education.

Stringer, J. (Ed.). (1998). *More science & technology ideas for the under 85.* Hatfield, Herts., UK: Association for Science Education.

Tickle, L., Lancaster, M., Devereux, M., & Marshall, E. (1990). Developing practical knowledge for teaching design and technology. In L. Tickle (Ed.), *Design and technology in primary school classrooms* (pp. 29–78). New York: Falmer Press.

Yager, R. E. (Ed.). (1992). *The status of science-technology-society reform efforts around the world.* Hong Kong: International Council of Associations for Science Education.

Yager, R. E. (Ed.). (1993). *What research says to the science teacher: The science technology society movement.* Arlington, VA: National Science Teachers Association.

Suggested Readings

Cross, G., & Szostak, R. (1995). *Technology and American society: A history.* Upper Saddle River, NJ: Prentice-Hall. (A text about the history of invention and the interaction of technology and society.)

Eggleston, J. (1996). *Teaching design and technology* (2nd ed.). Bristol, PA: Open University Press. (A text about design and technology and its role in the national curriculum of England.)

Forcier, R. C. (1999). *The computer as an educational tool: Productivity and problem solving* (2nd ed.). Upper Saddle River, NJ: Merrill/Prentice-Hall.

(A book on the application of computers in the curriculum to include problem solving.)

Kimbell, R., Stables, K., & Green, R. (1996). *Understanding practice in design and technology.* Bristol, PA: Open University Press. (A research-based text on technology education in England.)

Reynolds, K. E., & Barba, R. H. (1996). *Technology for the teaching and learning of science.* Boston: Allyn & Bacon. (A comprehensive resource on integrating technology into science education.)

Chapter 8

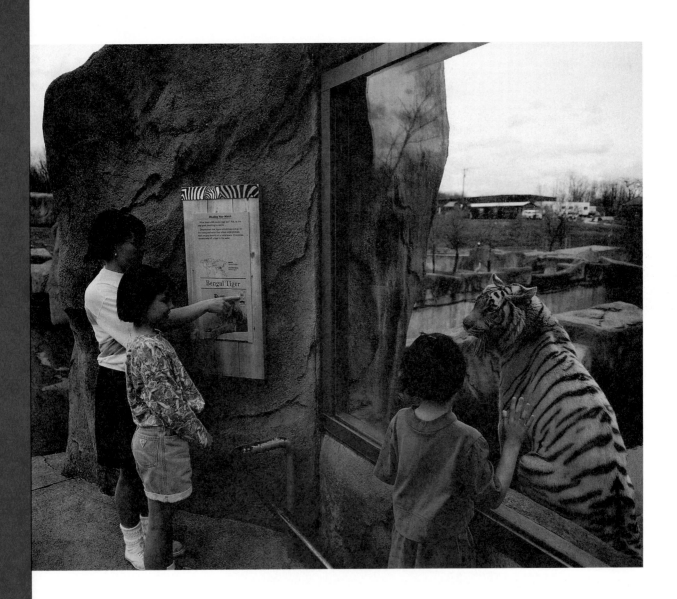

Science Learning Opportunities

VIGNETTE 8-1

Using the Zoo as a Science Education Resource

Dr. Sue Dale Tunnicliffe
ICASE Primary Projects and Homerton College
University of Cambridge, England

Visits to live animal collections can provide excellent opportunities for science learning if the teachers taking the students are familiar with the pedagogy of such visits and what opportunities are available. The knowledge that teachers need for zoo visits (and for visits to other animal collections such as natural history museums) includes the following:

- The stages of a visit in terms of the attention of students during the visit to the animals
- The features of anatomy and behaviors of the animals that the students are likely to notice spontaneously
- The colloquial or everyday names the students will use and any scientific names the teacher wants to be used
- The ability to identify and understand the concepts that the teacher wants the students to acquire

Otherwise, the content of the conversations generated replicates that of family groups who visit the zoo for leisure purposes.

Stages of a Visit

Students and accompanying adults do not focus on exhibits in the same manner throughout their visit. It is important to be aware of the different phases within a school visit and to plan activities for your students accordingly.

First, groups undergo an *orientation* phase, when they look around and find their way. The duration of this stage can be shortened if you provide orientation to the site beforehand. Such orientations can be achieved through showing slides or a video, providing the groups with a timetable, discussing opportunities for visits to the gift shop, telling when and where lunch is to be taken, and similar "housekeeping" arrangements.

Following orientation, the group embarks on the *concentration* phase of focusing on the tasks you have set, looking in a concentrated manner at exhibits, or participating in an educational activity provided by the zoo. It is unrealistic to expect the students to be involved in a focused task throughout the visit. After their concentration wanes, they move into the *leisure-looking* phase, during which their comments and observations are similar to those of "non-education" visitors. Finally, during the *leave-taking* phase, the attention of the group is concerned with gathering together for the journey home.

Spontaneous Observations of Students (and Accompanying Adults)

Elementary students, their accompanying adults, and family groups follow a fundamental pattern when looking at animal exhibits. It is important to be aware of this so that you can plan your activities for young students and the questions the accompanying adults or the activity sheets will ask of them; these are the starting points for science observations. Children spontaneously notice certain phenomena, so use these as the introduction to the topic you plan.

Names

Children spontaneously use everyday or colloquial names. Use these names when referring to the animals, but make it clear to everyone which additional name(s) you want them to use and where. You can then develop zoological classification with the students during the visit or back in school.

These everyday or colloquial names include the use of the term *animal* to mean only mammals. Within the class of mammals, people talk about cats, horses, zebras, rhinos, elephants, lions, tigers, hippos, bats, and seals. Visitors rarely use the specific names unless the animal is particularly well known or has captured the public's imagination (e.g., snow leopard). The identifying term *bird* is provided for any bird other than very memorable ones such as ostrich, eagle, penguin, vulture, and parrot. Reptiles are never referred to as such, unless this term is used by the zoo as a designation for a building, such as Reptile House. Reptiles are generally referred to individually as snakes, crocodiles (usually including the other crocodilians), turtles (for any of the chelonia), and lizards. I have never heard the term *reptile* applied by school groups to animals displayed in zoos.

Few zoos show amphibians, but the everyday terms *frog* and *toad* are used to refer to most of the specimens. Fish are called *fish* by the identifier except for sharks, piranhas, eels, and any particular species about which the visitor happens to have firsthand knowledge, such as chubb or perch. Young students, those under age 7, are unable to cope with two names for one animal; if they call a shark by that name, they deny that it is also a fish. Similarly, all insects and arachnids are "bugs" (in the everyday sense, not the zoological one) unless they know the name, such as ladybug. Spiders are just that unless they are a tarantula or black widow.

Anatomical Features and Behavior Spontaneously Noticed

When looking at the structure of the animals, the students will spontaneously comment on the shape, size, color, any particularly unusual feature, such as horns, and parts that disrupt the body outline and/or move, such as legs and tails. If the animal is performing some behavior, the students will notice it. The position of the animal within the enclosure or display case is important to the students and school. Groups also refer in about half of all conversations to other aspects of the exhibit, such as rocks and trees or feeding bowls. Very often, such nonanimal aspects are used in referring to the location of the animal.

If the animal is doing nothing, the students will query whether it is real, a common question posed about crocodilians in zoos. In museums, the students will be interested in the authenticity of the specimens and how they were prepared for display. Thus, the meaning of the word *real* depends on the context in which it is used. Often, children use the word *real* to refer to whether the animal is alive or not.

The science learning opportunities in a zoo for elementary students are *content* (science facts), *the process* (science method and inquiry), and *science language and communication skills.*

The science content can be biological or physical. The biological content is either botanical (which highlights the role of plants in the food chain and forming the natural habitats of animals) or zoological.

Zoological studies can focus on taxonomic studies or on adaptations to the environment, including adaptations for feeding. Animal behaviors are used to establish the taxonomy of a specimen, as well as to study adaptation and forms. Behavior is thus another important area of study, in which students can make, record, and interpret their firsthand observations of the animals. Such studies require the students to observe salient features of animals, such as form, number of locomotory organs, and body covering.

Elementary students should be able to group animals into their major groups—mammals, reptiles, birds, fish, amphibians, arthropods, mollusks, and annelid worms. They should also be able to say why they make these categorizations. Students should be able to use branching keys and picture keys at Grade 4, and by Grade 6 they should be able to use and construct dichotomous keys. Students should develop an understanding of the needs of animals and the essential life processes and should be able to identify how individual specimens meet them.

Zoos are often poor at providing realistic habitats, however, and visiting a zoo with the aim of learning about natural habitats is often unrealistic. Such studies may be more satisfactorily pursued in natural history museums with natural-looking dioramas.

Animal behavior studies can be frustrating if the students are looking for action. Inaction is just as important and should be used constructively. Find out before your visit which animals are likely to be active and visible within their enclosures. Ask about the pattern of the day of inactive and inaccessible animals so that the students can be given a time chart for these animals and can identify which part of their activity profile the animals are in when the students observe them. Ask the students to find the pattern of these animals' days so that the lack of activity is not a source of frustration, but an active learning experience.

Adaptation to the environment is a topic often well presented by zoo education programs. Decide which adaptations you wish your students to focus on. Very popular topics are birds' beaks (studying adaptations within this class of animals for different types of foods and, hence, different habitats), feet in mammals and birds, color of body coverings, and camouflage.

Planning and delivering the opportunities for experiences that involve your students is essential. Instead of replying with a name when a student asks "What is that animal?" ask the student to work out what it could be as far as she is able. Should a student identify an animal, ask him what features enabled him to make that identification.

Science is about communicating. If scientists don't communicate, no one else knows of their work. Encourage your students to share their observations and findings in a variety of ways: a science report, drama, art, journalist's report, or spoken address.

It is very important to communicate to the chaperones who accompany your students the aims and objectives in terms of education outcomes, as well as the "housekeeping" details. If this is not done, the experience that the students within the chaperoned groups receive is different from that experienced by the students with you. It is up to us, as teachers, to ensure that each student has equal access to an effective experience.

Opportunity to learn refers to quality of the instruction and curricular program that students are provided.

As you may infer from Vignette 8–1, trips to the zoo are an important science education "**opportunity to learn.**" Together with other forms of learning opportunities in the community, trips to a zoo will round out students' science experiences and help them construct understandings of biodiversity and conservation.

Mrs. Blackwelder's Class Trip

Mrs. Blackwelder and her class are excited today. They are planning a trip to the state park. Ranger Kellison will be discussing the wolf population and the recovery of a young wolf that was recently shot. She is glad to see the students' interest in learning about wolves.

The idea for this trip began 2 weeks ago as a social studies experience when the class read variations of the story of Little Red Riding Hood. Everyone became interested in comparing and contrasting accounts of this fable. Each story group read a different version. Will's group began with the traditional story *Little Red Riding Hood* (Schmidt, 1986). Erica's group read *Little Red Riding Hood: A Newfangled Prairie Tale* (Ernst, 1995), in which Grandma turns out to be the one surprising the wolf. Katelyn's group read *Red Riding Hood* (Marshall, 1987), a modern retelling of the tale. Tyler's group read a version from *Yo, Hungry Wolf!: A Nursery Rap* (Vozar, 1993), which is a retelling of three wolf-related stories in rap form.

The wolf theme is a good topic for integrated activities.

After discussing accounts of these tales, the class investigated versions of the Three Little Pigs story. This time, Alex read the traditional *Three Little Pigs* (Gay, 1997) tale. Celeste read *The True Story of the Three Little Pigs* (Scieszka, 1989), as told by "A. Wolf." Emerald read *The Three Little Wolves and the Big Bad Pig* (Trivizas, 1993), which is a role-reversal account of the allegory. Again, the class discussed the versions.

Following up on the stories, Mrs. Blackwelder asked her students what they really knew about wolves. The students had many misconceptions about wolves. These were mostly from the children's stories above and others like *It's So Nice to Have a Wolf Around the House* (Allard, 1997) or *Lon Po Po: A Red-Riding Hood Story From China* (Young, 1989). Television cartoons also provided misinformation. To provide an opportunity for her students to identify their misconceptions and develop a true understanding of the wolf, Mrs. Blackwelder encour-

See
http://www.prenhall.com/peters
for links related to wolves and the International Wolf Center.

aged the students to read more about wolves. She arranged a science center with wolves as the theme, made the Internet available, and bookmarked the International Wolf Center. Here, the students could see pictures of wolves and follow their migratory paths online.

Mrs. Blackwelder also put out a selection of other print resources on wolves. These included such books as *Julie of the Wolves* (George, 1972), *Call of the Wild* (J. G. London, 1993), *Baby Wolf* (Batten, 1998), *Look to the North: A Wolf Pup Diary* (George, 1998), *The Land of the Grey Wolf* (Locker, 1996), *Gray Wolf, Red Wolf* (Patent, 1990), *The Eyes of Gray Wolf* (J. London, 1993), *Wild, Wild Wolves* (Milton, 1992), and other reference books.

Mrs. Blackwelder began reading the book *Wolf Stalker* (Skurzynski & Ferguson, 1997) to discuss wolf restoration projects. This, of course, led to the students wanting to visit the wolf sanctuary at the state park and Ranger Kellison.

Later, Mrs. Blackwelder encouraged other science learning opportunities with her students. Some of her students will participate in "Journey North." This Annenberg/CPB Internet-based learning activity engages students in a global study of wildlife migration. Other students will visit the local natural history museum or engage in similar out-of-class experiences to develop an understanding of wolves and their habitats.

See *http://www.prenhall.com/peters* for links related to "Journey North."

Science Learning Opportunities in Support of the Formal Curriculum

We are familiar with the formal learning that takes place in the school, but if you look at Mrs. Blackwelder's activities, you will notice that she strives to go beyond the traditional teacher-student classroom setting. Her curriculum planning includes endeavors to integrate other learning opportunities as part of her students' knowledge construction about wolves and their environments.

Science learning takes place outside the classroom. One viewpoint is that these learning activities are voluntary and not developed primarily for school use or an ongoing school curriculum (Crane, 1994). Others see experiences outside the classroom as supportive of the existing curriculum (Landis, 1996; Tunnicliffe, 1992).

Science learning opportunities can be in the schoolyard, at home, or in any other social setting. They can also be brought into the classroom when traditional activities are suspended. The class trip to the state park is an example of science learning in support of Mrs. Blackwelder's curricular objectives. This learning is encouraged because it can be motivating for students, can enhance social interaction, and generally provides a rich observational experience.

Although it takes more time for you to arrange, children generally experience meaningful learning with out-of-school science learning opportunities.

Science learning facilities outside the classroom are generally supportive and provide programs and resources for working with your students and even for your own professional development. They can be especially helpful to new teachers who are having difficulty preparing science lessons and organizing activities (Melber, 2000). Another important reason for using these learning resources is that activities can support gaps in formal education where resources are not available to the teacher. Even if learning experiences were redundant, the crucial overlap can increase the opportunity to learn important science skills and concepts (Honeyman, 1998).

The National Science Teachers Association (NSTA) "strongly supports and advocates" out-of-school science learning opportunities for children (1998, p. 1). Figure 8–1 is a summary of the association's views related to this issue.

Do you think you need to go beyond the "traditional classroom" with your own science teaching? According to *National Science Education Standards* (National Research Council [NRC], 1996), "good science programs require access to the world beyond the classroom"

See *http://www.prenhall.com/peters* for links to NSTA's Position Statements.

- Informal science education complements, supplements, deepens, and enhances classroom science studies. It increases the amount of time participants can be engaged in a project or topic. It can be the proving ground for curriculum materials.
- The impact of informal experiences extends to the affective, cognitive, and social realms by presenting the opportunity for mentors, professionals, and citizens to share time, friendship, effort, creativity, and expertise with youngsters and adult learners.
- Informal science education allows for different learning styles and multiple intelligences and offers supplementary alternatives to science study for non-traditional and second language learners. It offers unique opportunities through field trips, field studies, overnight experiences, and special programs.
- Informal science learning experiences offer teachers a powerful means to enhance both professional and personal development in science content knowledge and accessibility to unique resources.
- Informal science education institutions, through their exhibits and programs, provide an effective means for parents and other care providers to share moments of intellectual curiosity and time with their children.
- Informal science institutions give teachers and students direct access to scientists and other career role models in the sciences, as well as to opportunities for authentic science study.
- Informal science educators bring an emphasis on creativity and enrichment strategies to their teaching through the need to attract their noncompulsory audiences.
- NSTA advocates that local corporations, foundations, and institutions fund and support informal science education in their communities.
- Informal science education is often the only means for continuing science learning in the general public beyond the school years.

Figure 8–1
NSTA declarations on informal science education.
Source: National Science Teachers Association, 1998, *Position Statements.* Reprinted with permission.

Standards Link

Inquiry Teaching Standard

Teachers of science design and manage learning environments that provide students with the time, space, and resources needed for learning science. In doing this, teachers:

- **Structure the time available so that students are able to engage in extended investigations.**
- **Create a setting for student work that is flexible and supportive of science inquiry.**
- **Ensure a safe working environment.**
- **Make the available science tools, materials, media, and technological resources accessible to students.**
- **Identify and use resources outside the school.**
- **Engage students in designing the learning environment.**

(Teaching Standard D, National Research Council, 1996, p. 43)

(p. 218). This idea is further reflected in the Inquiry Teaching Standard found in the Standards Link. The authors of this standard call for the identification and use of resources outside the school environment. They suggest that inquiry occurs as students engage in investigations, including those outside school. In this respect, the standards are used by teachers to bridge the gap between in-school and out-of-school experiences because they are common references for both types of learning (Hofstein, Bybee, & Legro, 1997; Katz & McGinnis, 1999).

The external resources offered generally require that you seek out community partners, parents, scientists, engineers, and business leaders in support of your goals for science education (National Research Council, 1998). This is exactly what Mrs. Blackwelder did with the wolf project and other thematic units throughout the year.

When planning her activities, Mrs. Blackwelder generally begins with the selection of a theme that her students have generated an interest in learning about and that would also be supportive of her learning goals. Next, she makes a mental list of what resources may be available for that theme. As she continues to plan activities related to the theme, she incorporates out-of-class learning possibilities. Sometimes she brainstorms with a listing of possibilities such as those contained in Figure 8–2.

Keep in mind that the listing in Figure 8–2 should be considered a starting point for ideas. This guide is not meant to be comprehensive for every theme. The resources in your community will vary, depending on the topic under study. Other important considerations are student interest, available time in your own teaching schedule, time considerations of other professionals involved, general availability of community resources, and most important, the opportunity to learn that the resource will provide.

Museum and Science Center Resources	Museums of Science/Science Centers/Hands-On Science Centers/Equipment Lending Centers Natural History Museums Military Museums Other Types of Museums
Zoo Resources	Zoological Parks Aquariums Specialized Zoos
Horticulture Resources	Plant Conservatories Herbariums Botanical Gardens County Extension Offices
Industrial Resources	Manufacturing Plants Television/Radio/Cable Stations Public Utilities Stores and Shops
Media Resources	Television Films
Park Resources	National, State, and Local Parks Animal Refuges Geologic Sites Dendrology Exhibits Aquatic Sites Bird, Butterfly, or Insect Areas
College Resources	Biological Exhibits Archeological Displays Astronomical Groups
Community-Based Resources	Professionals in the Community Scientists High School Student Volunteers
Home-Based Resources	Parent Educators Science-Related Toys Science and Nature Magazines

Figure 8–2
Areas of informal science education.

Science Learning Resources

See how a zoo, museum, or related resource would fit into your curriculum before proceeding with specific arrangements.

Where can your students see science-related objects and events in their community? There might be many places to explore, such as a zoo, wooded area, garden, nursery, greenhouse, pond, brook, bird refuge, observatory, natural history museum, road cut, construction site, waterworks, sewage treatment plant, dairy, airport, or weather bureau. Each of these places is a rewarding learning site for elementary school students to visit. Before you take a trip, however, some preparation will help make it worthwhile.

A school district catalog of suggested places to visit in the community may be available. It can furnish the necessary details for educational trips. In general, however, you will want to keep the following points in mind:

- Be clear about the purpose for leaving the classroom.
- Check with the principal about policies such as student supervision.
- Visit the site yourself.
- Plan with the children what to look for on the trip.
- Develop behavior and safety standards to be remembered.
- At the site, make sure everyone can see and hear adequately.
  - Develop a timetable of events and activities.
  - Ask questions if desired.

After returning to the classroom, help your students evaluate the trip. Allow them to tell whether the trip was a meaningful educational experience.

As you consider the above points, place special emphasis on the reason for the trip. Give your students an assignment during the trip so that they know the reason for the activity. This assignment does not have to be a written report; it should focus their observations and reduce behavioral problems. Be sure to select adults to help supervise students. These adult chaperones will need to be briefed to provide a better learning opportunity during the visit (Tunnicliffe, 1997). The following sections contain further explanation of some of the resources in Figure 8–2.

Museums and Science Centers ──────────

Mrs. Blackwelder began her investigation of wolves long before she guided her class into a unit on wolves. She read *Child of the Wolves* (Hall, 1996) and wanted to become more familiar with wolves and their travels. When she called a museum, she found out that she could work with a museum staff member to learn more about wolves. This situation is not uncommon.

In *Inquiry and the National Science Education Standards* (NRC, 2000), we find a story about a teacher named Joanna. She is participating in activities at a science museum. There, she finds that her own inquiry methods are enhanced as she participates in science *as a learner*. In cooperation with the museum staff, she is learning inquiry-based teaching methods such as the following:

- How both science subject matter and inquiry outcomes can be built into learning experiences.
- How a deeper understanding of scientific concepts can promote discussion and the formulation of productive questions.

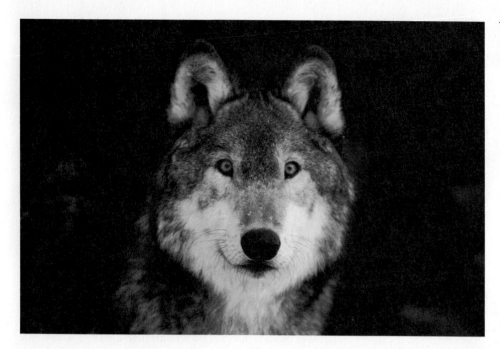

Wolves and children's misconceptions about wolves are good elementary science topics of study.

- How the essential features of classroom inquiry can be woven into a learning experience.
- What it feels like to learn this way, complete with frustrations and struggles.
- What roles and behaviors instructors can use that promote and support learning. (NRC, 2000, p. 101)

Joanna's experience represents a shift in the role of the museum as part of a **stakeholder** in science education as opposed to maintaining a curatorial function. Put another way, museums today are no longer static collections of humanmade or natural history. Rather, they function to develop public understanding of scientific and technological concepts and provide an interface between these concepts and related societal issues. Where once a staff scientist or curator provided a tour, we now have educational specialists or museum staff who have received special training in educational philosophy (Bitgood, Serrell, & Thompson, 1994). These professionals are better able to support state and national standards and science learning in general.

Stakeholders are those individuals or groups that have a "shared interest" in science education and scientific literacy.

This philosophy makes museums ideal sources of out-of-school education for your students as well as yourself. Another reason that museums are a beneficial experience for students relates to the nature of out-of-school education itself. In-school education is a well-ordered system. Knowledge and instruction are continuous, sequential, often guided by textbooks or a specified curriculum, and explicitly assessed (Templeton, 1988). Out-of-school learning, contrarily, is often freely chosen. Exhibits at museums or similar facilities are specifically designed to attract the viewer's attention. Here, the instruction is planned to promote easy understanding. Knowledge is represented in things, not in textbooks. This representation often promotes deeper learning and can be very motivating for students and teachers alike.

Museums are also important proponents of constructive principles. A report of one such elementary-level partnership contained this quote: "If children learn best when constructing their own meaning from their experiences, then indeed informal learning such as that occurring in science museums is an important model to become immersed in while learning to teach" (Nagel, Ault, & Rice, 1995, p. 34).

After reading Vignette 8–1 at the beginning of the chapter, you should have begun to understand the rich opportunity to learn provided by the zoo animals, the environment, and the zoo staff.

In sum, whether you personally take an entire class to the museum for predetermined activities in support of your curriculum, plan and encourage individual learning experiences, or provide external rewards for students who make visits on their own time, your students will certainly benefit from the experience. An analogous resource with many of the same learning benefits of the museum is the zoo.

Zoos

Observing animals, inquiring about their behaviors and habitats, and communicating observations provide excellent opportunities for science learning. Zoo experiences can also provide students a conservation-minded value system as they begin to appreciate the animals that are a part of the ecosystem (Harvey & Erickson, 1988).

Mrs. Blackwelder will provide enough time for her students to draw pictures and describe the animals that they find while on the visit. This will make the experience more meaningful.

Mrs. Blackwelder's class will arrange a visit to a zoo as a culminating activity for the wolf unit. After reading about arctic wolves in the book *To the Top of the World* (Brandenburg, 1993) and *Journey of the Red Wolf* (Smith, 1996), her students are particularly interested in looking at the physical characteristics of wolves and similar animals. They want to know what helps the wolves travel in the way that is discussed.

For a trip to a zoo to be a beneficial learning experience and not just an "entertaining outing," planning is important (Prather, 1989). You may want to try visiting only one area or ecosystem on each trip. The first step in using a zoo as a resource is to visit the zoo and contact the zoo staff to see what is available for you or your students. Today's zoos are changing and offer broader experiences than just observing animals. The zoo staff offers interactive learning experiences for children (Rennie & McClafferty, 1995). Some may even display animatronics (Tunnicliffe, 1999) so that an animated animal and its behavior can be studied in detail. Many zoos offer group tours, special programs designed just for children, career presentations, gifted or challenged student programs, or outreach programs during which the zoo staff bring animals to a class that is not able to travel to the zoo facility.

As you begin your career as a teacher, contact local zoos, museums, and other facilities to see what professional development opportunities are available there.

Keep in mind that not only is a zoo a resource for your students, but, like museums, many zoos provide professional development opportunities for teachers. Whether a curriculum development project, a summer workshop, or a paid internship, you can benefit from the experience provided by zoo educational specialists.

Horticultural Resources

Mrs. Blackwelder's class dialogue of what wolves eat from the book *Wolves* (Dudley, 1997) initiated a discussion of different types of edible mushrooms. Now, Mrs. Blackwelder is making arrangements for her class to talk with a horticulturalist. She will show interested students local varieties of mushrooms, including those that are edible and those that are poisonous.

Conservatories, herbariums, arboretums, and botanical gardens, like their animal counterparts, can be resources for indispensable science learning opportunities. These resources provide out-of-school learning education experiences such as schoolyard ecology programs for elementary students. Conservatories and arboretums also provide teacher education programs such as faculty development workshops. Examples of organizations that provide services or contact with experts are listed below:

- National Arbor Day Foundation
- North American Conservatories
- United States National Arboretum
- Ecological Society of America
- American Association of Botanical Gardens and Arboreta
- National Park Service
- Botanical Society of America
- National Association of State Foresters

As you can see, this is a diverse group of institutions and experts ready to assist you with your learning goals.

When looking for local botanical resources, it may be helpful to begin with your county extension office. You may also want to refer to the document *Resources for Teaching Elementary School Science* (National Science Resources Center, National Academy of Sciences, Smithsonian Institution, 1996) for contacts in your area.

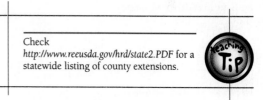

See
http://www.prenhall.com/peters
for links related to conservatories and arboretums.

Check
http://www.reeusda.gov/hrd/state2.PDF for a
statewide listing of county extensions.

Industrial-Based Resources

Alliances among business, industry, government, higher education, and the K–12 educational community are effective ways to supplement learning and bring the community together for science education improvement (American Association for the Advancement of Science [AAAS], 1998; International Council of Associations for Science Education [ICASE], 1990). Teachers who participate in industry-based work experiences report the following:

- Using new teaching strategies in their classrooms
- Introducing updated content into the curriculum
- Increasing the use of computers in the classrooms
- Seeking ways to work with other teachers and maintaining their connections to the businesses in which they worked
- Adding career information to the curriculum
- Gaining in self esteem
- Affirming their decisions to become teachers

Alliances and business partners can also contribute to effective standards-based reform (Business Coalition for Education Reform, 1998; Rigden & McAdoo, 1995; Triangle Coalition for Science and Technology Education, 1996). They provide support to elementary classrooms through a variety of means such as summer internships, minigrants to teachers or students, volunteers for tutoring, mentoring, guest lecturing, sponsoring clubs, judging contests, institutes for professional development, speaker bureaus, loans and donations of equipment, technical assistance, curriculum assistance, program development, public awareness campaigns, clearinghouses, databases, hotlines, projects for women and minorities, computer assistance, administrator training, and school restructuring (Triangle Coalition for Science and Technology Education, 1991).

To get a better perspective on which businesses in your area are supporting education, contact the Triangle Coalition for Science and Technology Education, 1201 New York Avenue, NW, Suite 700, Washington, DC, 20005. This organization provides information on the Scientific Work Experiences for Teachers (SWEPT) program. You may also want to refer to the document *A Business Guide to Support Employee and Family Involvement in Education* (Otterbourg, 1997).

To see what other resources are available in your area, your first step should be contacting your local Chamber of Commerce. You can begin by viewing the U.S. Chamber of Commerce Chamber Mall.

See *http://www.prenhall.com/peters* for links related the U.S. Chamber of Commerce.

Media Providers

See *http://www.prenhall.com/peters* for links to endangered species sites.

Mrs. Blackwelder encouraged her students to take a virtual tour of an endangered species site after reading the Ranger Rick book *Wolves* (Wolpert, 1990). This is one of many out-of-school learning resources available from the National Wildlife Federation. An ever-increasing supply of resources is available from media providers about wolves and many other elementary science topics. One place to begin looking for resources is with your local cable company.

See *http://www.prenhall.com/peters* for Cable in the Classroom links and for Discovery Channel School links.

The Cable in the Classroom program is a public service effort supported by the cable industry. Cable companies provide free cable connections to many classrooms in their area, as well as hundreds of hours of free programming to the schools. Videotaping of the shows is encouraged, allowing teachers flexibility in when they show the productions in their individual classrooms. Teachers can refer to *Cable in the Classroom* magazine, which lists the schedule and provides feature articles. The Cable in the Classroom program also provides a professional development institute that includes traveling and virtual workshops for teachers.

The Discovery Channel School lists programming previews, lesson plans to accompany shows, Web links, and discussions. *Discovery's Educator Guide* is a reference to the educational programming on Discovery Channel, The Learning Channel, Travel Channel, and Animal Planet and is free.

Nickelodeon currently provides *Mr. Wizard's World* and *Teacher to Teacher With Mr. Wizard* programming. A guide to the shows and teacher resources is available. The *Nick News* series also provides many science-related episodes.

See *http://www.prenhall.com/peters* for Nickelodeon links and for PBS, *Nova, Scientific American Frontiers, Newton's Apple, Bill Nye,* and *PBS Online* links.

The Public Broadcasting System (PBS) has many science-related series, including *Nova, Scientific American Frontiers, Newton's Apple, Bill Nye,* and *PBS Online*. PBS includes resources such as an online *TeacherSource* guide and program listings. The *Nova* series covers a variety of science topics that are useful to teachers and students. Lesson ideas, past show resources, and online activities are available on the Internet. A printed teacher's guide is also available.

Scientific American Frontiers, produced in association with *Scientific American,* has an online Web site. This Internet site includes "ask the scientists," "in the classroom," "cool science," and "resource" sections.

The *Newton's Apple* series is an excellent resource for science subjects. This is a family and classroom science show. Many *Science Try Its* are available on the related Web site, as are numerous activity guides for the past season's shows. New program guides are generally available a few weeks before the show, and a printed program guide is available for teachers.

Bill Nye's Web site is a gateway to episode guides for more than 100 shows. This site has "sounds of science" clips and home demonstrations of science phenomena.

One related but often overlooked resource for science is science fiction. It is a good beginning point for discussion of topics that are of student interest. Actual scientific principles used or misused in films and television can be better learned through the use of science fiction (Dubeck, Moshier, & Boss, 1988) because film or television series directors often use concrete ways to demonstrate abstract principles. Science fiction can be a tool for the elementary science teacher in identifying misconceptions.

Other Resources

See
http://www.prenhall.com/peters
for links to ICASE, NSTA, and
science clubs.

Resources such as state parks, local parks, colleges, community-based businesses, and home-based resources are also available to you as an elementary teacher. One specific example is the science club. Science clubs allow members to choose areas of study based on mutual interest as opposed to a specific curriculum (Tunnicliffe, 1998). For further information, see the International Association of Science Clubs, the International Council of Associations for Science Education (ICASE), or the National Science Teachers Association (NSTA) Web sites.

In planning to use resources, first identify your specific learning goals and then check for a local contact that will meet those needs. One way to begin is by contacting a curriculum specialist, elementary science specialist, or lead teacher within your local school or district. You can also try a general Internet World Wide Web search for resources in your area.

"Partners in education" can bring science into your classroom in special ways.

Individual Partners in Education

The story *The Boy Who Cried "Wolf!"* (Schecter, 1994) begins with a boy earning a living as a shepherd in his village. The villagers come to help the boy when he cries out, "Wolf!" *Peter and the Wolf* (Lemieux, 1991) is a similar story of villagers coming to the rescue when a wolf is present. Although these stories contain misinformation about wolves, they do illustrate how community members are willing to help out in difficult situations. This maxim is still true today. Parents and other community leaders are willing to help you out with your elementary science program.

Community resource individuals can be utility-based professionals; animal care technicians; earth, space, and weather experts; botanists and agriculture specialists; social science researchers; or scientists and engineers working in general industry.

When it is impossible to arrange visits away from the school, resource persons from the community may be able to visit your classroom. Many districts compile lists of informed persons who are willing to volunteer. Like the science education resources discussed in the previous section, individual partnerships can be an excellent source of assistance, ideas, and materials to support your elementary science program. Figure 8–3 lists some contacts within these categories.

Utility-Based Partners	Engineers
	Electricians
	Environmental Scientists
	Telecommunications Specialists
	Television/Radio Technicians
	Computer Systems Designers/Operators
Animal/Human Care Partners	Veterinarians
	Zoologists
	Entomologists
	County Health Department Employees
	Hospital-Based Professionals
Earth, Space, and Weather Partners	Weather Forecasters
	Pilots/Astronauts
	Geologists
	Surveyors
	Civil Engineers/Contractors
	Paleontologists
Botanists and Agriculture Partners	Forest/Park Rangers
	Farmers and Ranchers
	Horticulturists/Landscape Workers
	County Extension Employees
Social Science Partners	Psychiatrists/Psychologists
	Anthropologists
	Geographers
General Industry Partners	Chemists/Biologists/Physicists
	Inventors/Architects
	Engineers

Figure 8–3
Individual partner examples.

Some guidelines will help build success when developing partnerships on an individual basis. First, *contact the volunteer in advance* and arrange your first meeting outside the classroom. This will allow plenty of time to answer questions, explain general class procedures, determine any specific materials or equipment needed, and discuss the objectives of the visit. As the time approaches, *remind the volunteer* of her visit and provide the school's and your home telephone numbers for a return call. The schedules of many professionals change often, and mistakes can occur. You do not want to have a disappointed class or have future experiences jeopardized from a poor initial experience.

Do not forget to offer cold drinks or coffee to visitors. Also show all visitors where the restrooms are located.

When the visitor arrives, have someone there to greet her and make her comfortable with the experience. You can do this personally while another teacher or an administrator watches your class. You could also have a teacher aide or the room parent greet the visitor and bring her to the classroom. Arrange for a name tag if possible, and introduce the speaker to the class.

After the visit, follow up with a thank-you card or telephone conversation. Let the principal know something about the volunteer and the outcomes of the visit. The principal or you may want to alert the news media about positive experiences. If volunteers will be visiting on a continuous basis, do not forget to provide them your schedule changes. Meet with them periodically to see whether the objectives of the visits are still being met and whether they have any further suggestions.

Scientists as Professional Development Partners

A partnership with a scientist is a strategy suggested for professional development of teachers who may need to build their content knowledge or confidence in teaching science (Loucks-Horsley et al., 1999). Scientists are good partners in education, especially from a "real" science or equity standpoint. Scientists can provide real-world applications of science as they mentor teachers. Teachers, in return, allow scientists to see firsthand the condition of school science programs. Scientists also benefit by enhancing their own teaching effectiveness as they learn new strategies from educational professionals.

Here are some specific goals for having a scientist make a presentation or work with your class:

- To help students understand science
- To help students gain an understanding of the work scientists do
- To help students see scientists as real people
- To help scientists develop insight into today's schools and students (Shaw & Herminghaus, 1993)

If the scientist visiting your class is new to the educational field, it may be helpful to provide some initial suggestions, such as the elements of a successful presentation or things to do in the classroom.

As a classroom teacher, you should select a topic for the scientist to present. Call the scientist and explain your needs. Be sure to provide background information and how his presentation will support your learning goals. Make sure you discuss appropriate behavior with your students beforehand.

See the article "Scientists in the Classroom" (Shaw & Herminghaus, 1993) for ideas and a reproducible checklist of things the scientist should know and "do" as part of the presentation. This resource contains information that a teaching professional will understand but that a scientist may not be aware of before the presentation. A summary developed from the list is found in Figure 8–4. The book

Do	Because
Make eye contact with students	Students love personal contact
Have presentation materials organized	Students have a hard time waiting
Use student volunteers	Students love to feel important
Require students to raise their hands	Students will all want to talk at once
Make sure they understand the task	This avoids unnecessary questions
Face the students and move about	This will help maintain the interest
Ask the teacher for help with discipline	The teacher will know how to help
Use wait time	The students need time to think
Praise good behavior	This will encourage more good behavior
Enjoy the students	They have a unique perspective

Figure 8–4
Do and because list for scientists.
Source: From Shaw & Herminghaus, 1993, p. 119.

Science Education Partnerships: Manual for Scientists and K–12 Teachers is also a good resource for use in understanding how a scientist can support science learning in your classroom and how you can develop a partnership program in your school (Sussman, 1993).

Parents as Partners ————

Parents are essential to their children's success in school. Out-of-school time is an important opportunity for learning (Bergstrom, 1984). According to the National Science Teachers Association Board of Directors, parents can help their children by

- Seeing science everywhere
  Parents can help their children feel the excitement of observation and discovery. They can also promote growth in thinking, further develop problem-solving abilities, and encourage positive attitudes toward science.
- Doing science together
  Parents can share experiences and demonstrate that science learning is enjoyable.
- Developing a variety of skills
  Parents can assist their children in developing science process skills and comprehending scientific information.
- Finding the appropriate level
  Parents can assess the developmental level of their children and seek out appropriate strategies and ideas to assist their children with scientific understandings. (NSTA, 1994)

Parents can achieve the above goals by simply taking the time to listen to their child, building a resource collection, and co-investigating science at home and within the community on a daily basis. Parents should also become involved in the school to make sure that science-related experiences are ongoing.

Teachers can support parents by keeping 15 to 30 kits containing activities that the students can check out and take home. These kits can be stored in small plastic containers and are easy to prepare with help from a teacher aid or parents. Begin by looking through this text and other resources that may be available to you. Look for activities and investigations that might enrich your regular science program. Select any number of these activities and make one copy of each activity.

Bring these copies to Parents' Night or similar meetings early in the school year. Start by briefly introducing your science program. Next, discuss what topics your students will study and some of the materials they will work with throughout the year. Then, show your activity sheets and example kits and give their purpose. Hand out the duplicated activity sheets, have parents examine them, and then ask for volunteers to make the kits. Encourage the parent volunteers to do the activities with their children, discuss the results together, and return the completed kits.

Some teachers like to have parents experience firsthand a few children's activities across the curriculum. This puts the parents in better touch with their children's work. Parents who are involved with your program are typically willing to supplement your science supplies with discardable items from around the home. Some will volunteer to assist at science learning centers or will share their expertise in science or technology. But for these things to happen, parents need to hear details from you about what's needed.

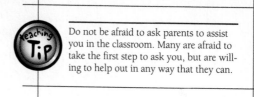

Do not be afraid to ask parents to assist you in the classroom. Many are afraid to take the first step to ask you, but are willing to help out in any way that they can.

Parents are usually more concerned about their children's progress in reading than in other subjects. Point out to them the value of parents reading aloud with their children, sharing books, and discussing concepts that come up in the reading. Show parents several kinds of science trade books available that correlate with upcoming units. The students may check out these books from several sources, including the school or district or public library. If your school has a newer multimedia science program, check out the science-related literature books that typically accompany these programs.

Show parents examples of useful articles from a newspaper, news magazine, *National Geographic,* or other sources they might share with their children who, in turn, might share the information at school. Explain that this material is easier to understand and remember when it relates to topics and concepts being studied at school. Stress the need to discuss the articles with the children, because these are seldom written in an age-appropriate style. Mention, too, some titles of science periodicals for children. They contain excellent current material, are more age-appropriate, and will help students learn what to look for when scanning newspapers and other publications.

Some parents and children will already have visited a local natural history museum, zoo, observatory, bird refuge, or botanical garden. Ask parents about these experiences and suggest additional places recommended by seasoned colleagues and school district publications. A school catalog will have descriptions and a listing of places for families to visit at different grade levels or for certain units of instruction. And if you intend to take your class on study trips to these places, a parents' meeting is a good time to solicit volunteers to accompany the class.

You probably realize that we have mentioned more things to inform parents about than you will have time for in one introductory meeting, especially if you discuss other subjects. Periodic newsletters, a classroom newspaper, individual conferences, and further parent–teacher meetings all present more chances to reach them. The content of your message is far more important than its forum. When you give parents specific ways to help their children study science and support your efforts, everyone gains.

Family Science Festivals

A Family Science Festival is a time when parents can share with their children without any fears of "failure," such as a low science grade.

A Family Science Festival is a recreational community event where families participate in science activities after school (MCCPTA-EPI Hands-On Science, 1985). They are not science fairs but community events where people can have fun while they increase their awareness of science. When planning and implementing a festival, keep the following five important considerations in mind.

1. Project Leader
   The project leader is the head of the committee and is in charge of areas such as recruitment of volunteers and keeping people on task.

2. Volunteers
   Volunteers make telephone calls and make arrangements for festival day such as reminder letters, name tags, and thank-you notes.

3. Publicity
   The publicity person develops the announcements or flyers to give to the graphics team, arranges photographic support, and seeks media coverage of the event.

4. Graphics
   The graphics people print the signs or flyers for the event, as well as any necessary table decorations or instructions needed for the event.

5. Activities/Materials
   The activities crew selects and makes arrangements for the activities, including arranging to have the necessary materials on hand to complete the events. (MCCPTA-EPI Hands-On Science, 1985, p. 4)

The important thing to remember about Family Science Festivals is that they should be indicative of your school or community's creativity and be fun. As with other out-of-school learning experiences, they should support science learning in a successful way.

Summary

1. Science learning opportunities that take place outside the classroom can support or supplement an ongoing school curriculum. This type of learning can be in the schoolyard, at home, or in any other social setting.
2. Museums and science centers, zoos, horticulture exhibits and experts, industrial resources, and various forms of media all provide learning opportunities for students and professional development opportunities for preservice and in-service teachers.
3. Utility-based partners; animal/human care partners; earth, space, and weather partners; botanists and agriculture partners; social science partners; and general industry partners are all available to support your elementary science program.
4. Parents can be essential learning partners for your students. One type of event that can involve parents is a Family Science Festival where families participate in science activities after school.

Reflection

1. Look at Chapter 9 of *Resources for Teaching Elementary School Science* (National Science Resources Center, National Academy of Sciences, Smithsonian Institution, 1996, Washington, DC: National Academy Press; Available: *http://stills.nap.edu/html/rtess/contents.html*) or *Science Fun in Chicagoland: A Guide for Parents and Teachers* (Sills, 1995, Chicago: Dearborn Resources). What are some out-of-school science education resources located near your community?

2. Read through *Helping Your Child Learn Science* (Paulu, 1992, Washington, DC: U.S. Department of Education; Available: *http://www.ed.gov/pubs/parents/Science/index.html*). Would you recommend this reading to parents? Why or why not? What does it say to you as a future teacher? Did you get any new ideas from the "Activities in the Community" section?

3. Obtain a copy of *Science Education Partnerships: Manual for Scientists and K–12 Teachers* (Sussman, 1993, San Francisco: University of California) and identify ways to develop and fund partnerships. These could be with your students or on an individual basis as a means to further your own scientific knowledge.

4. Using *Learning in Living Color: Using Literature to Incorporate Multicultural Education Into the Primary Classroom* (Valdez, 1999, Needham Heights, MA: Allyn & Bacon, pp. 60–79), develop lessons to integrate the wolf theme with multicultural themes such as Native American history. Also show the relationship between the nature of science (skepticism) and stereotyping. What facts are related to wolves, and what fiction has skewed our understanding of wolves?

5. Review the National PTA's *National Standards for Parent/Family Involvement Programs* at *http://www.pta.org/programs/invstand.htm*. Develop a presentation that you can use in the future to seek parental support for your science program.

References

Allard, H. (1997). *It's so nice to have a wolf around the house.* New York: Picture Yearling Books.

American Association for the Advancement of Science (AAAS). (1998). *Blueprints for reform.* New York: Oxford University Press.

Batten, M. (1998). *Baby wolf.* New York: Grosset & Dunlap.

Bergstrom, J. (1984). *School's out—now what? Creative choices for your child.* Berkeley, CA: Ten Speed Press.

Bitgood, S., Serrell, B., & Thompson, D. (1994). The impact of informal education on visitors to museums. In V. Crane, H. Nicholson, M. Chen, & S. Bitgood (Eds.), *Informal science learning: What the research says about television, science museums, and community-based projects* (pp. 61–106). Ephrata, PA: Science Press.

Brandenburg, J. (1993). *To the top of the world: Adventures with arctic wolves.* New York: Walker.

Business Coalition for Education Reform. (1998). *The formula for success: A business leader's guide to supporting math and science achievement.* Washington, DC: U.S. Department of Education.

Crane, V. (1994). An introduction to informal science learning and research. In V. Crane,

H. Nicholson, M. Chen, & S. Bitgood (Eds.), *Informal science learning: What the research says about television, science museums, and community-based projects* (pp. 1–14). Ephrata, PA: Science Press.

Dubeck, L. W., Moshier, S. E., & Boss, J. E. (1988). *Science in cinema: Teaching science fact thorough science fiction films.* New York: Teachers College Press.

Dudley, K. (1997). *Wolves.* Austin, TX: Raintree Steck-Vaughn.

Ernst, L. C. (1995). *Little red riding hood: A newfangled prairie tale.* New York: Aladdin Paperbacks.

Gay, M. L. (1997). *The 3 little pigs.* Buffalo, NY: Groundwood Books.

George, J. C. (1972). *Julie of the wolves.* New York: HarperTrophy.

George, J. C. (1998). *Look to the north: A wolf pup diary.* New York: HarperTrophy.

Hall, E. (1996). *Child of the wolves.* New York: Bantam Doubleday Dell.

Harvey, P., & Erickson, D. (1988). Making the most of the zoo. In M. Druger (Ed.), *Science for the fun of it: A guide to informal science education* (pp. 78–82). Arlington, VA: National Science Teachers Association.

Hofstein, A., Bybee, R., & Legro, P. (1997). Linking formal and informal science education through science education standards. *Science Education International, 8*(3), 31–37.

Honeyman, B. (1998). Non-formal and formal learning interactions: New directions for scientific and technological literacy. *Connect, 23*(1), 1–2.

International Council of Associations for Science Education (ICASE). (1990). *Industry-education liaison.* Hong Kong: Author.

Katz, P., & McGinnis, R. (1999). An informal elementary science education program's response to the national science education reform movement. *Journal of Elementary Science Education, 11*(1), 1–11.

Landis, C. (1996). Teaching science in the field. *ERIC/CSMEE Digest, EDO-SE-96–7.* Columbus, OH: ERIC/CSMEE.

Lemieux, M. (1991). *Peter and the wolf.* New York: Mulberry Paperbacks.

Locker, T. (1996). *The land of the gray wolf.* New York: Dial Books.

London, J. (1993). *The eyes of grey wolf.* San Francisco: Chronicle Books.

London, J. G. (1993). *The call of the wild.* New York: Scholastic Paperbacks.

Loucks-Horsley, S., Hewson, P. W., Love, N., Stiles, K. E., Dyasi, H. M., Friel, S. N., Mumme, J., Sneider, C. I., & Worth, K. L. (1999). Ideas that work: Summaries of 15 strategies for professional development. In A. Thorson (Ed.), *Ideas that work: Science professional development* (pp. 10–44). Columbus, OH: Eisenhower National Clearinghouse for Mathematics and Science Education.

Marshall, J. (1987). *Red riding hood.* New York: Dial Books.

MCCPTA-EPI Hands-On Science. (1985). *Putting together a family science festival.* (Available from author at 12118 Heritage Park Circle, Silver Spring, MD 20852).

Melber, L. (2000). Tap into informal science learning. *Science Scope, 23*(6), 28–31.

Milton, J. (1992). *Wild, wild wolves.* New York: Random House.

Nagel, N., Ault, C., & Rice, M. (1995). Learning to teach and the science museum. *Science Education International, 6*(2), 31–34.

National Research Council (NRC). (1996). *National science education standards.* Washington, DC: National Academy Press. Available: *http://books.nap.edu/html/nses/html/index.html*

National Research Council (NRC). (1998). *Every child a scientist: Achieving scientific literacy for all.* Washington, DC: National Academy Press.

National Research Council (NRC). (2000). *Inquiry and the national science education standards.* Washington, DC: National Academy Press. Available: *http://books.nap.edu/html/ inquiry_addendum/*

National Science Resources Center, National Academy of Sciences, Smithsonian Institution. (1996). *Resources for teaching elementary school science.* Washington, DC: National Academy Press. Available: *http://stills.nap.edu/html/rtess/ contents.html*

National Science Teachers Association (NSTA). (1994). *An NSTA position statement: Parent involvement in science education.* Arlington, VA: Author. Available: *http://www.nsta.org/handbook/ position.asp*

National Science Teachers Association (NSTA). (1998). *An NSTA position statement: Informal science education.* Arlington, VA: Author. Available: *http://www.nsta.org/handbook/position.asp*

Otterbourg, S. (1997). *A business guide to support employee and family involvement in education.* New York: Conference Board. Available: *http://www.ed.gov/pubs/BusinessGuide/*

Patent, D. H. (1990). *Gray wolf, red wolf.* New York: Clarion Books.

Prather, J. P. (1989). Review of the value of field trips in science instruction. *Journal of Elementary Science Education, 1*(1), 10–17.

Rennie, L. R., & McClafferty, T. (1995). Using visits to interactive science and technology centers, museums, aquaria, and zoos to promote learning in science. *Journal of Science Teacher Education, 6*(4), 175–185.

Rigden, D., & McAdoo, M. (1995). *Supporting the national education goals: A guide for business leaders.* New York: Council for Aid to Education.

Schecter, E. (1994). *The boy who cried "wolf!"* New York: Bantam Book.

Schmidt, K. (1986). *Little red riding hood.* New York: Scholastic.

Scieszka, J. (1989). *The true story of the 3 little pigs!* New York: Puffin Books.

Shaw, D., & Herminghaus, T. (1993). Scientists in the classroom. In G. Madrazo & L. Motz (Eds.), *Sourcebook for science supervisors* (4th ed., pp. 117–121). Arlington, VA: National Science Teachers Association.

Skurzynski, G., & Ferguson, A. (1997). *Wolf stalker.* Washington, DC: National Geographic Society.

Smith, R. (1996). *Journey of the red wolf.* New York: Cobblehill Books.

Sussman, A. (1993). *Science education partnerships: Manual for scientists and K–12 teachers.* San Francisco: University of California.

Templeton, M. (1988). The science museum: Object lessons in informal education. In M. Druger (Ed.), *Science for the fun of it: A guide to informal science education* (pp. 83–88). Arlington, VA: National Science Teachers Association.

Triangle Coalition for Science and Technology Education. (1991). *A guide for building an alliance for science, mathematics, and technology.* College Park, MD: Author.

Triangle Coalition for Science and Technology Education. (1996). *A look at industry and community commitment to educational systematic reform.* College Park, MD: Author.

Trivizas, E. (1993). *The three little wolves and the big bad pig.* New York: Aladdin Paperbacks.

Tunnicliffe, S. D. (1992). The school visit as a science learning opportunity. In *Annual proceedings of the American Association of Zoological Parks and Aquariums* (pp. 342–349). Toronto: AAZPA/American Zoo and Aquarium Association.

Tunnicliffe, S. D. (1997). The effect of the presence of two adults—chaperones or teachers—on the content of conversations of primary school groups during school visits to a natural history museum. *Journal of Elementary Science Education, 9*(1), 49–65.

Tunnicliffe, S. D. (1998). Science clubs. *Science Education International, 9*(3), 36.

Tunnicliffe, S. D. (1999). Use with care: Animatronics in museums and zoos—a new type of exhibit. *Science Education International, 10*(3), 34–37.

Vozar, D. (1993). *Yo, hungry wolf!: A nursery rap.* New York: Doubleday.

Wolpert, T. (1990). *Wolves for kids.* Minnetonka, MN: NorthWord Press.

Young, E. (1989). *Lon Po Po: A red-riding hood story from China.* Ossining, NY: Paper Star.

Suggested Readings

Committee on Biology Teacher Inservice Programs, Board on Biology Commission on Life Sciences, National Research Council. (1996). *The role of scientists in the professional development of science teachers.* Washington, DC: National Academy Press. Available: *http://stills.nap.edu/html/role/* (A comprehensive report and reading list on the topic of the use of scientists in teacher professional development.)

Kubota, C. (1993). Education-business partnerships: Scientific work experience programs. *ERIC/CSMEE Digest, EDO-SE-93-3.* Columbus, OH: ERIC/CSMEE.

National Science Resources Center, National Academy of Sciences, Smithsonian Institution. (1997). *Science for all children: A guide to improving science education in your school district.* Washington, DC: National Academy Press. (Provides examples of specific partnerships in support of elementary science education.)

Paulu, N., & Martin, M. (1991). *Helping your child learn science.* Washington, DC: U.S. Department of Education, Office of Educational Research and Improvement. (How parents can increase their children's science interests through home activities. Available at $3.25 from OERI Outreach Office, 555 New Jersey Ave., NW, Washington, DC 20208-5570.)

Pearlman, S., & Pericak-Spector, K. (1992). Helping hands from home. *Science and Children, 29*(7), 12–14. (Parent volunteers make active science more manageable.)

GENERAL SOURCES OF ACTIVITIES

American Association for the Advancement of Science, & Walthall, B. (Ed.). (1995). *IdeAAAS: Sourcebook for science, mathematics, & technology education*. Washington, DC: Learning Team.

American Chemical Society. (2001). *The best of wonderscience* (Vol. 2). Belmont, CA: Wadsworth.

Cothron, J., Giese, R., & Rezba, R. (1996). *Science experiments by the hundreds*. Dubuque, IA: Kendall/Hunt.

DeVito, A., & Krockover, G. H. (1997). *Creative sciencing: Ideas and activities for teachers and children*. Glenview, IL: Scott, Foresman.

Freidl, A., & Koontz, T. (2000). *Teaching science to children: An inquiry approach*. New York: McGraw-Hill Higher Education.

Goldsworthy, A., & Feasey, R. (1997). *Making sense of primary science investigations*. Hatfield, Herts., UK: Association for Science Education.

Sewall, S. (1990). *Hooked on science: Ready-to-use discovery activities for grades 4–8*. West Nyack, NY: Center for Applied Research in Education.

Stringer, J. (Ed.). (1996). *Science and technology ideas for the under 8s*. Hatfield, Herts., UK: Association for Science Education.

Stringer, J. (Ed.). (1998). *More science and technology ideas for the under 8s*. Hatfield, Herts., UK: Association for Science Education.

Strongin, H. (1991). *Science on a shoestring*. Reading, MA: Addison-Wesley.

Van Cleave, J. P. (1989–1991). *Science for every kid* (5 volumes: biology, chemistry, earth, astronomy, physics). New York: John Wiley.

OTHERS

Also visit the AIMS Education Foundation (*http://www.aimsedu.org/*), Great Explorations in Math and Science (*http://www.lhs.berkeley.edu/GEMS/gems.html*), National Science Teachers Association (www.nsta.org), and the Association for Science Education (*http://www.ase.org.uk/*) for new activity books and ideas.

TEACHER PERIODICALS

Discover, Time, Inc., 3435 Wilshire Blvd., Los Angeles, CA 90010. (Monthly. Interesting, up-to-date information about developments in science; *http://www.discover.com/*).

Frontiers, National Science Foundation, 4201 Wilson Blvd., Arlington, VA 22230. (Newsletter of the National Science Foundation; *http://www.nsf.gov/od/lpa/news/publicat/ frontier/start.htm*).

Journal of Elementary Science Education, contact Dr. Kevin Finson, Western Illinois University, Macomb, IL; Kevin_Finson@ccmail.wiu.edu. (Practical and theoretical articles related to elementary science teaching and learning.).

Journal of Research in Science Teaching, contact David Haury, National Association for Research in Science Teaching Executive Secretary, The Ohio State University, 1929 Kenny Rd., Columbus, OH; haury.2@osu.edu. (Scholarly articles on research and practice).

Journal of Science Teacher Education, contact Jon Pederson, Association for the Education of Teachers in Science Executive Secretary, University of Oklahoma, Norman, OK; pedersenj@ou.edu. (Practical and scholarly articles related to teacher preservice, teacher inservice, and science teaching).

Natural History, American Museum of Natural History, Central Park West at 79th St., New York, NY 10024. (Monthly, 10 issues a year. Interesting articles on a variety of natural subjects, including ecology; *http://www.amnh.org/*).

School Science and Mathematics, contact Donald Pratt, School Science and Mathematics Association Executive Secretary, Curriculum and Foundations, Bloomsburgh University, Bloomsburgh, PA; pratt@bloomu.edu. (Monthly, nine issues a year. Includes articles on methods and research).

Science, American Association for the Advancement of Science, 1515 Massachusetts Ave., NW, Washington, DC 20005. (Monthly, except bimonthly Jan./Feb. and July/Aug. Accurate, up-to-date nontechnical information about developments in science; *http://www.scienceonline.org/*).

Science Activities, Heldref Publications, 1319 Eighteenth Street, NW, Washington, DC. (Ten issues a year. Useful activities for teachers of the upper grades and beyond; *http://www.heldref.org/html/sa.html*).

Science and Children, National Science Teachers Association, 1840 Wilson Blvd., Arlington, VA 22201-3000. (Monthly, eight issues a year. Articles of interest and practical value to elementary school teachers; *www.nsta.org/*).

Science Education, John Wiley and Sons, Inc., 605 Third Ave., New York, NY 10158. For individual subscriptions contact Jon Pederson, Association for the Education of Teachers in Science Executive Secretary, University of Oklahoma, Norman, OK; pedersenj@ou.edu. (Reports of research and essays on the teaching of elementary and secondary school science).

Science News, Science Service, 1719 N Street, NW, Washington, DC. (Weekly. Brief, easy-to-read reports on current findings of scientific research; *http://www.sciencenews.org/*).

CHILDREN'S PERIODICALS

National Geographic World, National Geographic Society, Department 00481, 17th and M Streets, NW, Washington, DC 20036. (Monthly. Articles on environmental features of interest to children; *http://www.nationalgeographic.com/world/*).

Odyssey, AstroMedia Corp., 625 E. St. Paul Ave., P.O. Box 92788, Milwaukee, WI 53202. (Bimonthly. Full-color astronomy and space magazine for children 7–13; *http://www.odysseymagazine.com/*).

Ranger Rick Nature Magazine, National Wildlife Federation, 1412 Sixteenth St., NW, Washington, DC 20036. (Monthly, for children of elementary school age. Interesting stories and pictures on natural subjects, including ecology. *Your Big Backyard* is for preschool and primary-level children; *http://www.nwf.org/rrick/* and *http://www.nwf.org/ybby/*).

3–2–1 Contact, Sesame Workshop, P.O. Box 2933, Boulder, CO 80322. (Ten issues a year. Experiments, puzzles, projects, and articles for children 8–14; *http://www.sesameworkshop.org/*).

Wonderscience, American Chemical Society, 1155 16th St., NW, Washington, DC 20036. (Science activities for children; also includes *Best of Wonderscience*; *http://www.acs.org/education/curriculum/wondsci.html*).

PROFESSIONAL TEXTS

Abruscato, J. (1996). *Teaching children science: A discovery approach* (5th ed.). Needham Heights, MA: Allyn & Bacon/Pearson Education. (Methods, activities, and content for elementary school science.)

Barba, R. H. (1998). *Science in the multicultural classroom: A guide to teaching and learning* (2nd ed.). Needham Heights, MA: Allyn & Bacon. (Elementary science methods.)

Cain, S. E., & Evans, J. M. (2002). *Sciencing: An involvement approach to elementary science methods* (4th ed.). Upper Saddle River, NJ: Merrill/Prentice Hall. (A methods text organized into six broad units to develop teaching competencies.)

Carin, A., & Bass, J. (2001). *Teaching science as inquiry* (9th ed.). Upper Saddle River, NJ: Merrill/Prentice Hall. (Methods and activities, with emphasis on discovery teaching.)

Ebenezer, J., & Conner, S. (1998). *Learning to teach science: A model for the 21st century.* Upper Saddle River, NJ: Merrill/Prentice Hall. (Methods and activities, with emphasis on discovery teaching.)

Esler, W. K., & Esler, M. K. (1996). *Teaching elementary science* (7th ed.). Belmont, CA: Wadsworth. (Methods and subject matter. Exemplifies and applies three kinds of lessons.)

Gabel, D. (1993). *Introductory science skills.* Prospect Heights, IL: Waveland Press. (A laboratory approach to learning science and mathematics skills and basic chemistry.)

Harlan, J., & Rivkin, M. (1995). *Science experiences for the early childhood years: An integrated approach* (7th ed.). Upper Saddle River, NJ: Merrill/Prentice Hall. (Everyday science activities for younger children.)

Howe, A. C. (2002). *Engaging children in science* (3rd ed.). Upper Saddle River, NJ: Merrill/Prentice Hall. (Elementary science methods.)

Krajcik, J., Czerniak, C., & Berger, C. (1999). *Teaching children science: A project-based approach.* New York: McGraw-Hill.

Lind, K. K. (1996). *Exploring science in early childhood: A developmental approach* (2nd ed.). Albany, NY: Delmar. (Elementary science methods.)

Martin, D. J. (2000). *Elementary science methods: A constructivist approach* (2nd ed.). Albany, NY: Delmar. (Elementary science methods.)

Martin, R. E., Jr., Sexton, C., & Gerlovich, J. (1998). *Science for all children: Lessons for constructing understanding.* Needham Heights, MA: Allyn & Bacon. (Methods and content of elementary school science.)

Rezba, R., Sprague, C., Fiel, R. L., & Funk, H. J. (1995). *Learning and assessing science process skills* (3rd ed.). Dubuque, IA: Kendall Hunt. (Process skill development and assessment.)

Tolman, M. N., & Hardy, G. R. (1998). *Discovering elementary science: Method, content, and problem-solving activities* (2nd ed.). Needham Heights, MA: Allyn & Bacon. (Elementary science methods and content.)

Victor, E., & Kellough, R. (2000). *Science for the elementary and middle school* (9th ed.). Upper Saddle River, NJ: Merrill/Prentice Hall. (Methods, content, and activities. Features an extensive scope of subject matter in outline form.)

AGENCIES AND SOCIETIES

Association for the Education of Teachers in Science, contact Jon Pederson, Association for the Education of Teachers in Science Executive Secretary, University of Oklahoma, Norman, OK; pedersenj@ou.edu (*http://www.aets.unr.edu/*).

Computer Learning Foundation, P.O. Box 60007, Palo Alto, CA 94306-0007 (*http://www.computerlearning.org/*).

ERIC Clearinghouse for Science, Mathematics, and Environmental Education (ERIC/CSMEE), 1929 Kenny Rd., Columbus, OH 43210-1080 (*http://www.ericse.org/*).

ERIC Clearinghouse on Disabilities and Gifted Education, The Council for Exceptional Children, 1920 Association Dr., Reston, VA 22091-1589, (703) 264-9474, fax (703) 264-9494 (*http://ericec.org/*).

ERIC Clearinghouse on Elementary and Early Childhood Education (ERIC/EECE), University of Illinois at Urbana–Champaign, 805 W. Pennsylvania Ave., Urbana, IL 61801-4897 (*http://ericeece.org/*).

Foundation for Science and Disability, E. C. Keller, Jr., Treasurer, 236 Grand St., Morgantown, WV 26505-7509 (*http://www.as.wvu.edu/~scidis/organizations/FSD_brochure. html*).

The Franklin Institute Science Museum, 222 North 20th Street, Philadelphia, PA 19103, (215) 448-1200 (*http://www.fi.edu/*).

International Council of Associations for Science Education (ICASE), Jack B. Holbrook, Executive Secretary, ICASE, P.O. Box 6138, Limassol, Cyprus.

International Council of Associations for Science Education (ICASE), Stepping Into Science Project, Homerton College, Cambridge, CB2 2PH, England (*http://sunsite.anu.edu.au/icase/*).

National Audubon Society, 700 Broadway, New York, NY 10003-9562, (212) 979-3000, fax: (212) 979-3188 (*http://www.audubon.org/*).

National Energy Foundation, 5225 Wiley Post Way, Suite 170, Salt Lake City, UT 84116 (*http://www.nef1.org/*).

National Science Foundation, 4201 Wilson Blvd., Arlington, VA 22230 (*http://nsf.gov/*).

National Science Teachers Association, 1840 Wilson Boulevard, Arlington, VA 22201-3000, (703) 243-7100 (*http://www.nsta.org/*).

National Weather Service, 1325 East West Highway, Silver Spring, MD 20910 (*http://www.nws.noaa.gov/*).

Office of Indian Education Programs, Bureau of Indian Affairs, U.S. Dept. of the Interior, 1951 Constitution Ave., NW, Washington, DC 20240 (*http://obemla.ed.gov/offices/OESE/oie/*).

Society for Advancement of Chicanos and Native Americans in Science (SACNAS), University of California, 1156 High St., Santa Cruz, CA 95064, (408) 459-4272, fax (408) 459-3156 (*http://www.sacnas.org/*).

Technical Education Resource Center, 2067 Massachusetts Ave., Cambridge, MA 02140, (617) 547-0430, fax (617) 349-3535 (*http://www.terc.edu/*).

U.S. Environmental Protection Agency, Headquarters Service Branch, Public Information Center, 401 M. St., SW (3406), Washington, DC 20460, (202) 260-2080, fax (202) 260-7762 (*http://www.epa.gov/*).

U.S. Geological Survey, Information Services, P.O. Box 25286, Denver, CO 80225-9916 (*http://www.usgs.gov/*).

APPENDIX B | Science Curriculum Projects

ACTIVITIES FOR INTEGRATING MATHEMATICS AND SCIENCE (AIMS)

Grades K–8. This program, developed at Fresno (California) Pacific College, was originally funded by the National Science Foundation to train a group of teachers in the rationale and methods for integrating science and mathematics in Grades 5–8. The classroom testing of written materials produced such positive results that a full-fledged writing project was launched to develop additional teaching booklets. Materials are now available for K–8.

The rationale for AIMS includes these points: (a) Mathematics and science are integrated outside the classroom and so should also be integrated inside it; (b) as in the real world, a whole series of mathematics skills and science processes should be interwoven in a single activity to create a continuum of experience; (c) the materials should present questions that relate to the students' world and arouse their curiosity; (d) the materials should change students from observers to participants in the learning process; and (e) the investigations should be enjoyable because learning is more effective when the process is enjoyed.

For more information, write to AIMS Education Foundation, P.O. Box 8120, Fresno, CA 93747-8120 (*http://www.AIMSedu.org/*).

EDUCATION DEVELOPMENT CENTER INSIGHTS

Grades K–6. The Education Development Center is in Newton, Massachusetts. The program contains 17 activity-based modules that can be used separately within another science curriculum or as a full curriculum within the life, earth, and physical science areas. Each module is organized around four phases of instruction: Getting Started, Exploring and Discovering, Organizing and Processing for Meaning, and Applying and Extending Ideas. Six major science themes are incorporated into the program: systems, change, structure and function, diversity, cause and effect, and energy. Content and process skills are balanced across the curriculum. Material from other school subjects is integrated into many activities to give an overall understanding of how they normally relate.

The activities, often open ended, focus on experiences that draw on the urban environment. Playground apparatus, toys, and the students themselves may serve as resources for learning science concepts. Instructional materials are designed for both the inexperienced teacher and the veteran who seeks innovative strategies to develop critical and creative thinking in students.

An advisory group of teachers from seven major urban areas continually gave feedback to program developers about the quality of learning and assessment activities.

The commercial distributor is Improving Urban Elementary Science Project, Education Development Center, Inc., 55 Chapel St., Newton, MA 02158; (617) 969-7100, ext. 2430 (*http://www.edc.org/*).

ELEMENTARY SCIENCE STUDY (ESS)

Grades K–6. ESS was begun in the 1960s as a curriculum improvement project of the Education Development Center, a nonprofit organization devoted to generating new ideas for education.

The program consists of 56 units of instruction that cover a wide range of science subjects. Each unit has a teacher's manual, and most units have an accompanying kit of materials. No fixed master plan exists for scope and sequence. The developers thought that each school district was best qualified to assemble its own curriculum from the units to meet local conditions.

ESS is intentionally child centered. Activities are designed to reflect the wonder, curiosity, and natural play of childhood. Although the teacher guide for each unit suggests an overall structure, the students help determine the direction the activities take and how much time is spent on each activity. Most classroom procedures are exploratory and open ended. ESS believes that learning happens best when children are free to use their own styles without overstructuring and premature closing from adults.

Materials are available from Delta Education, Inc., P.O. Box 915, Hudson, NH 03051 (*http://www.delta-ed.com/*).

FULL OPTION SCIENCE SYSTEM (FOSS)

Grades K–6. The FOSS program is designed to serve both regular and most special education students in a wide cross section of schools. Developed at the Lawrence Hall of Science, in Berkeley, California, the program features several modules at each grade level that include science lesson plans in the earth, life, and physical sciences and extension activities in language, computer, and mathematics applications.

The laboratory equipment includes several package options, from complete kits to individual items. Materials assembly directions show how teacher and students can gather and construct equipment for many activities. A correlation table tells how to integrate activities with other programs and state department of education guidelines for science.

Much care is taken to have a suitable match between activities and students' ability to think at different ages. Further work has made the program easy to instruct and manage. Provisions for preparation time, ease of giving out and retrieving materials, cleanup, storage, and resupply have continually guided program developers.

The commercial distributor of FOSS is Delta Education, Inc., P.O. Box 915, Hudson, NH 03051 (*http://www.delta-ed.com/*, *http://www.lhs.berkeley.edu/FOSS/FOSS.html*).

GREAT EXPLORATIONS IN MATH AND SCIENCE (GEMS)

Grades Preschool–9. Gems is a growing resource for activity-based science and mathematics. Developed at the University of California at Berkeley's Lawrence Hall of Science and tested in thousands of classrooms nationwide, more than 50 GEMS Teacher's Guides and Handbooks offer a wide spectrum of learning opportunities from preschool and kindergarten through 10th grade. GEMS guides can be integrated into your curriculum or stand on their own as a stimulating way to involve students.

The GEMS series interweaves a number of educational ideas and goals. GEMS guides encompass important learning objectives, summarized on the front page of each guide, under the headings of skills, concepts, science themes, mathematics strands, and the nature of science and mathematics. Taken together, these headings help provide a summary of the unit objectives. These objectives can be directly and flexibly related to science and mathematics curricula, local and district guidelines, state frameworks, benchmarks, and the national standards. For more on flexible ways to build your own curricula using GEMS, contact the University of California, GEMS, Lawrence Hall of Science, Berkeley, CA 94720-5200 (*http://www.lhs.berkeley.edu/GEMS/GEMS.html*).

NATIONAL GEOGRAPHIC KIDS NETWORK

Grades 4–6. The National Geographic Kids Network is a program that has children gather data on real science problems and then use a computer network to share their data with a scientist and children in other locations. The developer is the Technical Education Resource Center (TERC) in partnership with the National Geographic Society, which publishes and distributes the program.

Each instructional unit is 6 weeks long and focuses on a central science problem. Children learn to ask questions and gather data in scientifically acceptable ways. The data are transmitted to an interested scientist who analyzes the data, answers children's questions, and then sends back an overview of all the collected information from cooperating schools.

Curriculum materials include children's handbooks that have background information on the topic of study, teacher guides, and computer software. The software is made up of a word-processing program,

data charts, and a computer map of North America, all of which are used to ready and transmit data.

For details, write National Geographic Society Educational Services, 17th & M Streets, Washington, DC 20036 (*http://www.nationalgeographic.com/kids/*).

OUTDOOR BIOLOGY INSTRUCTIONAL STRATEGIES (OBIS)

Ages 10–15. Developed at the Lawrence Hall of Science, University of California (Berkeley), OBIS is designed for use with community youth organizations and schools that want to offer outdoor laboratory experiences. Four activity packets offer a broad selection of interesting, firsthand activities for studying ecological relationships in different environments: desert, seashore, forest, pond and stream, city lots, and local parks.

Each activity card consists of background information for the leader, description of materials needed and any advance preparation required, a lesson plan, and several follow-up suggestions. Each activity can be used alone or as part of a developmental sequence. The commercial distributor is Delta Education, Inc., P.O. Box 915, Hudson, NH 03051 (*http://www.delta-ed.com/*).

SCIENCE FOR LIFE AND LIVING

Grades K–6. The full name for this curriculum is "Science for Living: Integrating Science, Technology, and Health." The developer is the BSCS Group, a nonprofit foundation for science education.

After readiness activities at the kindergarten level, these concepts and skills form the main curriculum structure: order and organization (Grade 1); change and measurement (Grade 2); patterns and prediction (Grade 3); systems and analysis (Grade 4); energy and investigation (Grade 5); and balance and decisions (Grade 6). Children build their own understanding of an integrated world of science, technology, and health as they work through activities that bring out the concepts and skills.

Each complete lesson contains five consecutive phases: (a) An engagement activity begins the lesson. Children connect what they know to the current material and reveal their prior knowledge, including misconceptions. (b) Exploration follows, in which students explore the materials or environment and form a common base of experience. (c) An explanation phase gives students a chance to describe what they are learning and gives the teacher an opportunity to state the intended learning. (d) Elaboration then provides activities that extend understandings and give further chances to practice skills. (e) The last phase, evaluation, allows students and teacher to assess what has been learned.

Published materials are available from the Kendall/Hunt Publishing Company, 2460 Kerper Blvd., Dubuque, IA 52001 (*http://www.kendallhunt.com/*).

SCIENCE AND TECHNOLOGY FOR CHILDREN (STC)

Grades 1–6. The developer of the STC curriculum project is the National Science Resources Center, established in 1985 by the National Academy of Sciences and the Smithsonian Institution to improve the teaching of science and mathematics in the nation's schools. The project's mission is to increase significantly the number of schools that offer hands-on science programs to children and to interest more females and minority members in science.

Teaching units include such titles as Weather and Me (Grade 1), The Life Cycle of Butterflies (Grade 2), Plant Growth and Development (Grade 3), Electric Circuits (Grade 4), Microworlds (Grade 5), and Magnets and Motors (Grade 6). They are designed to focus on easy-to-use materials and integrate science with other areas of the curriculum. Each unit includes a teacher's guide; pupil activity booklet; description of needed materials; and annotated lists of recommended trade books, computer software, and audiovisual materials.

The developers sought to make the management of materials and activities as practical as possible. In the field testing of units, evaluation procedures monitored how well the units worked under a wide variety of classroom conditions.

For details, contact the National Science Resources Center, Arts and Industries Building, Room 1201, Smithsonian Institution, Washington, DC 20560 (*http://www.si.edu/nsrc/pubs/stc/overv.htm*).

SCIENCE—A PROCESS APPROACH (SAPA)

Grades K–6. SAPA has a unique structure. It uses process skills rather than subject-matter content as the base for its scope and sequence. Subject matter is used mainly as an aid to developing the skills, although much content is presented.

Eight "basic" processes are taught in Grades K–3: observing, using space/time relationships, using numbers, measuring, classifying, communicating, predicting, and inferring. In Grades 4–6, five "integrated" processes are taught that build on and extend the basic processes: formulating hypotheses, controlling variables, interpreting data, defining operationally, and experimenting. The method used in organizing the development of the skills was to identify the process behaviors of scientists and then to break down the behaviors into logical sequences through which they could be learned by children.

SAPA II, a more recent version of this program, has a more flexible structure than the first edition. Alternative procedures have been provided to allow the teacher more leeway in meeting students' individual differences and organizing teaching.

The commercial supplier is Delta Education, Inc., P.O. Box 915, Hudson, NH 03051 (*http://www.delta-ed.com/*).

SCIENCE CURRICULUM IMPROVEMENT STUDY (SCIS)

Grades K–6. SCIS is organized on a base of powerful and modern science concepts. Each of 12 instructional units features a central concept, with supporting subconcepts and process skills integrated into the activities.

Lessons have three parts: exploration, invention, and discovery. In the exploratory part, children are given objects to observe or manipulate. At times, these observations are guided by the teacher; otherwise, the children observe and manipulate the objects as they wish.

Explorations allow firsthand contact with the material under study and provide a basis for children to use language. At the same time, the need arises for an explanation to make sense out of what has been observed. This is taken up in the second part of the lesson sequence. After discussion, the teacher gives a definition and a word for the new concept.

This "invention" of a concept sets up the third part of the lesson. Now, children are given a variety of further experiences within which they discover many applications of the concept. These extend and reinforce their knowledge and skills.

An updated version of this program, SCIS3, is available from Delta Education, Inc., P.O. Box 915, Hudson, NH 03051 (*http://www.delta-ed.com/*).

SCIENCE IN A NUTSHELL

Grades K–8. Real fun with real science. Discover how exciting real science can be with Delta's new Science in a Nutshell mini-kit series. Introduce or enhance specific science content areas in the classroom, at home, in a resource room, or in an after-school program. Clearly written, hands-on activities challenge young scientists aged 6–12 to investigate their world. Mini-kits are suitable for use with individuals or with small groups of two to three. Contact Delta Education, Inc., P.O. Box 915, Hudson, NH 03051 (*http://www.delta-ed.com/*).

WONDERSCIENCE

Wonderscience offers hands-on science activities for elementary school teachers and students. Wonderscience is published monthly from October through May as a joint effort of the American Chemical Society, 1155 Sixteenth St., NW, Washington, DC 20036, and the American Institute of Physics, One Physics Ellipse, College Park, MD 20740. The single-copy subscription price is $6.00/eight issues plus $3.50 handling for each address. For subscription information, call toll-free 1-800-333-9511 or write to Wonderscience at the ACS address (*http://www.acs.org/education/curriculum/wondsci.html*).

APPENDIX C Commercial Science Suppliers

The following classifications of suppliers may not be entirely accurate, because suppliers often change offerings with business conditions. A current catalog should reveal the full scope of materials for sale in each case. Use school stationery when requesting free elementary-level catalogs. An annual, comprehensive listing of suppliers accompanies each January issue of *Science and Children*.

GENERAL SUPPLIES

Bottle Biology, Wisconsin Fast Plants, University of Wisconsin-Madison, College of Agricultural and Life Sciences, Department of Plant Pathology, 1630 Linden Drive, Madison, WI 53706, 1-800-462-7417 (*http://www.fastplants.org/*).

Carolina Biological Supply Company, 2700 York Road, Burlington, NC 27215 (*http://www.carosci.com/*).

Delta Education, Inc., P.O. Box 915, Hudson, NH 03051 (*http://www.delta-ed.com/*).

Edmund Scientific Company, 101 E. Gloucester Pike, Barrington, NJ 08007 (*http://www.edsci.com/*).

Frey Scientific Company, 905 Hickory Lane, Mansfield, OH 44905 (*http://www.scienceiscool.com/*).

Ward's Natural Science Establishment, 5100 West Henrietta Road, P.O. Box 92912, Rochester, NY 14692 (*http://www.wardsci.com/*).

BALANCES

Ohaus Scale Corporation, 29 Hanover Road, Florham Park, NJ 07932 (*http://www.ohaus.com/*).

MICROSCOPES AND MICROPROJECTORS

Bausch & Lomb, Inc., 1400 North Goodman Street, Rochester, NY 14602 (*http://www.bausch.com/*).

Brock Optical, 414 Lake Howell Road, Maitland, FL 32751-5907 (*http://www.magiscope.com/*).

Ken-A-Vision Manufacturing Company, 5615 Raytown Road, Raytown, MO 64133 (*http://www.ken-a-vision.com/*).

Swift Instruments, Inc., P.O. Box 95016, San Jose, CA 95016 (*http://www.swift-optics.com/*).

AQUARIA, TERRARIA, CAGES

Carolina Biological Supply Company, 2700 York Road, Burlington, NC 27215 (*http://www.carosci.com/*).

Delta Education, Inc., P.O. Box 915, Hudson, NH 03051 (*http://www.delta-ed.com/*).

Frey Scientific Company, 905 Hickory Lane, Mansfield, OH 44905 (*http://www.scienceiscool.com/*).

KITS AND MODELS

Delta Education, Inc., P.O. Box 915, Hudson, NH 03051 (*http://www.delta-ed.com/*).

SOFTWARE

Scholastic Software & Multimedia, 2931 East McCarty Street, Jefferson City, MO 65101, 1-800-724-6527 (*http://scholastic.com/*).

Sunburst Educational Software, Department EG53, 101 Castleton Street, P.O. Box 100, Pleasantville, NY 10570, 1-800-321-7511 (*http://www.sunburst.com/*).

APPENDIX D   Environments and Nutrition for Classroom Animals

Animal[1]	Environment	Nutrition[2]
Ants	Glass terrarium or large jar with dirt (covered with black paper)	Small food scraps or dead insects
Birds	Bird cage (ensure cage is large enough for bird to move freely)	Birdseed (nutritional mix from pet store—not wild bird seed)
Butterflies and Moths	Butterfly "tent" (sold in kits) or large jar with wire screen on top with small branches	Sugar water solution
Caterpillars	Medium-sized jar with holes in lid; includes a small branch	Leaves (preferably near to where they were found)
Chameleons and Lizards	Aquarium with screened top; dirt, stones, and branches on bottom	Mealworms or live insects
Fish	Aquarium with gravel and filter (dechlorinate water before use)	Fish food from pet store (do not overfeed); brine shrimp
Frogs and Toads	Aquarium with shallow water and rocks to climb out of the water	Mealworms, small caterpillars, or live insects
Fruit Flies	Small jars with fine mesh covering	A small amount of overly ripe fruit
Guinea Pigs and Rats	Large animal cage with secure openings and an exercise wheel	Guinea pig food; small amounts of fresh fruit and vegetables
Hamsters, Gerbils, and Mice	Medium or large animal cage with secure openings and an exercise wheel	Hamster or gerbil food; small amounts of fresh fruit and vegetables
Mealworms	Wide jar or plastic bucket with screen or mesh cover	Oatmeal and small slices of fresh apple
Newts and Salamanders	Aquarium with shallow water and rocks rising above water line	Mealworms and live insects
Rabbits	Large animal cage (rabbits will chew on cage, so avoid wood)	Rabbit pellets, fresh vegetables (avoid too much lettuce)
Snakes	Terrarium with secure openings; heating device (contact pet shop)	Live mice or insects (contact pet shop for specifics)
Spiders	Glass jar covered with screen	Live insects
Tadpoles	Aquarium 1/4 filled with water and rocks above the water line	Small insects or finely chopped meat
Turtles (land)	Terrarium with nonpoisonous plants and water pool	Mealworms, insects, earthworms; finely chopped vegetables
Turtles (aquatic)	Aquarium which is mostly water-covered, but with small land area	Mealworms, insects, earthworms; finely chopped vegetables

[1]Contact the National Science Teachers Association (1840 Wilson Blvd., Arlington, VA 22201-3000 for the Guidelines for Responsible Use of Animals in the Classroom.

[2]All animals require plenty of fresh water. To remove the chlorine from water, leave it standing overnight.

APPENDIX E Summary of Children's Thinking

Thought Process	Intuitive Thought[1]	Concrete Operations	Formal Operations
Cause and Effect	Logic often contradictory, unpredictable. Events may occur by magic or for human convenience.	Contradictions avoided. Physical objects are linked to show cause and effect. Commonsense explanations may be wrong but logical.	Can separate logic from content. Systematic control of variables possible, as well as hypothetical "thought experiments," to test ideas.
Relative Thinking	Egocentric perceptions and language. Little grasp of how vertebrates interrelate. Physical properties viewed in absolute, not relative, ways.	Perceptions of position and objects more objective. Aware of others' views. Some understanding of interrelated variables, when connected to concrete objects and pictures.	Understand relative position and motion. Can define and explain abstract concepts with other concepts or analogies. May temporarily show some egocentricity in propositions.
Classifying and Ordering	Sort one property at a time. Little or no class inclusion. Trial-and-error ordering in early part of stage.	Understand class inclusion principle. More consistent seriation with diverse objects. Can follow successive steps, less discrete thinking.	Can recombine groups into fewer, more abstract categories. Can form hierarchical systems.
Conservative Thinking	Mostly do not conserve. Perceptions dominate thinking. Center attention on one variable and do not compensate. Little or no reverse thinking.	Can reverse thinking, consider several variables and compensate. Conserve most of the Piagetian test concepts.	Conserve all of the Piagetian test concepts, with displaced and solid volume usually last.

Table based on a format suggested by Robert Mele.
[1]Intuitive thought is the last period of the preoperational stage.

APPENDIX F   State Education Agencies

Alabama
Alabama State Dept. of Education
Gordon Persons Bldg.
Montgomery, AL 36130
(*http://www.alsde.edu/*)

Alaska
State of Alaska
Dept. of Education
801 W. 10th St., Ste. 200
Juneau, AK 99801-1894
(*http://www.educ.state.ak.us/*)

Arizona
Arizona Dept. of Education
1535 W. Jefferson St., Phoenix, AZ 85007
(*http://www.state.az.us/education.html*)

Arkansas
Arkansas Dept. of Education
4 State Capitol Mall
Little Rock, AR 72201
(*http://arkedu.state.ar.us/*)

Bureau of Indian Affairs
Dept. of Interior, BIA
1849 C St., NW
Mail Stop 3525, Code 521, MIB
Washington, DC 20240
(*http://www.doi.gov/bureau-indian-affairs.html*)

California
State Dept. of Education
721 Capitol Mall, 3rd Floor
Sacramento, CA 95814
(*http://goldmine.cde.ca.gov/*)

Colorado
Colorado Dept. of Education
201 E. Colfax Ave.
Denver, CO, 80203
(*http://www.cde.state.co.us/index_home.htm*)

Connecticut
State Dept. of Education
P.O. Box 2219, Rm. 369
Hartford, CN 06145
(*http://www.state.ct.us/sde/*)

Delaware
State Dept. of Public Instruction
Townsend Bldg.
P.O. Box 1402
Dover, DE 19903
(*http://www.doe.state.de.us/*)

District of Columbia
Education Program
D.C. Public Schools
415 12th St., NW, Rm. 1004
Washington, DC 20004
(*http://www.k12.dc.us/dcps/home.html*)

Department of Defense
4040 N. Fairfax Dr.
Arlington, VA 22203
(*http://www.odedodea.edu/*)

Florida
Florida Dept. of Education
Florida Education Center, Ste. 522
Tallahassee, FL 32399
(*http://www.firn.edu/doe/index.html*)

Georgia
Georgia Dept. of Education
1862 Twin Towers East
Atlanta, GA 30334
(*http://www.doe.k12.ga.us/index.asp*)

Hawaii
Education Program
189 Lunalilo Home Rd., 2nd Floor
Honolulu, HI 96825
(*http://www.k12.hi.us/*)

Idaho
Idaho State Dept. of Education
650 W. State St.
P.O. Box 83720
Boise, ID 83720-0027
(*http://www.sde.state.id.us/Dept/*)

Illinois
Illinois State Board of Education
100 N. First St.
Springfield, IL 62777-0001
(*http://www.isbe.state.il.us/*)

Indiana
Indiana Dept. of Education
Rm. 229 State House
Indianapolis, IN 46204-2798
(*http://www.doe.state.in.us/*)

Iowa
State of Iowa
Department of Education
Grimes State Office Building
Des Moines, IA 50319-0146
(*http://www.state.ia.us/educate/index.html*)

Kansas
Kansas Dept. of Education
120 E. 10th St.
Topeka, KS 66612-1103
(*http://www.ksbe.state.ks.us/*)

Kentucky
Kentucky Dept. of Education
Capitol Plaza Tower
500 Mero St.
Frankfort, KY 40601
(*http://www.kde.state.ky.us/*)

Louisiana
State Dept. of Education
P.O. Box 94064
Baton Rouge, LA 70804-9064
(*http://www.doe.state.la.us/DOE/asps/home.asp*)

Maine
Maine State Dept. of Education
State House Station #23
Augusta, ME 04333
(*http://janus.state.me.us/education/homepage.htm*)

Maryland
Maryland State Dept. of Education
200 W. Baltimore St.
Baltimore, MD 21201-2595
(*http://www.msde.state.md.us/*)

Massachusetts
Massachusetts Dept. of Education
350 Main St.
Malden, MA 02148-5023
(*http://www.doe.mass.edu/*)

Michigan
Michigan Dept. of Education
P.O. Box 30008
Lansing, MI 48909
(*http://www.mde.state.mi.us/*)

Minnesota
Minnesota Dept. of Education
Capitol Square Bldg., Rm. 922
St. Paul, MN 55101
(*http://www.educ.state.mn.us/*)

Mississippi
State Dept. of Education
Walter Sillers Bldg., Ste. 501
P.O. Box 771
Jackson, MS 39205-0771
(*http://www.mde.k12.ms.us/*)

Missouri
Missouri Dept. of Education
Dept. of Elementary & Secondary Education
P.O. Box 480
Jefferson, MO 65102
(*http://services.dese.state.mo.us/*)

Montana
Office of Public Instruction
State Capitol Bldg.
Helena, MT 59620
(*http://www.metnet.state.mt.us/*)

Nebraska
Nebraska Dept. of Education
301 Centennial Mall South
P.O. Box 84987
Lincoln, NE 68509-4987
(*http://www.nde.state.ne.us/*)

Nevada
Nevada Dept. of Education
Capitol Complex
Carson City, NV 89710
(*http://www.nsn.k12.nv.us/nvdoe/*)

New Hampshire
New Hampshire Dept. of Education
1010 Pleasant St.
Concord, NH 03301
(*http://www.ed.state.nh.us/*)

New Jersey
New Jersey Dept. of Education
Division of Standards and Assessment
CN 500
Trenton, NJ 08625-0500
(*http://www.state.nj.us/education/*)

New Mexico
State of New Mexico
Dept. of Education
300 Don Gaspar
Santa Fe, NM 87501-2786
(*http://sde.state.nm.us/*)

New York
New York State Education Dept.
Bureau of Professional Career Opportunity Programs
Empire State Plaza
Cultural Education Center, Rm. 5C64
Albany, NY 12230
(*http://www.nysed.gov/*)

North Carolina
Dept. of Public Instruction
116 W. Edenton St.
Raleigh, NC 27603-1712
(*http://www.dpi.state.nc.us/*)

North Dakota
Dept. of Public Instruction
State Capitol
Bismark, ND 58505
(*http://www.dpi.state.nd.us/*)

Ohio
Ohio Dept. of Education
65 S. Front St.
Columbus, OH 43266-0208
(*http://www.ode.state.oh.us/*)

Oklahoma
State Dept. of Education
2500 N. Lincoln Blvd.
Oklahoma City, OK 73105-4599
(*http://sde.state.ok.us/*)

Oregon
Oregon Dept. of Education
700 Pringle Pkwy., S.S.
Salem, OR 97310
(*http://www.ode.state.or.us/*)

Pennsylvania
Pennsylvania Dept. of Education
8th Floor, 333 Market Street
Harrisburg, PA 17126-0333
(*http://www.pde.psu.edu/*)

Puerto Rico
Office of Education
Office 809
Dept. of Education
Hato Rey, PR 00919
(*http://de.prstar.net/*)

Rhode Island
Rhode Island Dept. of Education
255 Westminster St.
Providence, RI 02902-3400
(*http://www.ridoe.net/*)

South Carolina
South Carolina Dept. of Education
Curriculum Section
801 Rutledge Bldg.
Columbia, SC 29201
(*http://www.state.sc.us/sde/*)

South Dakota
Dept. of Education and Cultural Affairs
700 Governors Dr.
Pierre, SD 57501-2291
(*http://www.state.sd.us/deca/*)

Tennessee
Tennessee Dept. of Education
4th Floor Northwing
Cordell Hull Bldg.
Nashville, TN 37243-0388
(*http://www.state.tn.us/education/*)

Texas
Texas Education Agency
1701 N. Congress
Austin, TX 78701
(*http://www.tea.state.tx.us/*)

Utah
Utah Dept. of Education
250 East 500 South
Salt Lake City, UT 84111
(*http://www.usoe.k12.ut.us/*)

Vermont
Vermont State Dept. of Education
120 State St.
Montpelier, VT 05602
(*http://www.state.vt.us/educ/*)

Virgin Islands
Dept. of Education
No. 44–46 Kongens Gade
Charlotte Amalie, U.S. Virgin Islands 00802
(*http://www.usvi.org/education/index.html*)

Virginia
Virginia Dept. of Education
P.O. Box 2120
Richmond, VA 23218-2120
(*http://www.pen.k12.va.us/*)

Washington
Office of Superintendent of Public Instruction
P.O. Box 47200
Olympia, WA 98504-7200
(*http://www.k12.wa.us/*)

West Virginia
West Virginia Dept. of Education
1900 Kanawha Blvd. East
Charleston, WV 25305
(*http://wvde.state.wv.us/*)

Wisconsin
Dept. of Public Education
125 S. Webster St.
P.O. Box 7841
Madison, WI 53707-7841
(*http://www.dpi.state.wi.us/*)

Wyoming
State Dept. of Education
241 Hathaway Bldg.
Cheyenne, WY 82002-0050
(*http://www.k12.wy.us/*)

Index